The Best Of Th

DOLL READER®

VOLUME III

Article Reprints — 1982 to 1985

Compiled and Edited by Virginia Ann Heyerdahl

Hobby House Press™

Published by   Cumberland, Maryland 21502

1

FRONT COVER: This small 12in (30.5cm) doll is marked on the head, in red, "Depose//Tete Jumeau//Bte. S.G.D.G.//3." Her body is stamped in blue, "Jumeau//Medaille D'OR//Paris." Made about 1890, she has fixed paperweight eyes, closed mouth, pierced ears. Jointed composition body. *Turner Collection*.

BACK COVER: Three early *Shirley* dolls in a Shirley Temple trunk. Left to right: 11in (27.9), 18in (45.7cm) and 15in (38.1cm) versions. The last two are from the *Stand Up and Cheer* movie.

Additional copies of this book may be purchased at $13.95 plus $2.25 postage
from
Hobby House Press, Inc.
Cumberland, MD 21502

ISBN: 0-87588-322-2

TABLE OF CONTENTS

Page 19

Page 49

Page 70

Page 117

Continued...

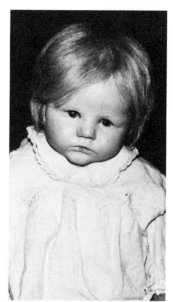

Page 132   Page 143   Page 124   Page 177

COLLECTIBLE

ANTIQUE

ABOVE: Doll with fabric head and painted features. When wound the tricycle zig-zags forward with the girl moving from side to side. Manufactured by Stevens & Brown, Cromwell, CT.

by **Margaret Whitton**

Photographs courtesy of
The Margaret Woodbury Strong Museum.

Hero, of Alexandria, in the second century B.C., used moving figures to demonstrate some of his theories. He described a mechanical theater in which the figures moved by an elaborate system of weights and pulleys. Variations of his techniques were used over and over again in order to move figures of all kinds. Birds and animals flew through the air when inflated, a lion was activated from wheels under his feet, a brass mechanical man who moved and spoke was created and metal birds sang in a golden tree.

In the latter part of the Renaissance period, the European clocks with their complex mechanisms ushered in the wonders of moving figures acting out dramas, either comic or tragic. Depending on the type of clock, they performed every hour, half hour or quarter hour.

By the 18th century, "one-of-a-kind" moving figures had reached their peak. These moving figures moved with amazing dexterity in a lifelike motion. Some performed magic tricks, played chess, told fortunes or danced.

BELOW: When wound, the music plays and the central figure raises cups from the table showing different objects underneath. The two musicians on either side move their arms as if playing their instruments. Manufacturer unknown. France. 1860-1880.

Automata and Toys with Movement

Doll at Dressing Table. When wound, the music plays and the bisque head figure raises her powder puff to and from her face and turns her head in different directions. Head marked Simon & Halbig Germany, 1900-1910.

Illustration 5. Drawing by the Maillardet automaton.

LEFT: Illustration 4. Bisque head with composition lower arms and legs, cardboard torso. A mechanism is concelaed within the torso and when wound the doll moves her head, arms and legs, and cries "Mama" and "Papa." Manufactured by Jules Steiner, France. 1880 to 1890.

Illustration 6. Writing by the Maillardet automaton.

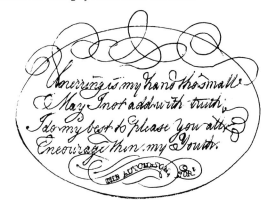

At first these figures appeared to have been made for royalty or the wealthy alone but eventually, through viewing at museums and traveling exhibits, the paying public obtained the privilege of seeing these fantastic and almost unbelievable machines in action.

Pierre Jaquet-Droz created three automata that are still performing for the public at the Neûchatel Museum in Switzerland. They were first introduced by Droz in Paris in 1794; a lady musician, a boy who writes and a boy who draws.

Another world famous automata maker was Henri Maillardet. He was born in Switzerland in 1745, the son of a clock-maker. As a young man he worked as an apprentice to Jaquet-Droz. Later he spent much of his time in London where he acted as an agent for Jaquet-Droz. During this period he himself created several automata, one of the most outstanding being the *Writing Child.*

The Margaret Woodbury Strong Museum exhibited Maillardet's *Writing Child* in its recent exhibition of auto-mata and toys with movement, through the generosity of the Franklin Institute of Philadelphia, Pennsylvania. This famous automaton had passed through many hands after being on exhibit in 1826 and its whereabouts was unknown for many years. Sometime in the late 1800s it came into the possession of Mr. John Penn Brock of Philadelphia. It was in poor condition, not operating and appeared to have been in a fire. Mr. Brock's grandchildren presented the automaton to the Franklin Institute in 1928. It was skillfully restored and put into working condition. After the restoration, the figure was able to write its own identification, "I am the automaton of Maillardet." The figure is programmed to write this example and six other sketches and writings.

The Strong's collection of automata and spring-driven toys includes both European and American examples with simple movement created either by pushing or pulling the toy, the use of levers, cranks, gravity, cord action, clockwork with or without music and spring-driven mechanisms. Clockwork automata is produced today in limited quantity. Automated figures are manufactured for store window displays. Jean and Annette Frakas of France are making copies of some of the early automata using, at times, bisque heads and antique fabrics. Michel Bertrand of Switzerland is one of the few master craftsmen left who can recreate a figure using an original automaton as a model. He also has designed and made "one-of-a-kind" automata to order. He creates the papier-mâché heads, bodies, beautiful clothing and remarkably intricate movements or action.

Making automata, whether it be copying the lovely antique pieces or designing and making originals, is really a lost art. Time and money does not permit the average individual the luxury of creating these wonders that many times took years to perfect.

Maillardet's Writing Child

LEFT: When wound the music plays, the clown sticks out his tongue and touches the table with a magician's wand changing the objects under the cone four different times. France, 1890-1911.

BELOW: A bisque head with a papier-mache body. When wound the music plays and the doll moves her head from side to side and up and down. She pulls a bucket out of the well and a frog jumps up in the bucket. Decamps. France, 1880-1911.

OPPOSITE PAGE: TOP LEFT: Bisque head dolls seated in a boat. The toy is pulled along and the boy's head turns as he rows the boat. Heads made by Schoenau & Hoffmeister. Germany, circa 1910.

TOP RIGHT: A figure with a papier-mache head representing Marie Antoinette. The five wooden levers on the base activate the figure in different ways. France, 1790-1810.

BOTTOM LEFT: Bisque head doll with crying expression standing on a base which holds the mechanism and music box. When wound the music plays and she raises her broken doll up and then lowers her head and raises the handkerchief to her eyes. Manufactured by Lambert. France, circa 1890.

BOTTOM RIGHT: Gypsy with tambourine. Bisque head doll stands on a base containing a clockwork mechanism and music box. When activated the music plays and the doll sways at the waist, her hand shakes the tambourine and she moves her head. France, circa 1880.

Plain Living and High Thinking

by **Betty Cadbury**

Illustration 1. A typical Quaker bonnet of the last century, perhaps for Sunday Meeting, as it shows little sign of wear. It is made of slate gray silk with matching ribbon ties. The lining is of white silk and the pleated crown and sides are stiffened. The bonnet size can be adjusted by a drawstring at the back of the neck. The owner would probably have had a straw bonnet for summer wear.

"Quakers" is the general usage name for the Society of Friends and their influence on early American history is important in many ways, particularly for the part they played in the colonization of New Jersey and Pennsylvania. Their ordered system and discipline was reflected in their simple and somber form of dress.

Colors were quiet -- black, dark brown and fawn, and, of course, "Quaker" gray. Fashions, too, were modest; often the dresses had high necklines, or, if low and square cut, they were filled in with detachable white muslin. Skirts were long and full and many photographs surviving in old records of Quaker families show that shawls were also an important part of the total outfit. The wearing of caps by women persisted through the Victorian period, with caps for day wear at home, more stylish caps for formal occasions and night caps. With the fashion of hooded cloaks,

the cap was a most useful accessory when the hood was thrown back. Caps, too, were part of customary Quaker costume -- muslin with high crown and frills and cotton caps in plainer style.

The Quaker bonnets were charming and **rumor** has it that their large brims and wide sides were supposed to stop the young men and women exchanging amorous glances during Meeting!

What a strange custom it was -- this wearing of hats and caps indoors. It survives even today at formal or official luncheons when the ladies still wear hats. Samuel Pepys, the great English diarist (1633 to 1703), writing in his diary suggests a possible reason ... "Got a strange cold in me head -- by flinging off my hat at dinner." Well, Quaker ladies certainly wore caps -- indoors and outdoors and sometimes two! The doll in *Illustration 2* wears two caps -- a black cap beneath the muslin cap -- beneath the bonnet!

Quaker children, just like any others, played with toys and games, but such play was not encouraged on the Sabbath. Indeed, their toys were sometimes altered. One devout Quaker father presented his young son with a toy steam battleship, and, with a fine disregard for realism, had all the guns removed! However, many cherished dolls still survive and naturally some are dressed as Quakers; this is where doll collectors are especially interested. When clothes belonging to previous generations become outmoded, they are sometimes kept and eventually handed to museums, but few entire ensembles are handed down intact -- dresses are separated from underwear -- hats from coats and shoes are usually discarded. Doll collectors, on the other hand, can offer the complete picture, for the antique doll dressed in original costume is authentic from top to toe and this is often a unique record. So, if you possess one of these rarities, it is vital that nothing is added or subtracted.

None of the dolls illustrated here has commercially made clothes. It is probable that the beautifully sewn garments were made by the same dressmaker who worked for the mother of the child who was to receive the doll. Examination of many adult garments of the period shows the care and expertise of the hand-sewing. The proliferation of dress shops as we know them was unknown: richer ladies had their favorite dressmakers and patronized establishments offering bespoke tailoring. No doubt many Quaker families, rich or poor, had the dolls dressed professionally or sewed the clothing themselves. The final achievement was to look "just like Mamma."

ABOVE LEFT AND RIGHT: Illustrations 2 and **3**. A fine and rare doll in mint condition. The glazed china face, bust and arms are flesh tinted. The black glazed hair has a center part with a coil at the back. The slim tapering body and legs are stuffed. She wears exquisite hand-sewn clothes of shift (no drawers), flannel petticoat, quilted cotton underskirt which exactly matches the dress of pale fawn taffeta. The dress has a pointed shaped bodice with attached skirt, opening at the sides and tied with silk ribbons. The neck is covered with a detachable crossover muslin shawl and the three-quarter sleeves are also edged with the same material. She wears a muslin cap with a drawstring at the nape of the neck. The lower legs have cotton stockings tied with ribbons, and black leather-soled boots with black ribbon ties. Her outdoor wear is equally fine -- a double thickness cloak (matching the quilted underskirt) and a black silk bonnet, stiffened and lined with white silk.

BELOW LEFT AND RIGHT: Illustrations 4 and **5**. A poured wax doll with head turned slightly to one side, wax limbs on a stuffed body. A good example of complete Quaker costume for everyday wear. The full-skirted fine woolen and lined dress has a rounded bodice and long sleeves edged with cream silk. The crossover bodice trim is also of matching cream silk. The dress fastenings are brass hooks with hand-sewn bars for the eyes. The underclothes are cotton drawers, flannel petticoat, cotton petticoat and she has socks and leather-soled satin shoes with metal and ribbon rosettes. Her outer wear consists of a gray silk cloak, lined with white silk, with cream silk collar and stiffened bonnet to match. The bonnet has an attached frilled muslin interlining and drawstring at the nape of the neck. She also possesses a matching drawstring bag (and a wooden box with glass front, which, no doubt, has helped to preserve her)!

13

There have been famous characters amongst the membership of the Society of Friends and Elizabeth Fry (1780 to 1845) was one of many. One must remember that she lived during the Regency period -- a time of great extravagance and ostentation. The young Elizabeth struggled between "plain" and "gay" (worldly) for she had a love of music and dancing, but she thought seriously about the problems and decided that as regards speech and dress " 'plain' appears to me a sort of protector to the principles of Christianity in the present state of the world."

Nowadays we send photographs of our nearest and dearest to relatives living abroad, but 150 years ago Joel Cadbury had no such choice. He had emigrated from England to America and wanted to show his mother and father what his little children looked like, so dolls were dressed in typical Quaker costume and taken to England on his next journey home. Here is an extract from the accompanying letter to her English grandmother written by one of the children, Mary Ann, aged eight and dated 1831.

"My Dear Grandmother,

I hope thee is well. I am now ready to send thee a doll [sic] of this country and I hope thee will be pleased with them and they are dressed just like brother john [sic] and Myself..."
Philadelphia. 9 mo 19 1831.

Doll collectors have a special responsibility as regards records and research. We all treasure items in our collections, but the temptation to "prettify" should be resisted. Necessary alterations and subtractions may have to be made, but they should be recorded as such. In days gone by, ladies had sufficient time to keep their journals -- to enter into their diaries all the day-to-day experiences which make such fascinating reading for later generations. Today we do not have this time; perhaps we do not have the inclination either, but at the very least, doll collectors can keep records with their dolls -- a help and encouragement to those who follow us.

ABOVE RIGHT: Illustration 6. This doll is reputed to represent "Mrs. Elizabeth Fry," but she is not a portrait doll and does not resemble paintings of the real Elizabeth Fry. However, although not as fine as the dolls previously illustrated, it is an example of a doll dressed in Quaker costume. The doll has a composition head with painted features and limbs on a stuffed body. She wears metal-rimmed spectacles and a gray mohair wig. Her dress is pale fawn, with lawn neck piece and the remains of a gray folded shawl. The bonnet is of stiffened gray silk, with white silk lining and a piece of net is folded under the brim to represent a cap. The underclothes are cotton drawers, shift and flannel and cotton petticoats. The doll is probably German in origin.

RIGHT: Illustration 7. Two dolls in Quaker costume of 1831 in America. LEFT: A boy doll of papier-mâché with long fawn trousers buttoned at the sides, short jacket with frilled collar and a straw, brimmed hat. RIGHT: A girl doll of papier-mâché with molded black hair, wooden arms and hands, wearing a long striped dress with cotton pinafore, shoulder cape, mittens and a straw bonnet with silk lining.

Cherishable China Dolls
Part I

by **Estelle Johnston**

Illustration 1. 17in (53.2cm) marked KPM with brown hair drawn into an extended bun; costumed in blue-gray silk taffeta trimmed with bias folds of brown silk and matching pelerine, brown straw bonnet in the style of the late 1830s.

Illustration 2. Close-up of KPM seen in *Illustration 1*, showing modeling and streaked two-tone painting of the hair. (Neck and shoulder repair without stray painting entire area.)

The lovely and much-needed book, *Chinas/Dolls For Study And Admiration,* by Mona Borger, has brought the charm of china dolls into focus for all of us. We celebrate this happening. For more than a century dolls have been made with glazed porcelain heads and, as in the large field of bisque dolls, the range of quality is extensive. Common china dolls are neither highly desired nor highly priced but the early, the rare and the unusual examples have always been elusive and expensive. In the process of glazing much sharpness of detail can be lost, so one searches not only for unusual hair styles and fine modeling and painting but a delicacy in the application of glaze which will not obscure comb marks or subtle planes of the features.

China dolls overlap the papier-mâchés of the 1840s and the bisques of the 1860s forming a bridge between these two other types...wax and wax-over papier-mâché dolls were also made in this period but were quite different in style and, in the early models, did not have modeled hair. As with papier-mâché and bisque dolls, fashions in hair styles are well reflected in the heads with molded hair. From the 1840s to the 1880s we can trace the changes in hair arrangements and also, to some extent, the changes in taste of the ideal in feminine beauty. Some of the same molds were used in all of these materials.

The western world finally discovered the ingredients for porcelain making in 1707 (or 1708, depending on which encyclopedia

Illustration 3. 11½in (29.2cm) china with peg-jointed wood body, china arms and legs, painted brown eyes and black hair looped in front of exposed ears with long ringlets in back; dress of sheer printed wool and silk fabric and straw hat with tiny flowers.

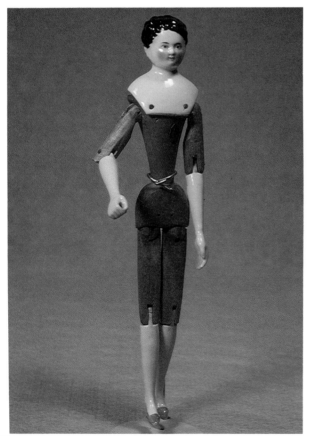

you read) and for most of the 18th century objects of porcelain were a luxury of high artistic merit and a valuable medium of exchange. Mechanical developments of the industrial revolution reduced both the quality and the value, but at last made this material available and economical for doll making. A number of porcelain factories began producing heads in the 1840s and by the 1860s and 1870s heads were made in quantity and in a variety of styles — to be purchased on commercial bodies with china arms and legs, or with leather arms and cloth bodies, or as a head only with the body and clothing made by loving hands at home. This, of course, put the china doll within the reach of more children and added greatly to the individuality and charm of the dolls.

By the end of the 19th century bisque dolls were in favor and were to be found in a wide range of price, but the china doll never completely disappeared. Indeed, the collectors of the 1940s and 1950s preferred chinas and fickle fashion will no doubt swing their way again. Toward this end, a few examples are presented with attention to chronology...and these are just a few of the many different heads yet to be discovered and enjoyed.

Illustration 5. 16½in (41.9cm) early china with stylized ringlets, white line between lips. oval nostrils, ringed and highlighted eyes; marked in old script "Fi" under shoulder; old cloth body with fine early china arms and legs.

Illustration 4. 11½in (29.2cm) china man similar to the doll seen in *Illustration 3,* showing body construction.

Illustration 6. 18½in (47cm) china with molded hair waved and winged back into braided chignon, old cloth body with china arms; contemporary dress of printed cotton with apron.

Illustration 7. Close-up of profile of the doll seen in *Illustration 6.*

Illustration 8. China dolls with variations of the braided chignon at the back of the head, the hair style of the doll on the right, 13½in (34.3cm), being at least a decade earlier than that on the left, 12in (30.5cm). The doll on the right has a molded bosom and is on a cloth body with wood arms and legs.

Illustration 9. Another view of the china dolls seen in *Illustration 8.*

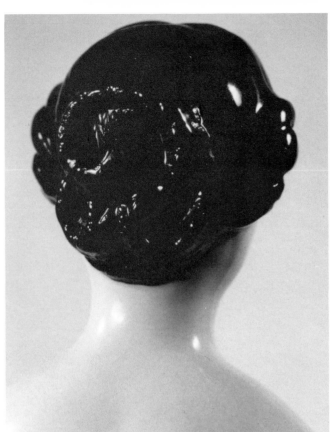

Illustration 10. 19in (48.3cm) china showing another variation of braided chignon with curls and brush-stroked hair at sides of the face, an exceptionally finely modeled head and deep shoulders; on a cloth body with china arms and legs.

Illustration 11. Back view of the doll shown in *Illustration 10*.

Illustration 12. On the left: 13½in (34.3cm) variation of that shown in *Illustration 10* with brush-stroked hair over covered ears and curls below the braided knot at back; dressed in a very fine old cotton print. On the right: 13½in (34.3cm) china lady with front hair rolled over a band and puffed over the ears before forming a coiled braided chignon at the back; lovely old dress of iridescent silk taffeta with black velvet trim.

Illustration 13. Back view of the dolls seen in *Illustration 12*.

18

Illustration 14. 7½in (19.1cm) small china with china arms and legs; original wool skating costume with matching bloomers, velvet hat and muff in setting with Currier & Ives "Skating by Moonlight" print.

Illustration 15. 16½in (41.9cm) glass-eyed china with blue glass eyes, open circle painting of the nostrils, white line between lips, very delicately painted eyelashes, exposed ears, plentiful comb marks in hair waved back from a center part to several layers of loose curls at the back; on an old cloth body with china arms.

Illustration 16. Two 31in (78.7cm) large chinas with similar mold. Doll on left with brown glass eyes and doll on right with painted brown eyes and fine deep modeling of features.

Part II

As mentioned in the first part of this article, by the second half of the 18th century china dolls were being made in a wide range of styles with the "fancy" heads displaying intricate and detailed hair arrangements, and sometimes gilding and floral decorations similar to the bisque heads with molded hair. Heads were also made without molded hair to accommodate wigs either pasted on a smooth crown or inserted in a slit in the top forming a center part. Although these wigged chinas were soon supplanted by the wigged bisque ladies they were elegant in their own right, the wig at times being handwoven with a naturalistic part, and on more than one occasion this type of doll was chosen as a Sanitary Fair treasure — as the lovely example at the Brooklyn Museum shown on the cover of *The Collector's Book of Dolls' Clothes* by the Colemans. China dolls certainly are to be cherished!

Illustration 17. 20½in (52.1cm) lovely lady with brush-stroked hair at the temples rolled to a braided chignon at the back and possessing patrician features and a partially modeled bosom.

Illustration 18. Doll on right: 17½in (44.5cm) showing a variation of the hair style seen in *Illustration 17;* dressed in a lovely silk taffeta with velvet trim by the late Estelle Winthrop of Dedham, Massachusetts. Doll on left: 15¾in (40.1cm) lady with molded snood touched with gold lustre and trimmed with gold band and bows; dressed in a similar silk.

Illustration 19. 15¼in (38.8cm) blonde china with painted black snood trimmed with a rose band and bows touched with gold lustre.

Illustration 20. 15¼in (38.8cm) china variation of the so-called Empress Eugenie mold showing high modeling of the black snood trimmed with a rolled rose-colored and fringe-ended scarf and a white feather plume touched with blue; the blonde hair is nicely shaded in from the hairline.

Illustration 21. Back view of the variation shown in *Illustration 20.*

Illustration 22. 21in (53.3cm) longer and slimmer-faced lady with black hair and molded snood with a bow over each ear and a band or comb across the back.

Illustration 23. 22½in (57.2cm) wigged china with brown painted eyes, deep flesh tinting and beautiful natural modeling of the neck and deep sloping shoulders and partial bosom on an old cloth body with china arms and legs; original dress of flecked lavender wool and silk weave with tie-on organdy sleeves.

Illustration 24. Pair of wigged chinas, so-called Biedermeiers. Doll on right: 15¾in (40.1cm) china with a fine long neck and partially modeled bosom, as well as a slimmer face; her dark brown human hair frizzed with snood at back and two long ringlets. Doll on left: 9in (22.9cm) small wigged china also with china arms and legs.

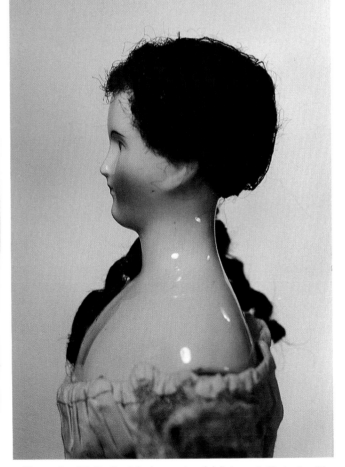

Illustration 25. Profile of the larger wigged doll shown in *Illustration 24.*

Illustration 26. 16¾in (42.6cm) china lady with a hair style of the mid 1860s waved and drawn back into a looped waterfall with exposed ears and brush-stroked temples, with a very long neck, old cloth body and arms of the Kintzbach patent with china hands. This lady is part of an interesting group of delicately modeled heads with small features, long necks and hair styles of about 1866 to 1868. Two other variations are shown in the Borger book on pages 118 and 119.

Illustration 27. Another view of the doll shown in *Illustration 26*.

Illustration 28. 18in (45.7cm) variation with blonde hair of these china ladies of the mid 1860s, the hair waved and drawn back from a center part into multiple puffs at the back topped with a small braid in coronet fashion and two long ringlets falling on either side of the neck; the ears are pierced and have old gilt earrings; the body is an old cloth one with white kid arms.

Illustration 29. Close-up of the head in profile of the doll seen in *Illustration 28* showing the modeling of the pale blonde hair.

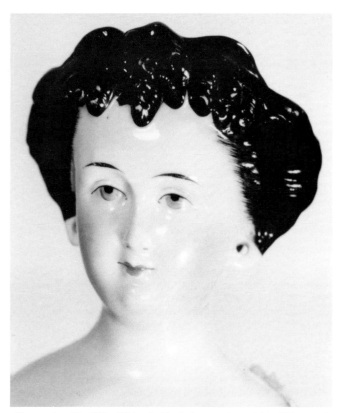

Illustration 30. 19¼in (49cm) gentleman china with molded side-parted curls and brush strokes at the temples, on an old cloth body with leather arms; dressed handsomely in a finely made old suit of tails, brocade vest and detailed shirt.

Illustration 31. 20½in (52.1cm) china lady sometimes dubbed "Dagmar" and also found in parian with clustered curls on the forehead and a band over which the brush-stroked sides are puffed and drawn into another large cluster of curls at the back held by a curved band or comb; the very large earlobes are pierced.

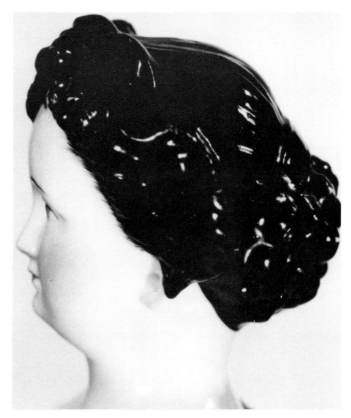

Illustration 32. Another view of the china shown in *Illustration 31.*

Illustration 33. 8in (20.3cm) very large and well-modeled china head with pronounced upper and lower eyelids, indented and oval-painted nostrils, brush-stroked hair rolled at the sides into four arranged puffs at the back held by a large curved comb with five raised beads. The china is thick and white and, as on page 116 of the Borger book, the left ear is partially exposed.

Dresser Dolls

by **Frieda Marion**

A dresser doll is a china figure for the dressing table, made to be both decorative and useful. In general, it is a container with the torso of a feminine figure composing the lid, and a voluminous skirt upon which the torso fits, actually being the section used as a box. There are endless variations on this theme, but basically a dresser doll may be defined as an ornamental china figure ingeniously designed to serve as a useful household article.

"Dresser dolls" is a legitimate term for these items because at least one manufacturer actually so marked his products. Thus, we may use it with impunity.

Of course, there is nothing unique about making pots and utensils in human form. In his book, *Dolls and Puppets*, Max von Boehn says that authorities assume that old Egyptian figures are among the earliest examples of utensils in human shape, and he states that in all parts of the world and in all cultures this has been done with diverse success. Von Boehn names ancient Greece, Africa, Peru, New Guinea and Mexico as areas where such crafts were distinctive, and, indeed, he devotes quite a bit of space telling us of the many materials other than clay which were used to produce all these varied items.

However, early flasks, pots, candlesticks and flagons are not our concern here. The dresser dolls of which we write are those charming, relatively inexpensive objects so popular during the last part of the 19th century and the first quarter of the 20th.

Most of the dresser dolls we collect today are in the shape of pretty ladies, although children were also popular subjects for the artist who modeled them. Of course, they were not made to be played with, but many of the dolls collected today were not really playthings, either. Creche figures, piano babies, artists' mannequins, fortune-telling dolls and half-figures are among other doll related items which were not actually playthings yet are included in many doll collections. Certainly they fascinated children and adults alike! Since dresser dolls had many uses, they can still be put to work if we so choose.

It was the development of hard paste porcelain and subsequent mass production of china ware which led to the proliferation of such articles as dresser dolls. As soon as purely ornamental figures could be priced within the range of the average householder, they found a ready market, but if a box, pin dish, perfume bottle or lamp base could be both ornamental *and* useful, it had infinitely more appeal to the thrifty working person than a purely decorative piece that simply sat on a shelf and was a constant reproach to extravagance.

By the first part of this century, the output of useful china items fashioned in human shape reached such dizzying proportions as to captivate today's most ardent collector.

While most of these dresser dolls were designed to be boxes for talcum powder or trinkets, there were jewelry boxes, shallow face powder dishes, pin trays and perfume and cologne bottles designed to portray persons. Figural lamps for the dressing table are also called dresser dolls, and porcelain half-figures sewn onto pincushions are near relatives.

As might be expected, most of these fancy china ladies were made in Germany and we are familiar with many of the manufacturers.

W. Goebel Porzellanfabrik, Oeslau, West Germany, producers of the famed Hummel figurines, made many delightful china powder boxes and other useful figurals. Ernst Bohne Söhne, Rudolstadt; Karl Schneider's Erben, Gräfenthal; Alfred Voigt, Sitzendorph; and Gebrüder Heubach, Wallendorf, all manufactured these novelties.

Unfortunately, we do not yet know the name of the factory that labeled a truly illustrious output of decorative china powder boxes, lamps, inkwells and the like with one or more of the following: "Erphila, E & R, Nancy Pert, Madame Pompadour, Ink Girls, Germany" and the indisputable phrase, "Dresser Dolls." A formidable collection of these "E & R" or "Erphila" pieces could be gathered if one wished to concentrate on a single manufacturer, and as these pieces are attractive and well made, such a collection would probably be worth considering as a modest investment.

A more diversified group would include those dresser dolls made in England and France and the many produced in Bavaria.

Japan contributed to this field, and often products from this country are difficult to distinguish from their European-made rivals. This is especially true in the case of the figural dresser or boudoir lamps. Those marked "Occupied Japan" are the most desired today, but a well-modeled, nicely decorated dresser doll of any make is a pleasure to own.

Perhaps their original purpose is still one of their greatest appeals, for while these pretty, colorful, amusing or beautiful ladies are highly ornamental, a dresser doll is still a very useful item to have around the house. □

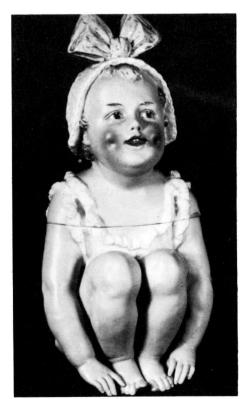

Illustration 1. An 8¼in (21cm) bisque powder box with the mark of the Heubach brothers incised on the lower back. A similar model was made by the same company as a Piano Baby. *Mary Griffith Collection. Photograph by Norma Werner.*

Illustration 2. A charming young lady playing a lute, this 5½in (14cm) porcelain powder box is incised: "Germany//3389." *Joyce Mineart Collection. Photograph by Norma Werner.*

Illustration 3. The classic design of an early 20th century powder box was that of a pretty young lady costumed in a fancy bodice and voluminous skirt. The skirt was essential to hold talcum powder or trinkets, while the lady's torso constituted the container's lid. The resulting variations of this motif, with added flowers, fans, wide-brimmed hats and other accessories, created a collector's paradise. *Eleanor Lar Rieu Collection.*

Illustration 4. An 8in (20.3cm) powder box marked: "Madame Pompadour//Dresser Dolls//E & R//Germany." *Norma Werner Collection. Photograph by Norma Werner.*

Illustration 6. This little dresser doll is not a complete figure; the china head is attached to a swansdown puff sitting in a powder box which forms the lady's shoulders. *Ruth Joyce Collection.*

Illustration 5. Matching 5in (12.7cm) high powder boxes marked: "Madame Pompadour// Dresser Dolls//Erphila//Germany." This classic style design has been found in several color schemes (blue, pink, yellow or green predominating) and, modeled in greater detail, 7½in (19.1cm). *Charlotte Bill Collection. Photograph by Gene Tuck.*

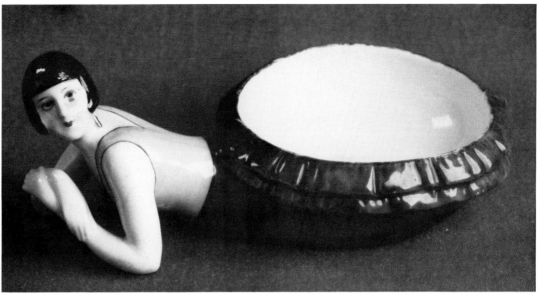

Illustration 7. What is missing here are porcelain legs fastened to a down puff which should rest in the shallow dish formed by the lady's ruffled skirt. On some similar models we find a china lid with modeled ruffles and legs making the cover, and a flat puff hidden inside the shallow powder box. *Charlotte Bill Collection. Photograph by Gene Tuck.*

Illustration 8. A striking dresser doll wearing a ruffled frock with a maroon skirt and black bodice set off by gleaming white bertha collar and white ruffled cuffs. Her short cut white hair is defined with black lines. Marked: "Roby//Paris" and also "MB" within a circle, with the added words "Boulogne//Seine//France." *Norma Werner Collection. Photograph by Norma Werner.*

Illustration 9. Purchased in New Zealand in 1975, this 4¾in (12.2cm) trinket box bears the mark of Alfred Voigt, Sitzendorf. An intrepid traveler in spite of her fancy dress! Its mark is shown in upper left-hand corner. *Photograph by Christopher Fraser.*

Illustration 11. Lid of a china powder box using the popular Spanish dancer motif of the 1920s. *Norma Werner Collection. Photograph by Norma Werner.*

Illustration 10. A charming 6½in (16.5cm) trinket box in a design that was rendered in a variety of colors. Unmarked. *Charlotte Bill Collection. Photograph by Gene Tuck.*

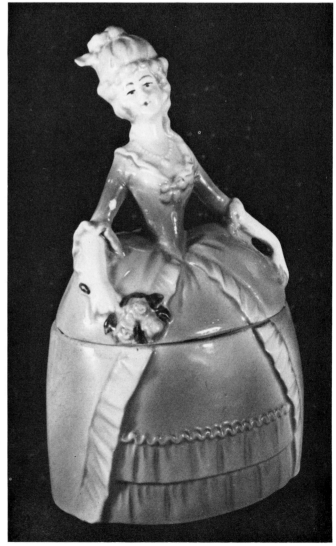

Illustration 12. A 6in (15.2cm) trinket box stamped "Madame Pompadour//Dresser Dolls//ERPHILA//Germany." *Norma Werner Collection. Courtesy of Dresser Dolls and Other China Figurals, Marion & Werner. Photograph by Norma Werner.*

30

The Palmer Cox Brownies

We, the Brownie Jury, do unanimously find:

That this book is the property of

Joe Binford

Bainbridge Ga

and that it was presented by

Mama

Illustration 1. Presentation page of the antique copy of Cox's *Another Brownie Book*.

by ANN BAHAR

Palmer Cox, the creator of the Brownies, was like most of us - - a product of the times in which he lived. As in our own jet powered age, the late Victorian's world was dominated by factory smog, increasing violence, unsightly industrial expansion and a confirmed faith in the practical. Like ourselves, our ancestors turned to escape literature to relieve the pressure of their high tension universe. Cox was the creator of a remarkably successful series of such books, intended originally for the nursery crowd but with tremendous appeal to the young at heart of all ages. Palmer Cox's Brownies investigate every 19th century invention, from the bicycle to the automobile, and their author's magic verses and pen drawings transform each gritty industrial manifestation into a refreshing, clean and astonishingly believable adventure.

The Brownie books, with their bustling crowds of impish illustrations, began quietly with an illustrated poem, "The Brownie's Ride," which was published in *St. Nicholas Magazine* in February 1883. The Brownies, having arrived, soon took the nation by storm. Indeed, by the time Cox died 40 years after their *St. Nicholas* debut, nearly every nursery in England and the United States had been touched by the Brownies. As a result of the books' popularity, the toy industry produced Brownie ninepins, rubber stamp sets, jigsaw puzzles and blocks. There were Brownie dolls galore, made of every conceivable material from paper to china, painted wood and cloth. The Arnold Print Works of Adams, Massachusetts, produced a very popular series of Brownie dolls

to cut, stitch and stuff from pre-printed cloth. An enquiry to the firm's present offices elicited the intriguing statement that Arnold Print Works believes "that the Japanese did this printing and it could be found in the Cape Cod gift shop area several years ago but since that time, [we] have not had any knowledge of the availablility." For interested readers and collectors, a number of these Arnold Print Work dolls, both made up and on the original printed cloth, are in the Margaret Woodbury Strong Museum collection.

German toy manufacturers leaped onto the Brownie bandwagon, and a German "nodder" doll styled along Brownie lines and produced between 1900 to 1910 is on display at the Perelman Antique Toy Museum in Philadelphia along with wooden American ones. In addition to dolls, nursery dishes, spoons, forks and potty chairs bore the Brownie motif. There was even a silver souvenir spoon sold at the 1893 Chicago World's Fair which had a Brownie etched in its bowl.

The American advertising industry seized the opportunity for profit which the Brownies offered. It was the age before "slick ads" and advertisements still displayed the naive charm of genuine folk art. Kodak produced its famous Brownie camera,

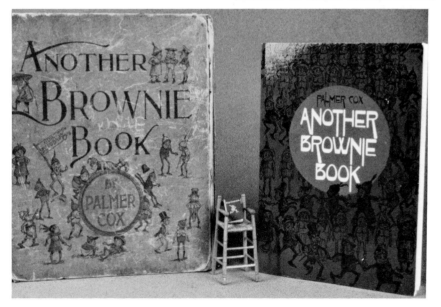

Illustration 2. Three generations of Brownie books: an antique original, a Dover reprint of the same volume and a tiny miniature book by Barbara J. Raheb, *The Brownies*, in size as well as vintage, a "newest addition!" Dover book reproduced courtesy of Dover Publications. Miniature book from *Barbara J. Raheb Collection*.

and Palmer Cox was commissioned to design the advertisements. An historical information specialist at the Eastman Kodak Company informed me that "there has been speculation that the Brownie camera got its name because it was manufactured by Frank Brownell and his camera works staff. It's also possible that the name was chosen with a bow to Palmer Cox." In either event, it is Cox's Brownies who clamber over Kodak's camera and romp through the advertisements, one of which is reproduced here. Cox also wrote delightfully illustrated doggerel verse to advertise Ivory Soap and designed manufacturer's premiums for Lion's Coffee. These were delightful Brownie paper dolls, the old-fashioned kind with interchangeable heads! All of the original books, dolls, toys and advertising material are now fascinating collectibles, rare but not impossible to find and relatively reasonably priced when available.

Palmer Cox (1840 to 1924) was born in Granby, Quebec, Canada. The community had a strong Scottish flavor, and Cox was reared to the accompaniment of endless tales of the wee folk of the Scottish hills and

Illustration 4. An uncut sheet of cloth Brownie dolls manufactured by the Arnold Print Works in 1892. *Margaret Woodbury Strong Museum Collection,* Rochester, New York. Reproduced courtesy of Crown Publishers, Inc., from *The Encyclopedia of Toys* by Constance King.

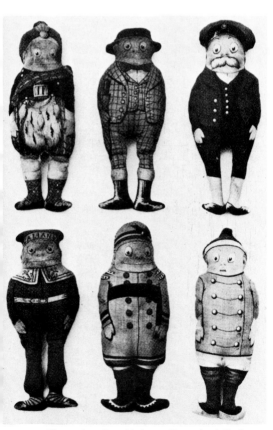

Illustration 3. Made-up Brownie dolls from the preprinted cloth by Arnold Print Works, 1892. *Margaret Woodbury Strong Museum Collection,* Rochester, New York. Reproduced courtesy of Crown Publishers, Inc., from *The Encyclopedia of Toys* by Constance King.

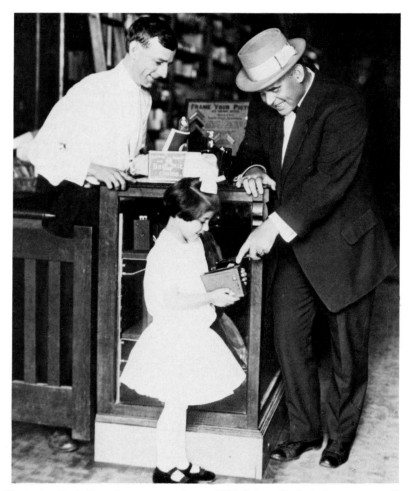

Illustration 5. A Brownie camera purchaser, 1900. Palmer Cox's design appears on the Brownie advertisement visible on the shop counter. *Eastman Kodak Company.*

32

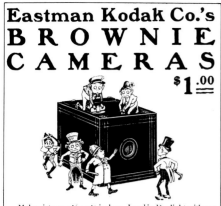
Illustration 6. Brownie camera ad, 1900. Cox was commissioned to design these advertisements, with delightful results! *Eastman Kodak Company.*

glens. The Scottish Brownies and their place in folk history were indelibly imprinted on his memory and he never forgot them. In young manhood Cox worked as a carpenter, builder of railway cars and a writer and traveled from Quebec, Canada, to San Francisco, California. However, it was as a creator of children's verse accompanied by delicious illustrations that he won fame. He developed this art form in middle life after returning to the East Coast to settle in New York City. It was there that "The Brownies' Ride" was published by Mary Mapes Dodge in *St. Nicholas* in 1883. The Brownies' success was meteoric. Success brought prosperity to Cox, a welcome change after nearly a quarter of a century of Bohemian artist poverty.

Aside from frequent appearances in *St. Nicholas* during the ensuing 30 years, Brownie poems with accompanying pen drawings appeared in other magazines. These include the *Ladies' Home Journal* which ran a fascinating series in 1893, eventually published in book form as *The Brownies Round The World.* For this series Cox wrote a short preface entitled "The Origin of the Brownies." This is a curiously-personal statement which stresses the antiquity, innate goodness and purity of soul of the traditional Scottish Brownies. He concludes with a poignant statement which endears Palmer Cox to us as much as it endears his mischievous elves. Writing of the Brownies in history, Cox states, "It is indeed

refreshing to learn that at a time when . . . every man's hand seemed to be against his brother, . . . the 'Brownies' through rain and shine were found at their post every night, aiding the distressed, picking up the work that weary hands let fall, and in many ways winning the love and respect of the people." (*Ladies' Home Journal,* November 1892, p. 8)

Late in life, Palmer Cox designed a residence for himself in his home town of Granby, Quebec, and his brother, William, built it for him. Cox named his house "The Brownie Castle," and his studio was at the top of a huge octagonal tower which dominated the structure. The adjacent barn was topped by a weathervane in the form of a Brownie in silhouette, running with outstretched arms. Curious indeed must have been the "Brownie window" which Cox had constructed along the main staircase inside his castle. One wonders in-

evitably whether Palmer Cox perhaps came to half accept the reality of the beings his pen had created. It is not beyond belief that this was so. Highly-gifted, imaginative authors have been known to fall under the spell of their own creations. The last reported words of L. Frank Baum, creator of the Oz books, "Now we can cross the shifting sands,"[*] implied that death would release him to cross the deadly desert separating reality from his fairyland. The same phenomenon appears in the case of Howard R. Garis, author of the Uncle Wiggly stories which have thrilled children for half a century. In a delightful biographical reminiscence, *My Father Was Uncle Wiggly* (McGraw-Hill, New York, 1966), Roger Garis describes the curious

[*]Cf. F. J. Baum and R. P. MacFall, *To Please a Child, A Biography of L. Frank Baum* (Reilly and Lee Co., Chicago, 1961), p. 275.

Illustration 7. Part of a set of paper doll premiums Cox designed for Lion's Coffee. Each stood 5in (12.7cm) to 6in (15.2cm) high and the possibilities for fun were infinite as the heads were interchangeable! Reproduced courtesy of Rizzoli from *Antique Toys and Dolls* by Constance King.

trust in Uncle Wiggly's protective kindness which pervaded his father's last years. That Palmer Cox, too, believed in his Brownies may explain the grip the Brownies held on the American imagination for half a century, both in the nursery and in the advertising world. To use a popular 19th century word, the Brownies were "sincere." The public sensed this and took Cox as well as his creations into its heart.

Only a shadow remains today of the Brownie world which Palmer Cox created and which played a major role in American domestic life at the end of the last century and the beginning of our own. I recently found a copy of Cox's second Brownie story, *Another Brownie Book,* published in 1890, in the attic of a Philadelphia antique shop. Although much worn, the dedication, reproduced here, echoes the popularity which the Brownies once enjoyed. The volume itself has been loved and read almost to shreds! Again, in The Attic Museum of Philadelphia's Strawberry Mansion, a historic house open to the public in Fairmount Park, there are several of the original cloth Brownie dolls. These were probably hand stitched from the Arnold Print Works patterns mentioned earlier, but they have been handled so much that they are as brown as their elfin Scottish prototypes. The Strawberry Mansion Brownies are in a large doll house and were clearly intended by the doll house's original owners to be mischievous protectors of the china doll family's official "residence." The whimsical cloth Brownie dolls peek out of attic windows and observe the maid in the dining room. Worn and faded, they still retain a curious charm.

Perhaps the Brownies are undergoing a revival today since the Hobbit and Gnome fantasies of our own decade mesh with the Brownie world of our grandparents. Dover Publications, Inc., began to reissue Palmer Cox's first Brownie books, *The Brownies, Their Book, Another Brownie Book* and *The Brownies At Home* (this last title is unfortunately out of print at the present time) in 1964. Roger W. Cummins, a descendent of Palmer Cox, has written a fascinating biography of his ancestor entitled *Humorous But Wholesome* (Century House, Inc., Watkins Glen, New York, 1973). Brownie toys are also beginning to trickle back into the modern marketplace. Shackman has a cloth nursery ball printed with four of the most familiar of Palmer Cox's Brownies, the "traditional" Brownie, the Indian, the Major Domo and

Uncle Sam. For antique doll and toy collectors, bibliophiles and lovers of all that is charming in history, a revival of interest in Palmer Cox and his Brownies would be a delightful event.

As in the old folk tales that fascinated Cox during his Scottish-Irish childhood on the farm in Granby, Quebec, the Brownies may never have deserted the American scene into

which their author's pen brought them. Instead, they may have been in hiding for decades. If they are indeed ready to reenter the world of American book and toy fantasy, they will be the acknowledged elderly relations of the Gnomes, Munchkins and Hobbits of our own time.

Illustration 8. An illustration which Cox drew for "The Brownies in The Studio," one episode in *Another Brownie Book* published originally in 1890 and reissued in 1966 by Dover Publications, Inc. This episode is particularly charming as the intimate bond between the author and his own creations is poignantly clear. Reproduced courtesy of Dover Publications, Inc.

The features, garments, and the style,
Soon brought to every face a smile.
Some tried a hand at painting there,
And showed their skill was something rare;
While others talked and rummaged through
The desk to find the stories new,

Illustration 9. 2½in (6.4cm) reproduction Brownie dolls from muslin, currently available from B. Shackman & Co.

Illustration 1. An unusual group of *Columbian Dolls,* left to right: a boy, a black doll, a doll painted by a local artist (note that the technique is not as fine as the others which were painted by Emma E. Adams), and one showing the beautiful and artistic work from the brush of Emma and the clothing by Marietta Adams.

Collectible Upstate New York Commercial Cloth Dolls: The Columbian Doll

by Mary Lou Ratcliff

COLUMBIA — QUEEN OF DOLLDOM

Almost every doll collection today contains a good old cloth doll, many times unknown as to origin, no longer in pristine condition, but standing out as a fine example of true Americana.

Few dolls are as charming and personable as these old dolls, which were generally referred to as "rag" and rightly so, for the very early ones were homemade and fashioned from the "rag bag" with whatever materials were available: patches of homespun linen, scraps from grandfather's "Union" suit, grandmother's fancy red silk petticoat, a hank of wool, flax, or cornsilk for the hair, shoe button eyes, embroidered and painted faces. Some were very crude, yet some were very lovely; it all depended on the talent of the artist. Crude as some were and many times lacking the beauty of the "store-bought" dolls, these dolls were made for loving.

In the last decade of the 19th century commercial cloth dolls were beginning to appear. These dolls were printed on sheets of cloth, a front and back, to be cut out like paper dolls, stitched and stuffed, and, when made up, the face and head were usually flat.

A fairly new invention, the sewing machine, was starting to be seen more frequently in the home. This invention, no doubt, would contribute to the success and popularity of commercial cloth dolls.

Though this was an easy and inexpensive way to mass produce dolls, they sometime lacked the imaginative materials and the individual touch previously shown in the homemade product. However, be that as it may, a group of young ladies within 75 miles of Syracuse, New York, were to design and create some of the most collectible and desirable cloth dolls of that era. Interestingly, the time frame was about the same for Ida Gutsell, Charity and Celia Smith of Ithaca, Julia Beecher of Elmira and Emma and Marietta Adams of Oswego Centre. Almost a century later some of these truly prized American cloth dolls are vying with the English waxes, French Jumeaus and the German characters.

Miss Emma E. Adams, born in 1858, of Oswego Centre, New York, was the originator of a much sought-after doll, which never lacked the individual touch. A talented young woman, she was well-known for her oil and crayon portraits. Her lovely and artistic floral paintings were captured on china, canvas and three-panel screens. As part of her early education she studied art at Oswego Normal School and later under private teachers.

Although much credit has been given to Emma, her younger sister, Marietta, was as important in the success of the dolls and would carry on the business in later years. Marietta attended business college in Oswego, and being a venturesome young lady took a secretarial position with a mining company in Chicago, Illinois.

Emma spent the year of 1891 and the first six months of 1892 in Chicago, visiting Marietta. While there a friend encouraged her to make a doll and paint the face, confident that Emma could make a more attractive doll than any previously made. Wishing to please her friend, she began to experiment and in Emma's own words, "In time made a doll which all pronounced a success." The faces of the first dolls were only tinted.

It occurred to Miss Adams that it might be a profitable business and when she took her doll to Marshall Field & Co., some were ordered immediately.

Emma returned home and with the help of her parents, Mr. and Mrs. William Adams, and Marietta, started a doll business. She continued to improve the design of the face with the use of oil paint, and perfect the overall construction of the body.

It was a family-type industry done in the home; however, neighbor ladies were engaged in sewing. An elderly lady, some years ago, recalled attending a party in the Adams' home when she was young. All the girls were given a needle, thread and a piece of material which they were to hem. It was more a test of skill than a game. Because of this young lady's ability, she was offered a job to work on doll clothes. She remembered using the money she earned to buy her own wedding finery.

The well-shaped bodies were made of a firm unbleached muslin. The construction with its darts and seams gave it lifelike flexibility, enabling the doll to sit very gracefully, rather than maintaining the rigid stance usually seen in the cloth doll.

The face was an off-white sateen with three small darts at the chin, the top of this material was fully gathered forming a rounded shape for the crown of the head and was attached to a piece of muslin with a seam down the back.

The successful method of stuffing the dolls was due to Mr. Adams' ingenious development of flexible wooden sticks made of spokes from his carriage shop. The sticks were designed in several shapes and sizes for various steps in the stuffing process. A fairly loose filling of fine excelsior was used, then cotton was introduced between the cloth and excelsior to give a smooth surface to form the natural curves of the chin and crown of the head. Sawdust was not used.

The head was stuffed first and ready for the artistic stroke of Miss Emma who hand-painted, in oil, all the faces. She would give the doll a flesh color face with rosy cheeks, eyes of brown or blue, a heart-shaped nose, a rosebud mouth and a hairdo of blonde or brown painted curls and waves. Then a coat of shellac was applied as a protective covering.

The arms and legs were stuffed with cotton only, to allow for the carefully stitched defined fingers and toes. A special sizing of glue and starch was applied and allowed to dry, then the lower portion of the limbs were oil painted with a soft warm pink, protecting them from the future scrubbing they were sure to receive from their young owners.

Light in weight, from 9 ounces to 24 ounces, the sizes varied from 15in (38.1cm) to 29in (73.7cm), Boy, girl and baby dolls were made, as well as a few black dolls.

Marietta was in charge of designing the wardrobe for the dolls. All the clothes were as skillfully and carefully

Illustration 2. Miss Emma E. Adams.

Illustration 3. Marietta Adams Ruttan.

THE COLUMBIAN DOLL.

PRICE LIST:

No.	1,	15 inch	Doll in	Gown, ...	$1.50
"	2,	15 "	" "	Dress, pink or blue Gingham,	2.25
"	2½,	15 "	" "	Baby dress, white, . .	2.50
"	3,	19 "	" "	Gown, ...	1.75
"	4,	19 "	" "	Dress, pink or blue, . .	2.75
"	5,	19 "	" "	Baby dress, white, . .	3.00
"	6,	19 "	" "	Boy's Suit, ...	2.75
"	8,	23 "	" "	Gown, ...	2.00
"	9,	23 "	" "	Dress, pink or blue, . .	3.25
"	10,	23 "	" "	Baby dress, white, . .	4.00
"	11,	29 "	" "	Gown, ...	3.25
"	12,	29 "	" "	Dress, white, . . .	5.00

ORDER BY NUMBER.

SEND ORDERS TO

MISS MARIETTA ADAMS,

OSWEGO CENTER, N. Y.

Illustration 4. An early price list published by Marietta Adams gives a good idea of some of the clothing that was made for the *Columbian Doll.*

made as they would have been for a baby, complete with buttons, buttonholes, trimmings of lace, and featherstitching. Even the royal blue and navy wool trousers for the boy dolls were lined with cambric and equipped with twill cross-over straps to hold them up.

The clothing dictated the price of the doll rather than the size. The footwear is generally missing from the dolls found today, but Mrs. Esther Ruttan Doyle, daughter of Marietta and niece of Emma, has a doll made by her aunt and wearing original, beautifully hand-sewn black kid slippers. The dolls also wore stockings and crocheted booties made by the local ladies, and, according to the fashion of the day, were never without their bonnets or hats.

In 1893, the doll gained admittance to the Columbian Exposition of the Chicago World's Fair. About 100 dolls were sold and at this time Emma named the doll *Columbian.* To the Adams' sisters delight, on June 1, 1894, a Diploma of Honorable Mention was awarded to Emma by the Columbian Commission.

The dolls were not patented. At this period of time, they were simply rubber-stamped with ink on the back of the lower torso, in the following manner:

"Columbian Doll//Emma E. Adams// Oswego Centre,//N.Y."

Wanamakers and other well-known department stores retailed the dolls; however, Marshall Field & Co. and Women's Exchanges throughout the country accounted for the majority of orders. Thorough in business affairs, Marietta did much of the corresponding; she was responsible for logging orders and shipments in a ledger which is still legible enough to be counted almost 100 years later.

The doll attracted the attention of a wealthy Boston, Massachusetts, doll collector, Mrs. E. R. Horton, and was destined to become a member of a great family of international dolls which Mrs. Horton exhibited to raise funds to benefit various charities, especially those devoted to aiding sick and needy children.

In December 1899, Emma put the last loving touches of rose color on one of her doll's cheeks, Marietta buttoned up her commonsense tan shoes, dressed her in a checked gingham dress, a brown covert traveling cloak, and tied her bonnet under her chin, no doubt with a hug and kiss sent her on her way. "Columbia" had a mission and arrived in Boston on New Year's Day in 1900 as a gift to Mrs. Horton.

In April, "Columbia" started her mission. Passport in hand, she would travel around the world, stopping wherever she might be invited to raise funds for the benefit of children. She traveled in a splendid telescope trunk donated by a leading trunk manu-

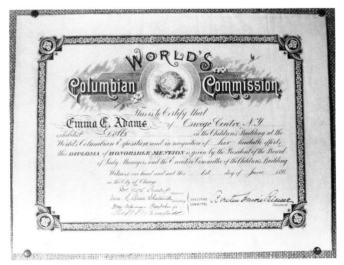

Illustration 5. Diploma of Honorable Mention awarded to Emma E. Adams by the Columbian Exposition. *Courtesy of Oswego County Historical Society, Oswego, New York.*

Illustration 6. A body of a *Columbian Doll* showing the stamp of Emma E. Adams.

THE COLUMBIAN DOLL
MANUFACTURED BY
MARIETTA ADAMS RUTTAN
OSWEGO, N. Y.

Illustration 7. A copy from the original rubber stamp that was used by Marietta Adams Ruttan on the *Columbian Doll* after 1906.

facturer. The Adams Express Company was in charge of her travels, the expressmen of America extended free carriage, the agents took excellent care of her. Pinned on her traveling cloak was a card which read:

> "I am taking a long journey through the kindness and courtesy of the express companies of America. I hope to go around the world, and if possible, help to aid children's charities."

Boston newspapers gave her a good send off. Across the land, through the mountains and over the plains, "Columbia" traveled, stopping in major cities, where the press gave glowing accounts of her arrival and activities.

In Denver, Colorado, she was warmly received and was probably the first doll to be given a reception on Sunday by a Sunday School of nearly 800 members, the largest in Colorado. There she took up a collection for the suffering children of India. "Miss Columbia" was taken to the top of

Illustration 8. A *Columbian Doll* by Emma E. Adams.

Illustration 9. A dream come true — a room of *Columbian Dolls*. At least 100 dolls ready for shipment by the Adams sisters.

Pike's Peak, over the famous loop of Georgetown and then to the Ute Indian Reservation, where she was hospitably and curiously entertained by famous Chiefs Buckskin Charley, Severra and Ignacio; a ceremonial dance was also given in her honor.

The *San Diego* (California) *Union,* dated July 22, 1900, reported among the notables arriving at Hotel del Coronado were "Miss Columbia" and "Uncle Sam" who had joined her in Los Angles, California. The two dolls were to be guests at a reception by Women's and Children's Home in San Diego with the proceeds to be turned over the Home. There was some talk "Uncle Sam" would accompany "Columbia" on her trip around the world, however, his presence might take on a political air. This was not the mission of "Columbia," she would travel alone and unchaperoned. He would return to Boston back to the

International Doll Collection.

For a year "Columbia" traveled up and down the Pacific Coast from Mexico to Alaska visiting children's homes and hospitals.

With a small American flag in her hand and a patriotic sash of red, white, and blue, she bade farewell to her native land on July 23, 1901. Since there were no express companies beyond the sea, she sailed on the United State Transport,"Thomas," as a guest of her real "Uncle Sam." According to a press release at this time she traveled with 600 teachers the United States sent to the Philippine Islands. On "Columbia's" arrival she was greeted by the newly appointed Civil Governor, William Howard Taft, who later became President of the United States. She became a charge of one of the teachers and had an extended stay of a year in the Islands.

She traveled to Hong Kong, Canton

and was a favorite in Singapore. One remarkable card attached to her cloak was inscribed: "If J. Pierpont Morgan does not permit you to walk the earth, please walk into Raffle's Hotel, Singapore, where the proprietor will be pleased to see you," On the other side of the card is printed, "Please permit the bearer to walk about the earth," signed J. Pierpont Morgan. She was particularly invited to an impromptu dance at Raffle's held by the women and officers of the United States Transport "Mc Clellan." This Transport was to take "Columbia" to many foreign ports and eventually bring her home.

In October 1902, she was taken on board the United States Transport "Mc Clellan" as guest of Capt. W. E. Nye and came by the way of Ceylon, the Mediterranean and Suez to New York.

The globe circling doll arrived "bag and baggage" in Boston on Christmas morning 1902 after almost three years of traveling.

One could readily fill a good size volume with the experiences set down in "Columbia's" diary and scrapbook filled with autographs and pictures which traveled with her. At one of the schools where she was exhibited, when told her name, a little boy asked if she was the wife of Columbus. The Collector of Customs at Zamboanga certified "Columbia" had complied with customs regulations at that port and he found nothing to indicate any intention on her part to defraud the government; however, one word of advice was given. Should she ever make another trip to these islands she carry more suitable clothing adding, "It doesn't snow here very often."

Perhaps most interesting of all are the souvenirs given to her. A Moqui papoose presented her with his picture and a cottonwood doll, a Pueblo Indian made her a gourd rattle which the medicine man gave her for protection on her journey. In Palestine she was presented with an elaborately embroidered costume. Children everywhere bestowed curious and childish treasures as tokens of their love.

"Columbia" and her souvenirs are part of the doll collection at Wenham Historical Association and Museum, Inc. at Wenham, Massachusetts.

While "Columbia" was busily making others happy, she was unaware that Miss Emma had suddenly died at the age of 42, July 26, 1900. Marietta continued to operate the doll business

Illustration 11. A rare black *Columbian Doll* with original clothing, a nice blue flannel wool sacque with featherstitching.

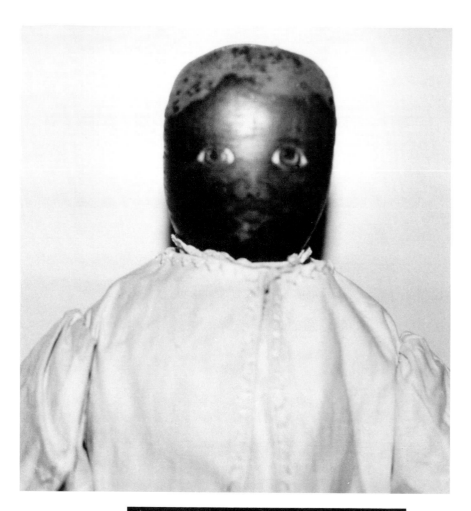

she and her sister had established. She published an interesting advertising circular with information about the dolls, along with testimonials from ladies of the press who visited the home where the dolls were made.

Commercial artists were employed to paint the faces of the dolls; however, nice as they were, the artists never acquired the distinctive touch that Emma had achieved.

In 1906 at the age of 36, Marietta married William Ruttan.

The manufacture of dolls continued and were now stamped: "Manufactured by//Marietta Adams Ruttan."

The most prolific years were 1900 to 1910. After 1910, Marietta was busy raising a family; however, the ledger shows 412 dolls were shipped to Marshall Field & Co. in 1911. The business was carried on successfully on a smaller scale for a number of years until a fever epidemic broke out with the children and operations were stopped for sometime. A few dolls were made as late as 1923 and 1924.

Much of this history would have never been recorded had it not been for Marietta's daughter, Esther Ruttan Doyle. Fortunately Esther became interested in the early history of the *Columbian Doll* and was able to document firsthand information from her mother. We are gratefully indebted to her.

In 1942, Mrs. Doyle arranged a special reception in Oswego Centre for "Miss Columbia" to be the guest of honor. From the Wenham Museum she returned back to her birthplace. She was reunited with open arms by Marietta who had so lovingly prepared her for her journey around the world. Marietta never had a chance to visit Uncle Sam and the other two *Columbian Dolls* which were a part of the Horton International Doll Collection at the Wenham Museum. She died May 15, 1944.

The press acclaimed the *Columbian Dolls* as "Queens of Dolldom," likewise, the title "Queens of doll makers" should go to Emma and Marietta, their creators. Certainly everything about these dolls were synonymous with the name "ADAMS," truly American. □

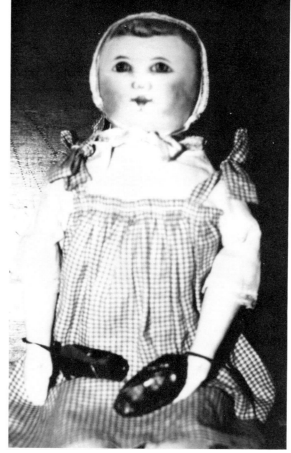

Illustration 12. *Columbian Doll* in pristine condition. Note the black kid slippers. This doll was painted by Emma, the clothing was made by Marietta and the doll was given to Marietta's daughter.

Editor's Note: All photographs are courtesy of Esther Ruttan Doyle, the daughter of Marietta Adams Ruttan.

MARTHA JENKS CHASE

Turn of the Century
American Doll Manufacturer

by **Margaret Whitton,** Curator of Dolls, Margaret Woodbury Strong Museum

Illustrations courtesy the **Strong Museum**

Doll with a patented snap bow on her head; 16in (40.6cm) tall.

During the 1890s and into 1900, American doll manufacturers still could not compete in a profitable way with the European market. The most popular dolls had, for years, been dolls manufactured in Germany and France. These were bisque head dolls with composition jointed bodies strung together with elastic. For some reason the American manufacturers were not able to perfect bisque heads, the quality was poor and the cost high.

American doll designers such as Rose O'Neill and Grace Storey Putnam, worked under contract for doll distributors in the United States and these same distributors had the dolls made and sometimes assembled in European factories, the bisque heads in particular. The distributors established offices in Germany and France.

During this period doll manufacturers in the United States were concentrating on new ideas that would stem this flow of imports from Europe. Emphasis was placed on dolls made of composition that were advertised as unbreakable and dolls made of cloth. The European bisque head dolls were, of course, breakable and this made them dangerous and costly to replace. They also were sometimes quite heavy and difficult for small hands to hold. The idea of a soft, cuddly doll and one that was unbreakable appealed to both mothers and children. They gained quick acceptance as the years went by. Our story of Martha Chase begins during this period of time.

Martha Chase was born in Pawtucket, Rhode Island, in 1851. Her father, Dr. James R. Wheaton, was a well-known physician in Rhode Island and, as was the custom in those days, had young doctors training under him in his office. One of his students was Julian A. Chase, a graduate of Harvard Medical School. In 1873, Dr. Chase and Martha were married. They had seven children, three of whom were girls.

Mrs. Chase was not happy with the bisque head dolls that her girls had to play with, feeling that a soft cuddly doll would be more appealing to them. In her imagination she pictured a doll that would be easy to handle and possibly washable. She designed such

Martha Chase dolls created from a German bisque lady-type head; 15in (38.1cm) tall.

"Mammy Nurse," 27in (68.6cm) tall.

a doll for one of her daughters and it became so popular with her daughter's friends and their mothers that Martha found herself busy making dolls for them. In 1891 she took one of these dolls to Jordan Marsh in Boston to be fitted for shoes. The buyer for the doll department happened to see it and asked her who had made the doll. When Mrs. Chase told him that she had made it herself he wanted to give her an order on the spot. She decided to discuss this proposed project with her family and they agreed that she should try it. The dolls were an immediate success and she set up her doll factory at the rear of her home in Pawtucket. The factory was known to everyone in the town as "The Doll House."

Martha Chase's dolls were promoted by skilled advertising such as brochures that read, "If Stradivarius had made dolls he would have made the Chase Stockinet Doll," and "The Chase Stockinet Doll adheres to the age-old tradition of perfection of design combined with the best materials and fine craftsmanship. It takes its place beside the works of the Christopher Wren, Sheraton and Stradivarius. It is built for all times, not just for the moment." In 1909, Chase dolls were advertised by R. H. Macy & Co. and in 1913 by F.A.O. Schwarz. Advertising for her dolls also appeared at this time in the *Ladies Home Journal* and *Vogue* magazine. The early style of Chase dolls was manufactured during the late 1890s possibly up to 1910. The dolls were made of a stockinet material especially worked out by Mrs. Chase and the manufacturer of the material. The idea for using stockinet probably came from the use of this material as a medical practice for placing it around broken limbs before a plaster cast was applied. Stockinet worked well for the dolls because it was soft, pliable and could be stretched in any direction. The heads, arms and legs were painted and a Princess Sateen covering, similar to a slip-cover, was applied over the bodies. The heads of the dolls were designed with raised features, similar to bisque head dolls, and were formed and hardened by a special secret process.

Martha Chase never revealed the secret of how she made the masks for her dolls and even managed to keep this a secret from the women who worked in her factory. One worker was quoted as having said, "the masks Mrs. Chase made herself and never let any of us know how she did it." This mystery was solved in 1981 when the Margaret Woodbury Strong Museum acquired from members of the Chase family, a revealing collection of dolls and molds they had found in the factory. Evidently Mrs. Chase had purchased bisque heads from Europe and made molds from these heads. She then took her stockinet material, wet it, pressing it into the mold and partially filled the inside of

A doll listed in Chase records as an Indian, showing the original hanging strings still on the shoulders 24in (61cm) tall.

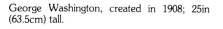

George Washington, created in 1908; 25in (63.5cm) tall.

The original bust used to create the George Washington doll.

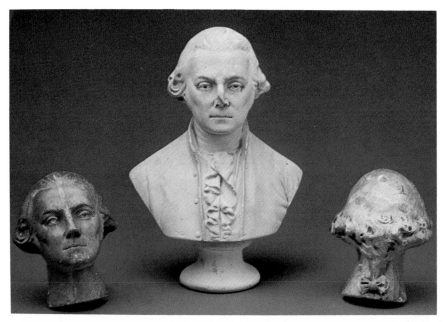

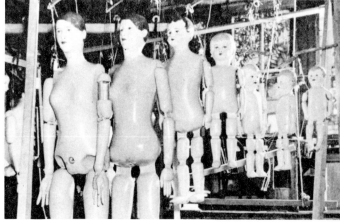

Martha Chase's first factory at the rear of her home on Park Place in Pawtucket, Rhode Island.

the stockinet material with a mixture that appears to be both plaster and glue or possibly papier-mâché. When this hardened, the stockinet was removed from the mold and the mask was formed, complete with raised facial features and a solid underbase, making the face strong and unbreakable. Balls of cotton and excelsior were made on 1/2in (1.3cm) sticks, 8 or 10 inches (20.3 or 25.4cm) long, according to the size of the doll to be made, and the masks were fitted on these balls. The heads were then attached at the neck to the torso of the doll. Separate molded ears and thumbs were applied, and the arms and legs were sewn on. Now the doll was ready for painting and waterproofing.

An early brochure advertising the Chase Stockinet Doll states: "The dolls of this style have bodies that are covered with Princess Sateen. They have a 'finished' appearance that can be secured in no other way." Six sizes were advertised:

#0	12in (30.5cm)	for $3.50
#1	16in (40.6cm)	for $4.50
#2	20in (50.8cm)	for $5.50
#3	24in (61.0cm)	for $7.00
#4	27in (68.6cm)	for $8.00
#5	30in (76.2cm)	for $9.00

Prices for repairing the dolls were listed, and a nice selection of doll clothing for girls, boys and babies were offered. Directions for washing the dolls recommended any mild soap and warm water, then rinsing thoroughly and wiping them dry as quickly as possible.

I would like to mention at this point that Martha Chase also made an 8in (20.3cm) doll that to the best of my knowledge was never advertised by the company. Two of these dolls are in the Strong collection.

In 1905, Martha Chase designed a series of character dolls. These dolls represented the "Alice in Wonderland" characters, including Alice, Tweedle-dee, Tweedle-dum, the Mad-Hatter, the Duchess, the Frog-Footman and the Rabbitt. From a book by Joel Chandler Harris, she made Mammy Nurse and two Pickaninnies. The final group was from Charles Dickens representing Little Nell, Mrs. Gamp and other Dickens characters.

The Alice in Wonderland set seems to be the most difficult to obtain. Martha Chase may have used the heads from figurines to make the molds for this set. The

Late Chase dolls made of molded vinyl plastic 16in (40.6cm) tall.

The German bisque lady-type head used to make the molds and the stockinet mask made from that mold.

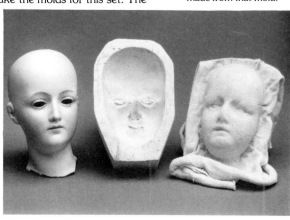

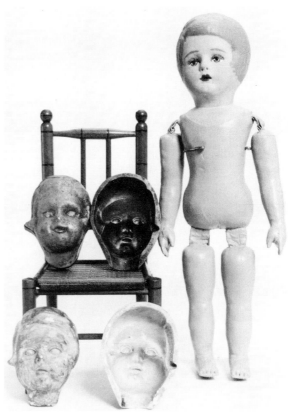

Girl with side part and original molds. The side curl shown on the mold seems to have disappeared in the making; 16in (40.6cm) tall.

Martha Jenks Chase in her studio.

molds are in the Strong collection but unfortunately we do not have the dolls. Hopefully they will be available to the museum at some time.

In 1908, a doll was made to represent George Washington. The doll was made from a bust of President Washington that Mrs. Chase found, and clothing was carefully designed for the completed figure. The doll was constructed in the same manner as her other dolls and stands 25in (63.5cm) high. The original patterns for the clothing of George Washington are in the Strong collection.

No patent has been found issued to Martha Chase, but one of the dolls acquired by the museum and listed as having belonged to her daughter, Anna, had "M J C Stockinet Doll Pat Applied For," stamped on the back of the torso. Evidently she had intended to patent the doll, but for some reason never did.

The Chase dolls were marked with a trademark showing a round baby face with the name "Chase" on top of the head and "Stockinet Doll" written on a band across the forehead. The words "Trade Mark" appeared under the head. Another type of label used was a paper label sewn on the back of the dolls that reads as follows: "The Chase Stockinet Doll made of Stockinet and Cloth, stuffed with cotton, made by hand, painted by hand, made by especially trained workers."

By 1910, the construction of the dolls had changed to some degree. The sateen covering over the torso was discarded and the dolls were painted overall making them completely washable. After the doll parts were assembled, the completed dolls were sized, the hands and feet were dipped in hot glue and shaped a little to look more lifelike, then with a brush, a paste was applied to the head, arms, legs and neck. Loops were attached to the shoulders that would allow the doll to be hung on a rack to dry. Then the paint was applied, as many as four or five coats, and the doll was ready to have the features and hair painted on. The final step seems to have been a waterproof paint that has been referred to in information given by the Chase family as a "complexion paint." This gave the dolls a lifelike appearance and an additional waterproof covering.

In 1911, Martha Chase created an adult figure for the purpose of training nurses. Her close association with the medical profession, a father and a husband who were both doctors, helped to turn her talents toward health care. This adult figure became known all over the world. The idea developed from a request by a nursing instructor at the Hartford Hospital in Hartford, CT.

This figure was over 5 feet (152.5cm) tall, made with a durable stockinet material which was finished with oil paints, making it waterproof. It was jointed so that it could be placed in any position desired. It was used as a substitute for a living model in teaching the handling of patients, positions for examinations, bathing and bandaging.

A later model was manufactured with an internal copper reservoir having two tubes leading into it in the location of the natural passages of a human being. This allowed the giving of instruction in methods of internal care. On this model the left arm and buttocks were fitted with removable sections of latex foam rubber for the practice of hypodermic injections. When the units were saturated they could be removed, squeezed dry and replaced. Martha Chase's son, Julian, designed and patented this internal mechanism in 1939. During the Second World War over two hundred of these figures were bought by our government to train army and navy medical corpsmen in hospital techniques. Many hospitals are still using this figure in the training of nurses.

In 1913, Martha Chase developed the Chase Sanitary Doll which was used extensively for teaching Infant Hygiene to health departments, mothers' clubs and baby clinics. This baby doll was made of stockinet material and stuffed with cotton batting, waterproofed from head to foot with four thick coats of durable waterproof paint. The advertising brochure tells us that they are easily kept clean and last for years. A quote from a brochure advertising the sanitary dolls is as follows: "If more babies are to live mothers must be taught the facts of Infant Hygiene. All over the country efforts are being made to produce a generation of Better Babies. Women's Clubs, High Schools and Colleges, Baby Clinics, District Nurses, and Hospitals are teaching the mothers of today and the mothers of tomorrow how to protect and care for the little ones. For not only do healthy babies make strong men and women but the health and happiness of the household, of the community, and the whole nation is improved by everything done to protect children."

Two of Martha Chase's daughters, Anna and Elizabeth, were involved in the doll business after the First World War. Elizabeth painted the faces and Anna seemed to have the business mind and was active in running the company with her mother. A son, Robert, did the advertising and, as has been mentioned before, her son Julian patented the internal mechanism for the hospital doll in 1939.

Anna Chase Sheldon was issued a patent in 1922 for the application of a snap on the top of a doll's head. This allowed a child to snap on different bows or barrettes.

Martha Chase died in 1925 and the business was run for many years by her daughter Anna Sheldon. When she retired it was taken over by Martha Chase's grandson, Robert D. Chase, Jr. Soon the company was producing fewer and fewer playdolls, concentrating on the hospital dolls instead.

A less expensive new style of playdoll and sanitary doll was constructed that did not prove to be successful. It was made of molded vinyl plastic, waterproof as the early dolls had been but losing all the charm of the original Chase dolls.

In 1978, Robert D. Chase, Jr., retired and the doll business was sold to a medical supply company in Chicago, Illinois.

Martha Chase achieved her goals through imagination, hard work and a great deal of that wonderful thing called "Yankee Ingenuity," and she also contributed an important training aid in nursing education by creating the Chase Hospital Doll that was used and is still being used in so many of the hospitals throughout the world. □

Rare 8in (20.3cm) Chase dolls with an original stockinet mask and mold.

The Many Faces of Georgene Averill

The Many Faces of Georgene Averill

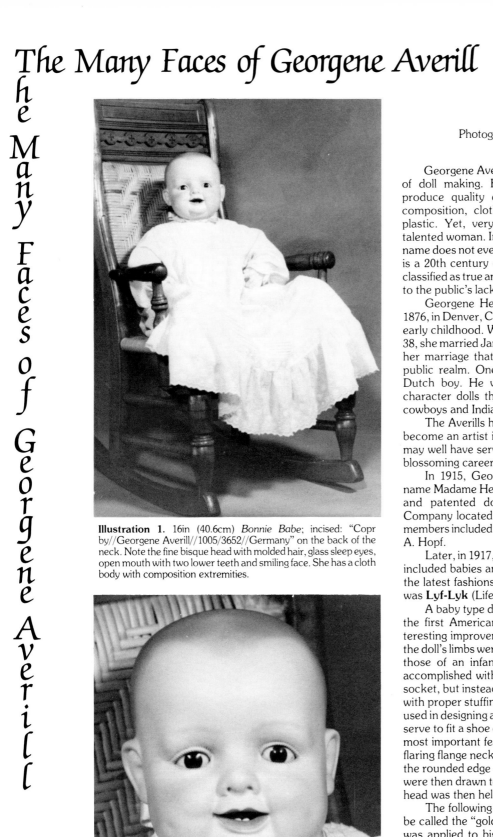

Illustration 1. 16in (40.6cm) *Bonnie Babe*; incised: "Copr by//Georgene Averill//1005/3652//Germany" on the back of the neck. Note the fine bisque head with molded hair, glass sleep eyes, open mouth with two lower teeth and smiling face. She has a cloth body with composition extremities.

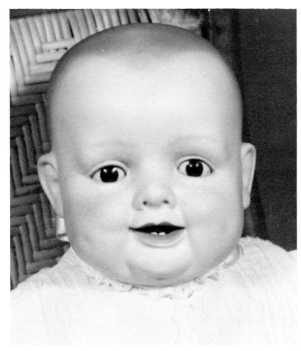

Illustration 2. Close-up of *Bonnie Babe* seen in *Illustration 1*, showing the finely molded facial features.

by **Ann Hays**
Photographs by **Kenneth S. Hays**

Georgene Averill was a creative genius in the realm of doll making. Her artistic talents inspired her to produce quality dolls in a multiplicity of mediums: composition, cloth, celluloid, bisque and even hard plastic. Yet, very little has been written about this talented woman. In fact, in some current doll books her name does not even appear. Perhaps this is because she is a 20th century doll maker and her dolls are not yet classified as true antiques. This omission may also be due to the public's lack of knowledge of her many creations.

Georgene Hendren Averill was born on May 21, 1876, in Denver, Colorado. Very little is known about her early childhood. We do know that in 1914, at the age of 38, she married James P. Averill. It was just a year before her marriage that she started producing dolls for the public realm. One of her first was an attractive little Dutch boy. He was part of a series of felt-dressed character dolls that later included international dolls, cowboys and Indians.

The Averills had but one daughter who was also to become an artist in her own right. This pretty little girl may well have served as an inspiration for her mother's blossoming career.

In 1915, Georgene Averill began using the trade name Madame Hendren. Under this name she designed and patented dolls for the Averill Manufacturing Company located in New York, New York. The firm's members included her husband and her brother, Rudolph A. Hopf.

Later, in 1917, she designed a new line of dolls which included babies and little girls claimed to be dressed in the latest fashions. The trade name given to this series was **Lyf-Lyk** (Life-Like).

A baby type doll was patented in 1918, being one of the first American "Mama Dolls." One of several interesting improvements claimed in this patent was that the doll's limbs were made seemingly jointless to simulate those of an infant. Movement of the limbs was not accomplished with mechanical joints, such as ball and socket, but instead by a *plurality* of fabric combinations with proper stuffing methods. This same technique was used in designing a foot with a projecting heel that would serve to fit a shoe or sock better. The third and possibly most important feature of this patent was an outwardly flaring flange neck. The cloth casing of the body fit over the rounded edge of the neck flange. These cloth pieces were then drawn together by means of drawstrings. The head was then held tightly to the body.

The following years in Georgene Averill's life could be called the "golden years of her genius." Her artistry was applied to bisque dolls produced by the German firms of Alt, Beck & Gottschalck and Gebrüder Heubach. A favorite with the doll collector is *Bonnie Babe*. The workmanship and detail in this smiling baby face is quite evident. A close-up illustration shows the doll's molded hair, glass sleep eyes, open mouth with two lower teeth and molded tongue. The head is attached to a cloth body with composition extremities. There is also a smaller all-bisque version of this doll. This or a small composition-bodied version would be a real prize for any collection.

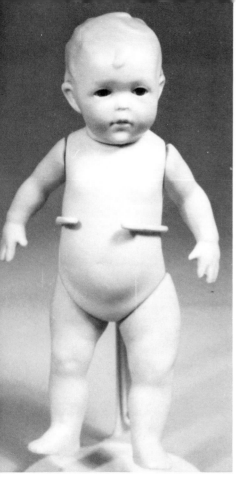

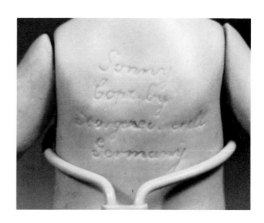

LEFT: Illustration 3. 6½in (16.5cm) all-bisque boy marked: "Sonny//Copr by//Georgene Averill//Germany" on his back.

RIGHT: Illustration 4. Close-up of *Sonny* in *Illustration 3* showing incised marking on his back.

Illustration 5. 13½in (34.3cm) all-cloth boy, tagged "Georgene's Nu-Art doll," with a yarn wig.

Illustration 6. 13½in (34.3cm) all-cloth girl, tagged "Georgene's Nu-Art doll," with yarn wig.

A very fine example of an all-bisque doll designed by Mrs. Averill can be seen in *Illustration 3*. This extraordinary 6½in (16.5cm) little fellow is incised: "Sonny//Copr by//Georgene Averill//Germany" on his back. He has molded hair, glass sleep eyes, swivel flange neck fitting over a neck socket and a closed mouth. The overall workmanship is excellent in both facial and body detail. Unlike the all-bisque *Bonnie Babe*, who wears molded shoes, *Sonny* has beautifully molded feet. He is seldom found offered for sale at auction or doll shows.

Using her creative skills, Georgene Averill also produced bisque-headed and all-bisque character animals. These, too, are becoming rare and their prices are usually in the four figure range.

It appears that in the early 1920s Georgene Averill and her husband became disassociated with the Averill Manufacturing Company and formed Madame Georgene, Inc. It was under this name that her *Wonder Dolls* were trademarked. George Borgfeldt held the exclusive right of distribution for these dolls.

Georgene Averill's list of accomplishments continued to grow with the multiplicity of her doll faces and designs. In 1933, she was granted a patent for a breathing doll. The important feature of this doll was the fact that when pressure was applied to the body, air was expelled through the nose and mouth passages, simulating the breathing process of a real baby.

At this point in her career, it is worth mentioning that another line of dolls was being produced by Georgene Novelties of New York, New York. The captivating felt dressed boy in *Illustration 5* was part of an international series produced by this firm. The sweet little miss in *Illustration 6* was also part of this group. Mrs. Averill was thought to have designed many of these dolls. Most of the dolls in this series were produced in boy and girl pairs wearing the native costumes of the country represented and holding a flag.

As with many gifted people, Mrs. Averill was always expanding her horizons. Probably unknown by many collectors was the fact that Mrs. Averill also patented

in 1935 a collapsible exercising apparatus. Even then physical well-being was emerging. The design of this exercise equipment enabled the user to recline on his back while his feet engaged a ball-like object in revolving action.

It would be impossible to mention all that Georgene Averill has designed in one brief article. It is hoped that this article has given the collector an insight into the many contributions of Mrs. Averill in the realm of doll artistry. Her death in Santa Monica, California, in 1961 has created a vacuum in the doll world. The many faces she has produced will serve as a beautiful memory of a very talented lady. □

Who Are You, Mr. Marque?

by **Francois Theimer**

Strange as it may seem, the Marque doll was unknown to the majority of collectors, as well as many specialists. However, in the No. 2 *Polichinelle*, page 34, I indicated that the Marque doll was beyond appraisal and that a prudent evaluation would be a minimum of 45,000 French francs. Indeed, there is a very limited number of examples in France (3) that are known to me. None of these have passed through the auction rooms, so I cannot estimate what value French collectors would place on them. If an absolute record price for this doll was attained on March 19th, 1982, the day before the Congress, this record is explained by the following.

At the Denver Convention in the United States in 1978, a Marque doll brought the record price of $32,000 (180,000 FF). Two others followed and fetched $30,000; and in 1979 this doll reached $35,000 (210,000 FF).

Thus in three years, across the ocean in France, this doll fetched 240,000 French francs, or 30,000 French francs more in three years time. If this is not really a world record, it is in any event a European record.

What does the Colemans' *Encyclopedia* tell us? On page 247 we read:

"MARQUE, A. Inscribed on dolls with bisque heads and composition bodies that appear to be French. Most of the faces are similar and appear to be of the character type, which suggests a 20th century doll probably early because of pierced ears. In 1916 Mr. Marque made a head for a Paris shop."

This description appears to be too rudimentary, and leaves us still lacking a full explanation. As for the suggestion that it has a resemblance to character babies, we are in complete agreement.

"What is so particular about this doll?" Thanks to some friends I was able to examine one at leisure. Others would say, "But what is so exceptional about this doll? It is not antique. It is ugly," and so forth.

Here we have an extremely complex question, which extends into the framework of a doll manufacturer. In the case of the Marque doll it is a question of an original piece of work, the work of a sculptor, a known sculptor — Albert Marque.

Albert Marque was born in Nanterre (Seine), France, July 14, 1872. He was a sculptor of the French school. From 1899 to 1904, he exhibited at the National Society Salon, the Autumn Salon and the Independant Salon.

At the Autumn Salon, in 1905, he exhibited a small head of a child which had a Florentine influence. A chance placement brought this bust to the room where such artists as Vlaminck, Derain, Matisse and other artists of their ilk were exhibiting. The art critic, Louis Vauxcelles, spoke of a "Donatello" being amongst a *milieu des fauves*. This appelation was adopted by this group of artists and thereafter their movement became known as "Fauvism."

In 1937, Albert Marque exhibited at the Exposition of the Masters of Independent Art. The Museum of Modern Art in Paris has a terra cotta bust of a little girl in their collection. This bust measures 13in (33cm) tall. It is signed on the left arm "A. Marque" and dated "1913." It is certain that this bust served as the model for one of his dolls.

It is unlikely that the doll modelled after this bust was made before 1916, since the war years of 1913 to 1916 would have precluded it being made. The doll modelled after Marque's bust is about 21in (54cm) tall, has glazed fixed eyes, closed mouth,

Illustration 1. 22in (55.9cm) tall A. Marque doll. *Photograph by Vernon Seeley.* © HHP 1980.

FOLLOWING PAGE: Illustration 2. Bisque head doll with glass eyes, composition jointed body, bisque lower arms and hands, original costume. Head incised "A. Marque". Country of origin France, 1916. 22" high. *Photograph courtesy of the Margaret Woodbury Strong Museum.*

poured bisque head, composition body with bisque arms that are fixed at the wrist, and wears a mohair wig. There is a very visible signature, but no size mark, which would indicate it was made in only one size. The dresses are always made by a known couturier — that is, the original dress, of course. We have found costumes bearing the label of "Margaine-Lacroix," 19, bd Haussmann, Paris, and another bearing the label of "Worth," another famous Parisian designer.

I am convinced that without proof to the contrary, this doll was made by the artist himself, as did Jean Saint-Martin when he did dolls for the fashion theatre. There is no reason for not believing that Albert Marque, for reasons we will call "elementary," actually made a small series of dolls using his child's bust as a model. Having made the molds for the head and forearms, he had them produced by a porcelain maker. For the rest of the body he called upon a maker of carton-paste. There was no lack of suppliers for the eyes and the wig. The doll was then assembled by him or an assembly worker.

Having the dresses made by well-known couturiers voices the possibility that he was filling an order for a large store, an opportunity for the sculptor to present his production with the best possible visage.

In Constance Eileen King's book, page 90, one reads:

"A very rare series carries the mysterious 'Marque A,' that one can attribute to no known enterprise." On page 68 of the same book there is an illustration of the Albert Marque doll. In the caption, the author speaks of the natural eyelashes, like those found on the beautiful dolls made by Casimir Bru. This confirms my conviction that this series of Marque dolls were made piece by piece, and that the artist permitted himself variations from one to another.

"How many Marque dolls exist in the world?"

This particular doll is not comparable to another doll. This is a case of an artist doing original work on a limited production basis. The number must have been extremely limited.

So far we have been able to locate the following examples:

One is in the Margaret Woodbury Strong Museum, Rochester, New York.

Two are found in The Old Dolls and Toys Museum, Winter Haven, Florida.

One is in the collection of the Wee Lassie Museum, Homestead, Florida.

One is in the collection of Sylvia Brockman, an American collector.

One is in the Doll in Wonderland Museum, Brighton, England. Three are in France; one was sold at a sale on March 19th, 1982. Another was brought to the World Congress of Dolls on March 21,

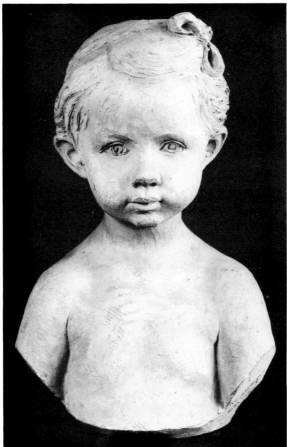

PREVIOUS PAGE: Illustration 3. Full length view of doll in *Illustration 2. Photograph courtesy of the Margaret Woodbury Strong Museum.*

Illustration 4. Terra Cotta bust of a small girl, by Albert Marque. *Cliche des Musees Nationaux. Musee: Orsay.*

original creations and in a limited edition. As in the case of Francisque Poulbot who created a model for the French Society of Baby Dolls and Toys (S.F.B.J.), or, of the same period, the painter Adolphe Willette who designed Pierrot and Columbine for the editors J. P. Gallais et Cie of Paris, so, too, Albert Marque created a doll that stands out from the usual dolls made commercially.

These factors evoke speculation concerning the originality and rarity of Marque dolls, rather than the quality of them.

A Jumeau, Bru or other doll is a doll made by a manufacturer. An Albert Marque or Adolphe Willette doll is an artist-made creation.

In conclusion, I will ask collectors and doll authorities to please contact me should they have anything concrete to add to this report about Albert Marque and his beautiful dolls. ☐

(*) These figures do not include the five A. Marque dolls in the collection of the Carnegie Museum, Pittsburgh, Pennsylvania, purchased from a shop in Paris, France, in 1916 according to an original bill of sale in the museum's records. These dolls are illustrated on the following pages. Also, some of the dolls mentioned by the author may have changed hands since the article first appeared in *Polichinelle* (April 1982).

1982. And another is in the private collection of a large Paris dealer.

If the total number of those just listed are added to the four sold at auctions in the United States we count only 13 known examples of Marque dolls. However, the sale of dolls between collectors that may never be recorded does present a problem. Consequently, we must assume that the total number of Marque dolls probably does not exceed 50.

Regarding copies!

At the beginning of 1980, The Seeley Society in New York State reproduced 500 Marque dolls. The misinterpretation of the "A" to mean "Andre," instead of "Albert," in their initial advertisement, easily identifies this reproduction. Also, there is a difference in size between the originals and the reproductions. The originals are 20in (54cm) and the reproductions slightly smaller at 19in (48.6cm). This discrepancy in size is the result of shrinkage when the doll's head and other parts were fired after being formed from molds made from the original parts of the doll.

CONCLUSION.

The Albert Marque dolls enter the sector of dolls made by artists that are

Illustration 5. An Albert Marque doll. *Photograph courtesy Marion Valentine.*

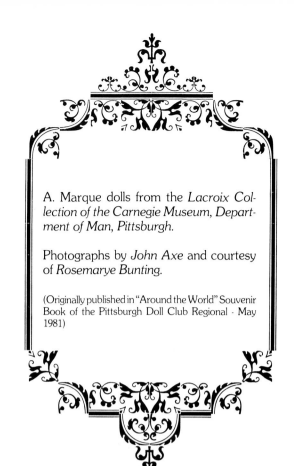

A. Marque dolls from the *Lacroix Collection of the Carnegie Museum, Department of Man, Pittsburgh.*

Photographs by *John Axe* and courtesy of *Rosemarye Bunting.*

(Originally published in "Around the World" Souvenir Book of the Pittsburgh Doll Club Regional - May 1981)

Illustration 6. A close-up of an A. Marque doll with underwear labeled "Mme. Lacroix."

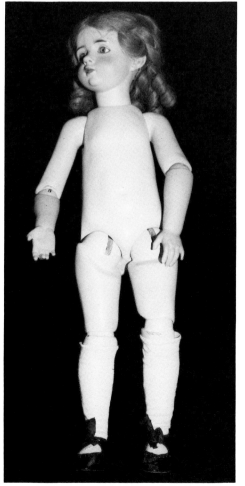

LEFT: Illustration 7. An undressed A. Marque doll showing the detailed body structure.

RIGHT: Illustration 8. A. Marque doll wearing underwear labeled "Mme. Lacroix."

LEFT: Illustration 9. A. Marque doll costumed as Queen Isabeau de Baviere of France.

RIGHT: Illustration 10. A. Marque doll costumed as Queen Marie Leszczynska of France.

Illustration 11. A. Marque doll dressed to represent Queen Marie Antoinette of France.

Illustration 12. A close-up of the Marie Antoinette doll.

MONSIEUR BRU'S NOVELTY DOLLS

by Sybill McFadden

All photographs by **Author** from her Museum of Antique Dolls and Toys

Illustration 1. 19in (48.3cm) *Bébé Teteur* or nursing baby dressed in pale green fine cashmere wool detachable cape and coat with matching bonnet edged in swansdown. The baby dress displays a ruffled panel of cutwork with 12 rows of tucking above.

ABOVE LEFT: Illustration 2. Close-up of *Bébé Teteur,* the nursing Bru, showing her blonde mohair wig in ringlets over a cork pate, gray-blue fixed eyes, open and pursed lips to receive the nursing bottle and pierced ears.

ABOVE RIGHT: Illustration 3. The *Bébé Teteur* was purchased with 11 pieces of her original infant clothing, handmade by the first owner's grandmother. Here she wears her white cambric gown tucked and decorated with pierced eyelet work at bodice and hem.

BELOW RIGHT: Illustration 4. Under her gown, *Bébé Teteur* wears a starched cambric overslip which gives the gown fullness. The slip is embroidered in matching eyelet.

Antique dolls with mechanical innovations are always fascinating. To the uninitiated non-collector, however, an antique doll which can *do* something is always a source of amazement. The general impression is that only in recent years have dolls been invented which can walk, talk, creep, cry, eat and drink.

Nevertheless history records that mechanical toys existed as far back as the 3rd century BC when an inventor named "Hero" of Alexandria used hydraulic and pneumatic action to devise "magical" figurines and little birds that "sang." Historic references to clocks begin in the 13th century and it was inevitable that in only a few years the

56

Illustration 5. *Bébé Teteur* is seen here in her number one white lawn petticoat.

same clockwork mechanisms would be found to be ideal for propelling dolls and toys. With the winding of a key and the addition of a wheel or two, animals could run in circles and dolls could walk off on their own, as independent as you please! If this was "magic" in those long ago days, the aura still lingers to fascinate and amuse us today when we view the performance of a 100-year-old doll motivated by a mysterious interior!

In 1783 a German inventor of automata, Johannes Malzel, was credited with making the first talking doll. He used a bellows action pumped through a reed to a voice box behind the doll's mouth.

Nearly 100 years later, Casimir Bru Jeune, in 1881, went on record as claiming "The firm of Bru is continually making novelties." He interpreted novelties to mean dolls which could perform in any manner other than the standard jointed doll. And indeed it was so. The firm of Bru Jeune & Cie, constantly on the alert to keep a step ahead of competition in this heyday of the French Bébé, turned out more "novelties" than any of the other doll manufacturers, with perhaps the exception of the Societe Steiner which was equally innovative.

Unfortunately many of the Bru dolls did not find favor in the French, American or European nurseries of the day. Consequently they were discontinued in a few years, and today they are very hard to find, if they exist at all.

One of these is an early musical doll patented by Madame Bru in 1872. She called it a "Surprise" doll and fitted it with a key to wind the mechanism and a lever to change the tunes. In 1874 Casimir Bru Jeune took a turn at inventing musical dolls himself. He listed his as "Magical" dolls. There were also crying dolls and talking dolls. The firm of Bru also invented a two-faced doll, one awake and one asleep, which may have been the forerunner of Germany's three-faced dolls, with the German addition of the crying face.

Two of the most amazing of Bru's novelty dolls were the breathing Bru, advertised in 1881, in which a mechanism inside the doll's chest pumped up and down in imitation of breathing, and the *Bébé Gourmand* or eating doll which could be fed. The food traveled down through the body and was removed through an opening in the foot.

Perhaps the most popular of the novelty dolls and the one we see more often than the others, is the *Bébé Teteur* or nursing baby. Patented in 1878 by

Casimir Bru Jeune, this doll had a simple but ingenious method for drinking its "formula." More about the remarkable formula later. Let us first see how the baby "drank" it. When the bottle was put in the baby's mouth it fit into a tube leading into a rubber ball in the back of the doll's head. When a key in the back of the neck was turned to the left, the compressed rubber ball was released, drawing the liquid out of the bottle, through the mouth, and into the ball in the head. There it could be kept in this receptacle until the next feeding, at which time the little mother simply turned the key to the right which re-compressed the ball and the milk flowed back into the bottle! In the directions which accompanied every doll it was suggested that the "milk" be made by adding a few drops of cologne to water, thus giving a cloudy-appearing liquid which the child could pretend was milk. No mention was made, however, as to how important it might be to follow those directions *exactly*. Milk, itself, was not practical as it would have soured in the rubber ball. One can not help wondering, then, how many times the little ones, desiring more realism, experimented with real milk and gummed the whole mechanism, perhaps permanently. Once the milk curdled in the rubber ball, it would be well-nigh impossible to return it to the bottle!

The author's *Bébé Teteur* is on a pristine all-wood body with the Bru label and has a cry box opening with two pull strings which produce a crying sound. While most *Bébé Teteur* dolls are seen on the kid body, this body is thought to be an early one, as the patent papers showed the doll on a ball-jointed body. Also, the early doll's directions mention the turning of a key, whereas later advertisements state that the doll is operated with an ivory button in back of her head.

With this wooden-bodied doll, however, we run, once more, into Bru confusion. We know from the name alone, *Bébé Teteur*, that the doll is intended as a baby. Yet the jointed all-wood body, while exceptionally beautiful, gives one the impression of a toddler or child doll. So, for that matter, does the kid body on which this baby is most commonly found. Since the Bru firm, however, did not make any type of bent-limb baby body, we have come to accept naturally the *Bébé Teteur* on the kid body. The name implied it was a baby, and the accompanying nursing bottle clinched it. The confusion, then, arises

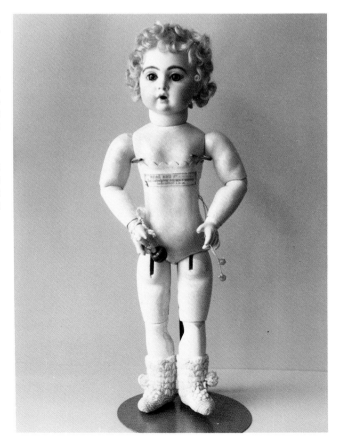

ABOVE LEFT: Illustration 6. *Bébé Teteur*'s first undergarments consist of a featherstitched navel band and a knitted wool underskirt. A French white cotton diaper buttons around the baby with four buttons. She wears fancy knitted booties.

ABOVE RIGHT: Illustration 7. Here is seen *Bébé Teteur's* original glass nursing bottle. The nipple emerges from an ivory top fitted with a cork through which a glass tube is suspended. In raised glass letters at the bottom of the bottle are the words "BEBE TETEUR" on one side and "BRU JEUNE" on the other side. She also holds her original brass rattle with an ivory handle.

BELOW RIGHT: Illustration 8. 19in (48.3cm) *Bébé Teteur* seen on her pristine all-wood body with label intact and pull strings to make her cry. This body is considered earlier than the kid body usually seen on this doll, as the all-wood body was shown on the first patent for the nursing baby.

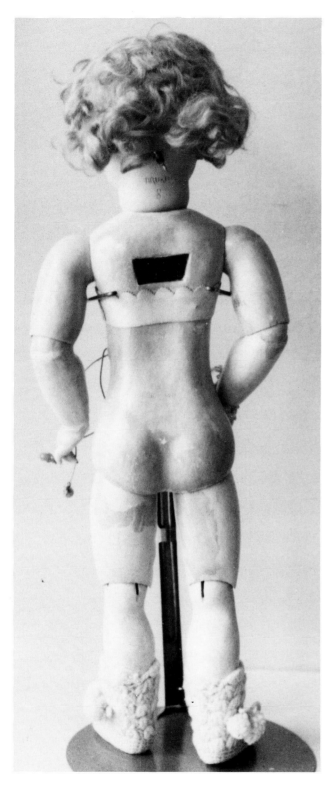

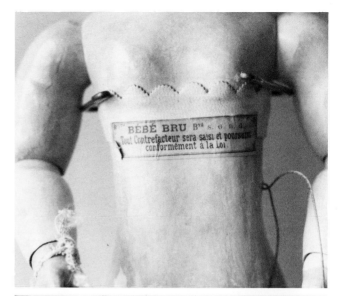

LEFT: Illustration 9. Back view of the *Bébé Teteur* showing the opening for the cry box. She holds the two motivating strings in her left hand. They have their original blue beads and when pulled, she cries.

ABOVE: Illustration 10. Close-up of the Bru label on the *Bébé Teteur* and of the brass rattle with the ivory handle. Strings emanate from her side and terminate in the original blue beads which, when pulled, make her cry.

MIDDLE: Illustration 11. Close-up of the key in the back of the doll's head which, when turned, causes her to "drink" the "milk" in the bottle, or turned in the opposite direction, causes the liquid to be returned to the bottle. The incised marking on the back of her neck are also seen.

BELOW: Illustration 12. Back view of the *Bébé Teteur's* body stamped "BEBE BRU//No. 8." The number "8" corresponds with the "8" incised on the head, absolute proof that this bébé is on her original body.

when we see this doll, as many of us have, factory-gowned in a French child's dress. The *Bébé Teteur* was most usually presented in its original white lawn baby gown and bonnet, sometimes lying tied to a pillowed couch, but it is also sometimes found in an original Bébé child's dress. A *Bébé Teteur* dressed as a child is most naturally displayed on a stand, and it all makes for a most confusing concept of a nursing baby.

The author's *Bébé Teteur* came from a one-owner family with 11 pieces of its original clothing. The infant garments were designed and hand-sewn by a relative of the first owner. There was no doubt that in this family, despite the beautiful child's body, this doll was understood to be a baby.

Another popular Bru novelty doll is the walking, talking, kiss-throwing doll patented in 1891 by Paul Eugene Girard,

the last head of the firm and the first president of the French society known as S.F.B.J. formed in 1899 to meet German competition. Paul Girard Bru dolls carry an incised R after the "Bru Jne" on the back of the head.

This 23in (58.4cm) doll has a fine quality pale bisque head. When held to the light it is translucent. Her blonde wig is on a cork pate. She has pierced ears, blue-gray glass eyes and an open

ABOVE: Illustration 14. Close-up of the kissing, walking, talking Bru with a blonde human hair replacement wig over a cork pate, gray-blue sleep eyes under feathered eyebrows, an open mouth (she is, after all, a talking doll) with molded porcelain teeth, pierced ears and head of the finest pale transparent bisque.

BELOW: Illustration 15. Close-up of the kissing, walking, talking Bru showing the cork pate and the incised marking "BRU. JNE R//9" which is the mark of Paul Eugene Girard in 1891 when this doll was patented. The incised "9" is the size number.

Illustration 13. 23in (58.4cm) kissing, walking, talking Bru dressed in her blue and ecru satin and lace gown and matching chapeau. Tiny garlands of ribbon flowers trim the bonnet and gown. Unfortunately the creation is frail and "melting."

mouth with four molded porcelain teeth. She is on a quality composition body with wooden arms jointed at the elbows and wrists, and wooden unjointed walking legs bolted to her body with heavy maneuverable wires which aid the walking movement. When a string in her side is pulled, (the original pink bead is still attached to string) she raises her

hand to her lips. When the string is released she blows a kiss.

Holding an exalted position in today's doll world, we collectors can be grateful that the Bebe Bru comes down to us in usually well-preserved condition. It attests to the fact, we think, that perhaps she was held in high regard even more than 100 years ago. ◊

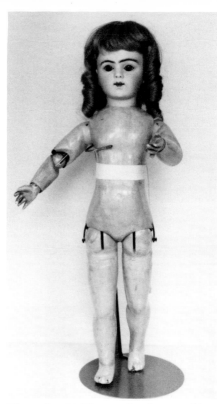

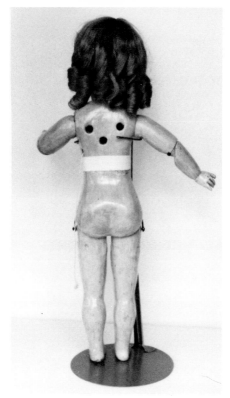

Illustration 16. The wood and composition body of the kissing, walking, talking Bru which is fashioned in two pieces to allow for access to the talking and kissing mechanisms. Her original kidskin strip which joined the two pieces was missing and has been replaced.

Illustration 18. Back view of the kissing, walking, talking Bru displaying three holes out of which the talking and walking strings originally emanated. Here can be seen the two bolts at the sides of the legs and the unjointed walking legs. The head also turns when she walks.

Illustration 19. When a string in the side of the 23in (58.4cm) kissing, walking, talking Bru is pulled, she raises her hand to her lips preparatory to blowing a kiss.

Illustration 20. When the string in her side is released, the kissing, walking, talking Bru throws a kiss.

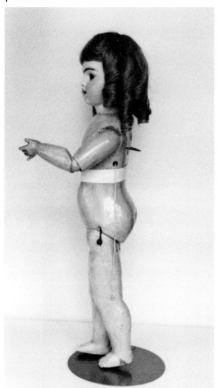

Illustration 17. Side view of the kissing, walking, talking Bru showing the string which, when pulled, causes her to raise her hand to her mouth and blow a kiss. Also shown is one of the two metal bolts at the top of her leg which allows the leg to swing forward in order to walk. Note the unjointed walking legs.

The Collector's Mini-Digest on French Dolls, Part I

by **Robert & Karin MacDowell**

Photographs by the **Authors**

Spanning the approximate period 1860 to 1925, a number of French concerns produced a wide-ranging selection of dolls, using numerous materials and assembly methods.

The format of this series of short articles follows that used in our full-length book *The Collector's Digest on German Character Dolls,* recently published by Hobby House Press, Inc., and offers un-retouched photographs illustrating details of construction and actual makers' marks.

Société Française de Fabrication de Bébés et Jouets, Paris, France.

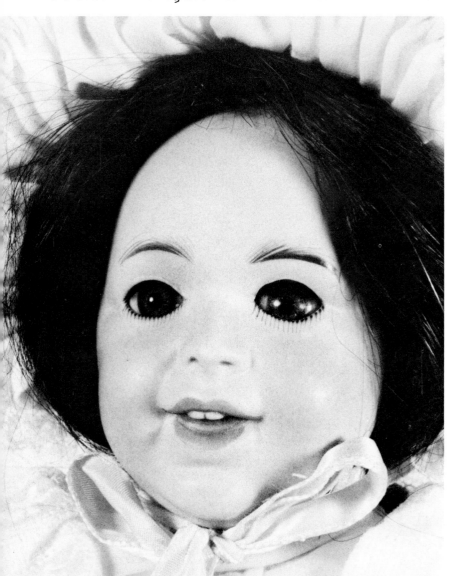

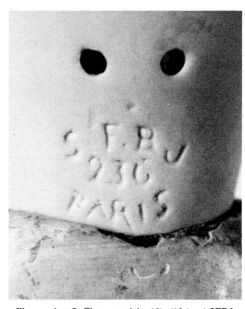

Illustration 1. 15in (38.1cm) SFBJ 236.
Head marked:

S. F. B. J.
236
Paris

Bisque socket head; blue sleep eyes with lashes; open/closed mouth with two upper molded teeth. *Carol Kitchens Collection.*

Illustration 2. Close-up of the 15in (38.1cm) SFBJ 236 showing the mark on the back of the head. *Carol Kitchens Collection.*

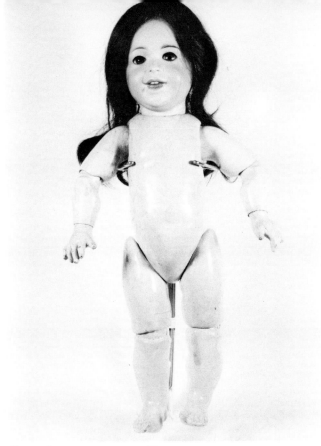

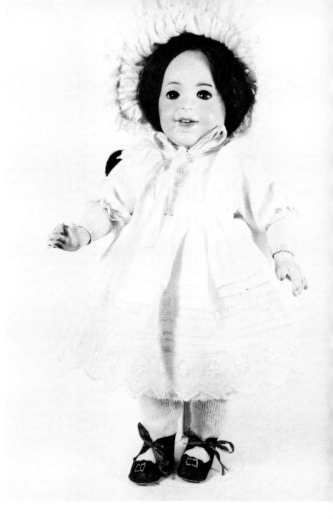

Illustration 3. 15in (38.1cm) SFBJ 236 head on French Composition toddler body. *Carol Kitchens Collection.*

RIGHT: Illustration 4. 15in (38.1cm) SFBJ 236 in white eyelet dress and hat. *Carol Kitchens Collection.*

Unknown Maker.

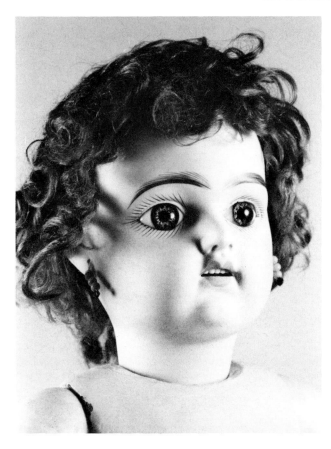

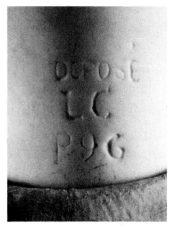

LEFT TO RIGHT: Illustration 5. 20in (50.8cm) doll by unknown maker. Head marked:

$$\text{DEPOSÉ}$$
$$\text{L C}$$
$$\text{P 9 G}$$

Bisque socket head, original auburn mohair wig; blue paperweight eyes; open mouth with upper molded teeth; pierced ears; jointed composition body with Jumeau sticker. *MacDowell Doll Museum.*

Illustration 6. Close-up of the 20in (50.8cm) doll by unknown maker showing the mark on the back of the head. *MacDowell Doll Museum.*

Illustration 7. Close-up of the paper sticker on the back of the 20in (50.8cm) doll by unknown maker. *MacDowell Doll Museum.*

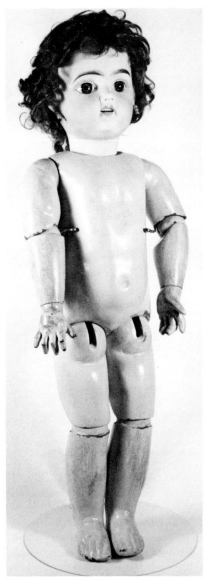

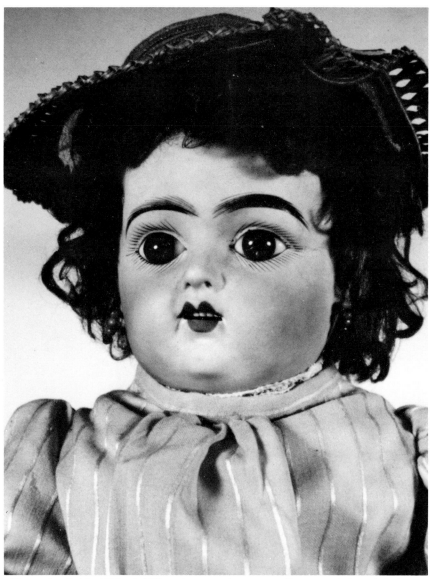

Illustration 8. 20in (50.8cm) doll by unknown maker shown undressed. *MacDowell Doll Museum.*

Illustration 9. 20in (50.8cm) doll by unknown maker, seen in *Illustrations 5 through 8,* shown wearing her original pale pink wool dress and straw hat with cloth orchid and ribbons. *MacDowell Doll Museum.*

Of all the unique distinguishing features, the "paperweight" eyes used in the earlier dolls warrant special mention. The following photographs graphically illustrate the differences between the French and typical German eyes.

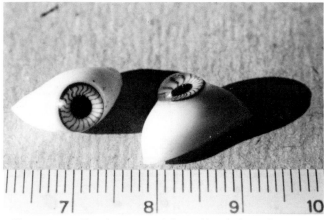

Illustration 10. German round eyes mounted on "sleep" assembly with lead weight which causes eyes to move when doll is reclined or set upright. Note roundness and nearness of iris details to surface of glass.

Illustration 11. French "paperweight" eyes. Note the basic white portion appears to be capped with a clear glass dome of pronounced depth and radically different curvature; iris details seem to be at the junction of the glass components, yielding a very realistic depth and character in the finished product.

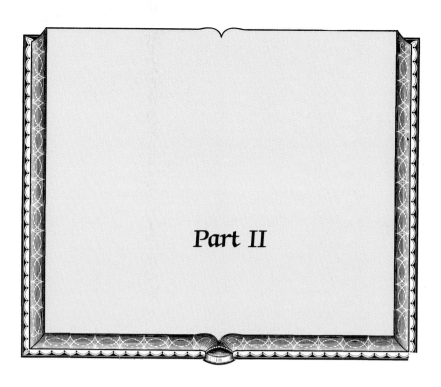

Part II

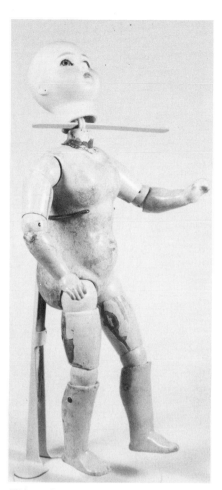

Belton-type (so-called).

These dolls were made by French (and also some German) firms. Collectors consider as Belton-type heads those made of bisque with two or more holes on top of the head for stringing. ☐

Illustration 3. 11½in (29.2cm) Belton-type shown with head removed slightly from top of body which has a wooden protrusion to which the head is attached by string. Note also the neck of the head which is straight and not flanged. The torso, lower arms and lower legs are of composition while the balls, upper arms and legs are of wood. *Blanche B. Hecht Collection.*

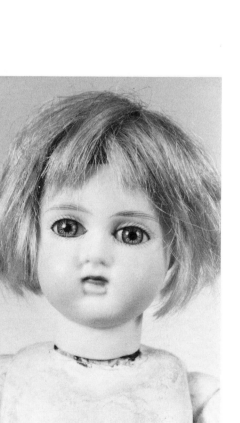

Illustration 1. 11½in (29.2cm) Belton-type. Head marked:

926
3

Bisque head with two holes for stringing; blue stationary eyes; closed mouth with tiny molded tongue; pierced ears; wood and composition body with straight wrists. *Blanche B. Hecht Collection.*

Illustration 2. Close-up of the 11½in (29.2cm) Belton-type showing the mark on the top of the head and the two holes for stringing. *Blanche B. Hecht Collection.*

RIGHT: Illustration 4. 11½in (29.2cm) Belton-type, seen in *Illustrations 1* through *3*, shown fully dressed. *Blanche B. Hecht Collection.*

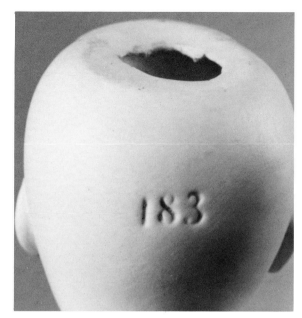

Illustration 6. Close-up of the 13in (33cm) Belton-type showing the mark on the head.

LEFT: Illustration 5. 13in (33cm) Belton-type. Head marked:
183
Bisque solid dome head with three holes on top for stringing, replaced human hair wig; brown paperweight eyes, feathered eyebrows; closed mouth; pierced ears; composition and wood body with straight wrists.

RIGHT: Illustration 7. 13in (33cm) Belton-type shown undressed on wood and composition body.

FAR RIGHT: Illustration 8. 13in (33cm) Belton-type, seen in *Illustrations* 5 through 7, shown wearing her original pink silk dress trimmed with lace and pink ribbon. She also has on lace stockings and Bru marked shoes.

Illustration 10. Close-up of the 17½in (44.5cm) Belton-type showing the mark on the head.

RIGHT: Illustration 9. 17½in (44.5cm) Belton-type. Head marked:
TR.
809.X
Bisque solid dome head with three holes on top for stringing, replaced human hair wig; brown paperweight eyes, feathered eyebrows; closed mouth, dimple in chin; pierced ears; wood and composition body with straight wrists. The mark on the head is by an unknown maker.

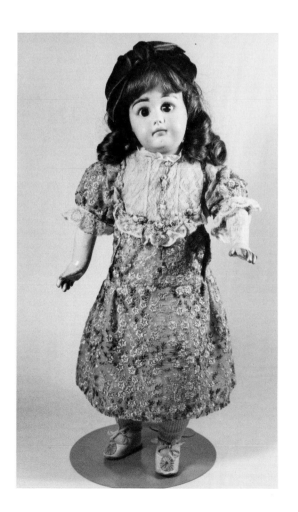

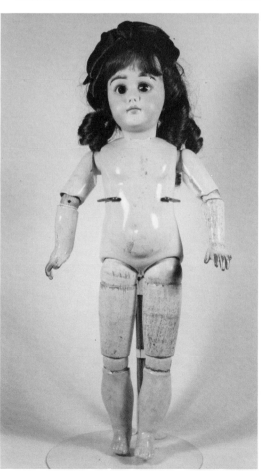

LEFT: Illustration 11. 17½in (44.5) Belton-type shown on wood and composition body with straight wrists.

FAR LEFT: Illustration 12. 17½in (44.5cm) Belton-type, seen in *Illustrations 9* through *11*, shown wearing a flowered silk dress with tiny applied silk flowers and ecru lace, cotton socks and leather shoes and a red velvet bow in her hair.

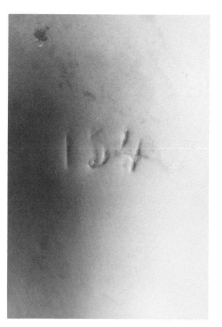

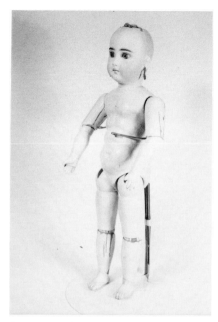

Illustration 13. 16½in (41.9cm) Belton-type. Head marked:

154

Solid dome bisque socket head with three holes on top for stringing, bisque is very pale; blue paperweight eyes, feathered eyebrows; closed mouth, dimple in chin; pierced ears; wood and composition body with straight wrists.

Illustration 14. Close-up of the 16½in (41.9cm) Belton-type showing the mark on the back of the head.

Illustration 15. 16½in (41.9cm) Belton-type 154 shown on wood and composition body with straight wrists.

Illustration 16. 16½in (41.9cm) Belton-type 154, seen in *Illustrations 13* through *15*, shown wearing a cotton dress with tiny blue, red and yellow printed leaves, trimmed with ruffles, lace and blue ribbons. She also wears lace stockings and beige leather shoes.

RIGHT: Illustration 17. 12½in (31.8cm) Belton-type. Head marked:

S

Solid dome bisque head with stringing holes on top of head, almost white bisque; pale blue paperweight eyes, single stroke eyebrows; closed mouth; five-piece composition body with painted socks and shoes. The head has a straight flange which fits over a dowel on top of the torso.

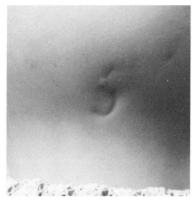

Illustration 18. Close-up of the 12½in (31.8cm) Belton-type showing the mark on the back of the head.

RIGHT: Illustration 19. 12½in (31.8cm) Belton-type shown undressed on her five-piece composition body with painted socks and shoes. Note attachment of head to torso.

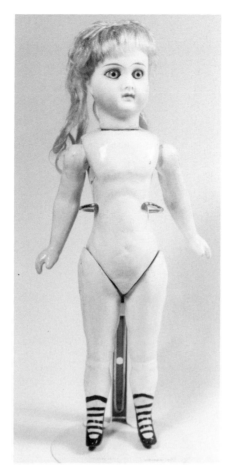

Illustration 21. 9in (22.9cm) Belton-type. Head marked:

G.K.
89.20

Bisque solid dome socket head with holes on top for stringing, human hair wig which appears to be original; blue paperweight eyes, single stroke eyebrows; closed mouth; pierced ears; five-piece composition body with white painted socks and yellow painted strap shoes.

Illustration 20. 12½in (31.8cm) Belton-type, seen in *Illustrations 17* through *19,* shown wearing lace-trimmed cotton underwear, a jacket with a skirt made of cotton in blue and white stripes trimmed with lace and blue velvet ribbon.

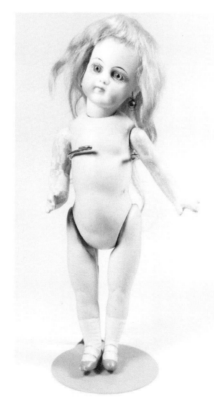

LEFT: Illustration 22. 9in (22.9cm) Belton-type shown undressed on her five-piece composition body.

RIGHT: Illustration 23. 9in (22.9cm) Belton-type, seen in *Illustrations 21* and *22,* shown wearing a checkered blue cotton dress trimmed with black lace over lace-trimmed cotton underwear. Her socks and shoes are painted.

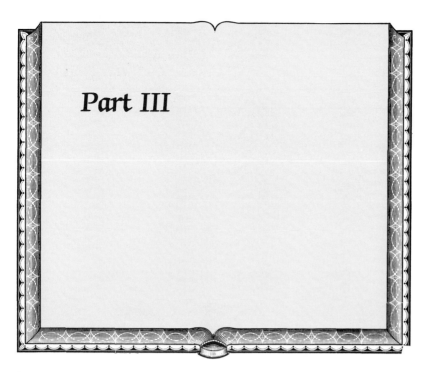

Part III

Maison Jumeau, Paris, France, 1842 on.

Illustration 2. Close-up of the inside of the head of the 22in (55.9cm) Tête Jumeau showing the original attaching hardware.

Illustration 3. Close-up of the 22in (55.9cm) Tête Jumeau showing the mark on her head.

Illustration 1. 22in (55.9cm) Tête Jumeau. Head marked (with fired-on red stamp):

▲ DÉPOSÉ
TÊTE JUMEAU
B^{TE} S.G.D.G.
10 VVII

Bisque socket head of very smooth and pale bisque, original cork pate and human hair wig; blue paperweight eyes; closed mouth; pierced ears; jointed composition body with paper label reading: "Bébé Jumeau// Diplome d'honneur."

Illustration 4. 22in (55.9cm) Tête Jumeau, seen in *Illustrations 1 through 3*, shown wearing a pink satin and ecru lace dress with her original socks and shoes.

Illustration 6. Close-up of the 14½in (36.8cm) Tête Jumeau showing the mark on the back of the head.

ABOVE: Illustration 5. 14½in (36.8cm) Tête Jumeau. Head marked (in red stamp):

˄ DÉPOSÉ
TÊTE JUMEAU
B^TE S.G.D.G.
(incised) 6 LV

Bisque socket head, original cork pate and blonde mohair wig; blue paperweight eyes; closed mouth; pierced ears; jointed composition body with paper label reading: "Bébé Jumeau//Diplome D'honneur."

BELOW: Illustration 7. 14½in (36.8cm) Tête Jumeau, seen in *Illustrations 5 and 6*, shown sitting in the high chair wearing a very dark lavender velvet jacket, skirt and tam and cream blouse. The doll standing is a 19in (48.3cm) open-mouth 1907 Jumeau shown in *Illustrations 8* through *10*.

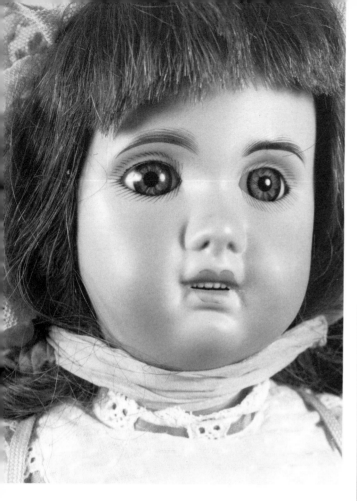

LEFT: **Illustration 8.** 19in (48.3cm) Jumeau. Head marked:

1907
•
8

Bisque socket head; blue sleep eyes; open mouth with upper molded teeth; pierced ears; jointed composition body with red stamp reading: "Déposé//Tête Jumeau." The bisque is much redder looking than the earlier Jumeaus.

BELOW: **Illustration 10.** 19in (48.3cm) 1907 Jumeau, seen in *Illustrations 8* and *9*, shown wearing a white dotted swiss dress with lace trim, a little muff of blue satin, white net and real fur; hat of blue silk, white net and flowers.

Illustration 9. Close-up of the 19in (48.3cm) Jumeau showing the mark on the back of her head.

RIGHT: Illustration 11. 26in (66cm) Jumeau. Head marked:

V
611
V
12 (out of sight on neck socket)

Bisque socket head of very smooth and pale bisque; blue paperweight eyes, feathered eyebrows; closed mouth; pierced ears; composition body with straight wrists. *Millie Eckert Collection.*

BELOW LEFT: Illustration 12. Close-up of the 26in (66cm) Jumeau showing the mark on the back of her head. *Millie Eckert Collection.*

BELOW RIGHT: Illustration 13. Close-up of the 26in (66cm) Jumeau showing the mark on her body: "JUMEAU//MEDAILLE D'OR//PARIS." *Millie Eckert Collection.*

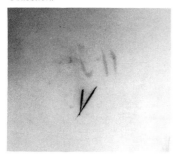

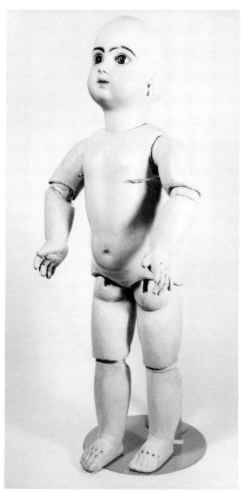

FAR LEFT: Illustration 14. 26in (66cm) Jumeau shown undressed. Note her nice and chunky body with the straight wrists. *Millie Eckert Collection.*

LEFT: Illustration 15. 26in (66cm) Jumeau, seen in *Illustrations 11* through *14,* shown wearing a brown and beige silk and moirée dress accented by ecru lace with a pert looking hat. *Millie Eckert Collection.*

Part IV

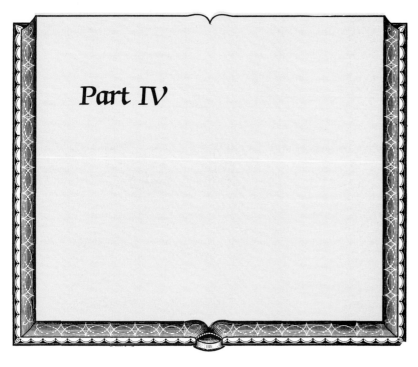

*Jules Nicholas Steiner
Paris, France, 1885 on.*

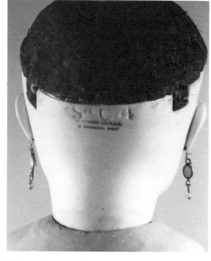

Illustration 1. 22in (55.9cm) Jules Steiner. Head marked:

**S^{TE} C 4
J. STEINER S.G.D.G.
BOURGOIN, SUCO**

Body Marked:

**Le Petit Parisien
J. St. Ste. S.G.D.G.
Paris**

Bisque socket head, original cardboard pate and auburn mohair wig; blue paperweight eyes; open mouth with two rows of tiny teeth; pierced ears; jointed composition body with mark. *Private Collection.*

Illustration 2. Close-up of the 22in (55.9cm) Jules Steiner showing the mark on the back of the head. *Private Collection.*

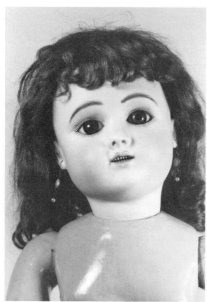

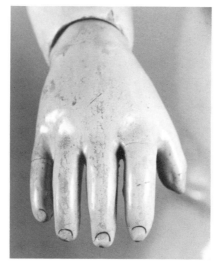

Illustration 3. Close-up of the hand of the 22in (55.9cm) Jules Steiner. *Private Collection.*

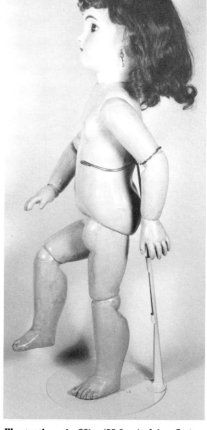

Illustration 4. 22in (55.9cm) Jules Steiner shown undressed. Note faint mark on her lower part of torso. *Private Collection.*

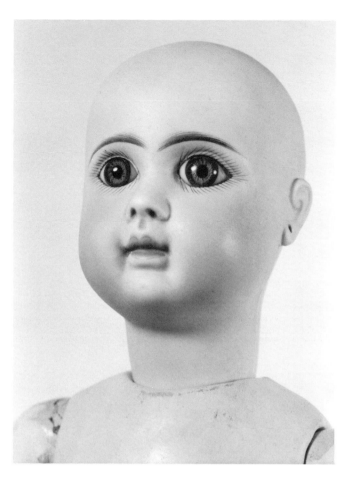

Illustration 5. 22in (55.9cm) Jules Steiner, seen in *Illustrations 1* through *4*, shown wearing a dark red silk dress with matching velvet yoke, red straw hat with feathers and flowers. She has one of the most beautiful faces we have ever seen. *Private Collection.*

Illustration 6. 18in (45.7cm) Jules Steiner. Head marked:

11
PARIS
Le PARISIEN

Bisque socket head; blue paperweight eyes; closed mouth; pierced ears; composition body with straight wrists. *Helen Read Collection.*

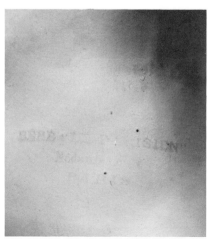

FAR LEFT TOP: Illustration 7. Close-up of the 18in (45.7cm) Jules Steiner showing the mark on the back of the head. *Helen Read Collection.*

FAR LEFT BOTTOM: Illustration 8. Close-up of the 18in (45.7cm) Jules Steiner showing the mark on the front of the lower part of the torso. The stamped mark reads: "BÉBÉ 'LE PARISIEN'//Médaille d'hor// PARIS." *Helen Read Collection.*

Illustration 9. 18in (45.7cm) Jules Steiner shown undressed. *Helen Read Collection.*

75

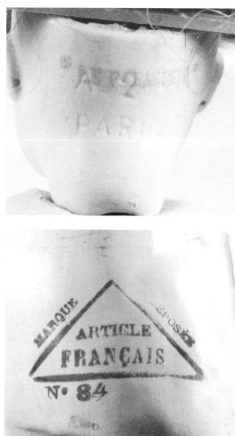

Illustration 11. Close-up of the 10in (25.4cm) Jules Steiner showing the mark on the back of the head. *Helen Read Collection.*

Illustration 12. Close-up of the 10in (25.4cm) Jules Steiner showing the stamp on the body. *Helen Read Collection.*

ABOVE: Illustration 10. 10in (25.4cm) Jules Steiner. Head marked:

"LE PARISIEN" (red stamp)
A 2 (incised)
PARIS

Bisque socket head, human hair wig in braids; blue paperweight eyes, feathered eyebrows (note the rather careless painting of the eyebrows); closed mouth; pierced ears; composition straight limb body marked in black. The bisque is not of the finest quality. *Helen Read Collection.*

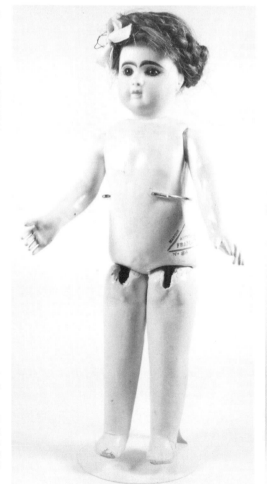

Illustration 13. 10in (25.4cm) Jules Steiner shown undressed. Note the stamp on the body. *Helen Read Collection.*

FAR RIGHT: Illustration 14. 10in (25.4cm) Jules Steiner, seen in *Illustrations 10* through *13*, shown wearing a pale green silk and ecru lace dress with matching silk ribbons, black cotton socks and black leather shoes. *Helen Read Collection.*

Illustration 15. 22in (55.9cm) Jules Steiner. Bisque head, original human hair wig; blue paperweight eyes, feathered eyebrows; open mouth with upper row of tiny teeth; pierced ears; cloth covered cardboard torso, kid upper legs, composition arms and legs; brass key for mechanism. When wound, she says; "Mama, Papa" and kick her legs, turns her head from side to side and waves her arms.

Illustration 16. 22in (55.9cm) Jules Steiner shown undressed.

Illustration 17. 22in (55.9cm) Jules Steiner, seen in *Illustrations 15* and *16,* shown wearing an old brown silk dress trimmed with cotton, cotton socks and one remaining pale green shoe, straw hat with flowers and net.

Part V

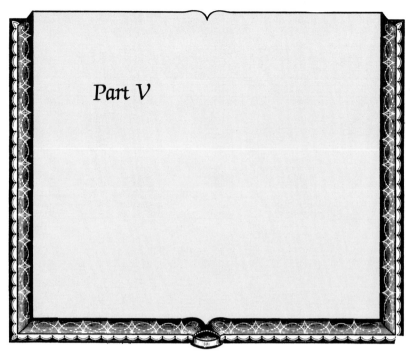

Jules Nicholas Steiner
Paris, France, 1855 on. □

Illustration 2. Close-up of the 22½in (57.2cm) Unis France showing the mark on the back of her head.

Illustration 1. 22½in (57.2cm) Unis France. Head marked:

UNIS

FRANCE

71   149
301
10

Bisque socket head; blue sleep eyes with original eyelashes, lower painted eyelashes, molded eyebrows; open mouth with molded teeth; jointed composition body.

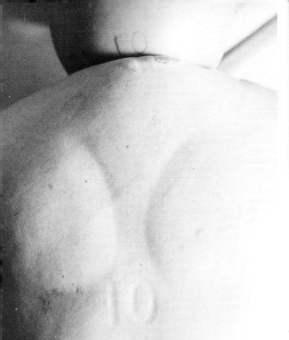

Illustration 3. Close-up of the back of the 22½in (57.2cm) Unis France showing the mark "10" on the back of the neck which corresponds to the mark "10" on the back of the body.

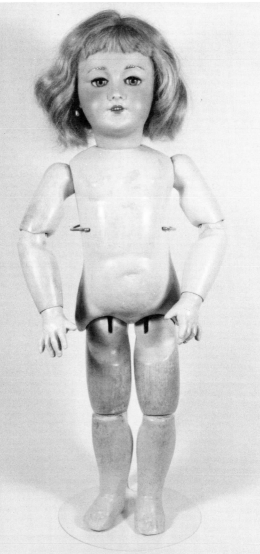

Illustration 4. 22½in (57.2cm) Unis France shown undressed.
RIGHT: Illustration 5. 22½in (57.2cm) Unis France, seen in *Illustrations 1* through *5*, shown wearing her original red silk dress with satin ribbon, matching red hat with cloth flowers, red cotton socks and a replaced shoe.

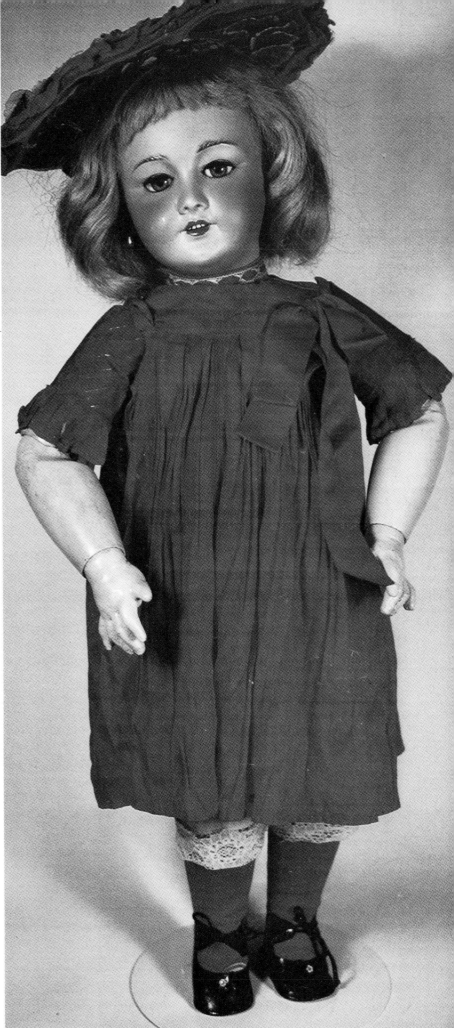

Illustration 6. 7in (17.8cm) Unis France. Head marked:

UNIS
FRANCE

7.   149
301

Bisque socket head, original blonde mohair wig; cobalt blue sleep eyes, single stroke eyebrows; open mouth with tiny upper molded teeth; straight limb composition body with pale yellow painted socks and brown strap shoes. The bisque is not as highly colored as on most dolls of this period.

Illustration 7. Close-up of the 7in (17.8cm) Unis France showing the mark on the back of her head.

ABOVE: Illustration 8. 7in (17.8cm) Unis France shown with her straight limb composition body.

RIGHT: Illustration 9. 7in (17.8cm) Unis France shown in her original trunk with three layers of clothes.

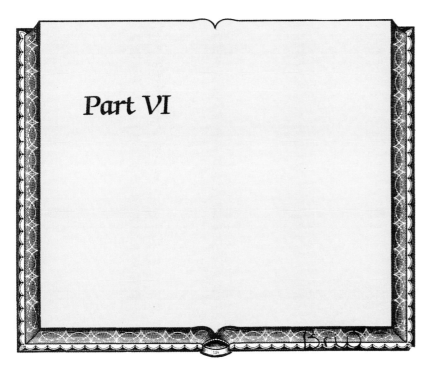

Part VI

Fashion-type

These dolls were made by various French firms from circa 1860 to 1925. Many of them have lovely bisque heads and are dressed in fashionable costumes.☐

Illustration 2. 13½in (34.3cm) Fashion-type.
Head marked: **1.**
Bisque shoulder head with swivel neck, original cork pate and braided blonde mohair wig; blue paperweight stationary eyes, feathered eyebrows; closed mouth; pierced ears; kid body with straight legs. The bisque is very pale and smooth and the cheeks are quite rosy.

Illustration 1. 14in (35.6cm) Fashion-type.
Head and shoulder marked: **2.**
Bisque shoulder head with swivel neck; cobalt blue stationary eyes; closed mouth; pierced ears; kid body; wearing her original organdy dress and hat.

Illustration 3. Close-up of the 13½in (34.3cm) Fashion-type showing the mark on the back of her head.

Illustration 4. 13½in (34.3cm) Fashion-type, seen in *Illustrations 2* and *3*, shown wearing a replaced dress of pale lavender velvet accented with ecru lace and silk ribbons. Her hat, which appears to be original, is made of the finest white leather trimmed with silk ribbons and cloth flowers.

Illustration 5. 15in (38.1cm) Fashion-type. Bisque shoulder head with swivel neck, original cork pate and blonde mohair wig; cobalt blue eyes, feathered eyebrows; closed mouth; pierced ears; gusseted kid body with wired fingers.

Illustration 6. 15in (38.1cm) Fashion-type, seen in *Illustration 5*, shown wearing her original white organdy dress trimmed with ruffles and ribbons, hat of pale gray silk and pink silk ribbons.

CLOCKWISE:

Illustration 7. 10in (25.4cm) Fashion-type.
Marked on back of shoulder: **F. G.**
Bisque shoulder head with stiff neck, original wig of blonde mohair; blue paperweight eyes, feathered eyebrows; closed mouth, painted with a darker red line between the upper and lower lip; very rosy cheeks; pierced ears. The bisque is very pale but it has a large amount of tiny black dots (kiln dirt) fired on.

Illustration 8. Close-up of the 10in (25.4cm) Fashion-type showing the mark on the back of the shoulder head.

Illustration 9. 10in (25.4cm) Fashion-type on a kid body with straight arms and individually stitched fingers which are wired inside. The kid around the shoulder is attached by nails to her shoulder plate which has sew holes. She wears her original regional costume: cotton pantaloons and chemise, white linen blouse under a brown and blue striped overdress. The trim on the dress is dark green rickrack and black silk ribbon tied in bows on top of the shoulder. Her bonnet is made of net-covered cardboard trimmed with ecru lace and pink silk ribbon. A golden cross completes her attire.

Part VII

A. Lanternier & Cie. Limoge, France, 1891 on.

Illustration 2. Close-up of the 15in (38.1cm) A. Lanternier *Cherie* showing the mark on the back of the head.

Illustration 1. 15in (38.1cm) A. Lanternier *Cherie*. Head marked:

> FABRICATION
> FRANCAISE
>
> AL & Cie
> LIMOGES

Cherie 4

Bisque socket head, original human hair wig; blue paperweight eyes; open mouth with upper molded teeth; pierced ears into the head; jointed wood and composition body. The bisque on this doll is not of the finest quality. It is highly colored. The eyebrows, eyelashes and lips are glossy. Her paperweight eyes are of outstanding quality.

Illustration 3. 15in (38.1cm) A. Lanternier *Cherie* shown undressed on her jointed wood and composition body. ▷

85

Danel & Cie., Paris, France, 1889 to 1895.

Illustration 4. 15in (38.1cm) A. Lanternier *Cherie*, seen in *Illustrations 1 through 3*, shown wearing a blue dress with white lace and a straw hat.

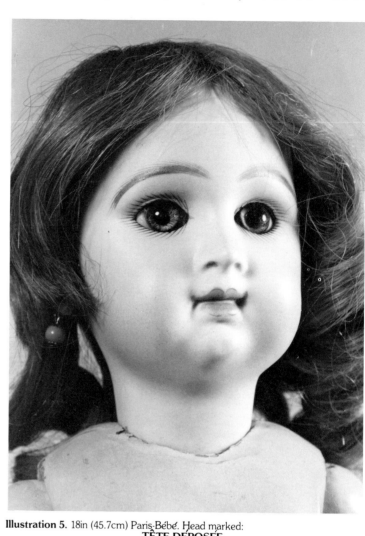

Illustration 5. 18in (45.7cm) Paris-Bébé. Head marked:
TÊTE DÉPOSÉE
PARIS-BÉBÉ
8
8 (incised)
Bisque socket head, replaced human hair wig; blue paperweight eyes, feathered eyebrows; closed mouth; pierced ears. The bisque is very pale and the cheeks have very little coloring. Note the long and slender nose and the dimpled chin. The jointed composition body is stamped in blue on the back of the torso: "PARIS BÉBÉ// DÉPOSÉ."

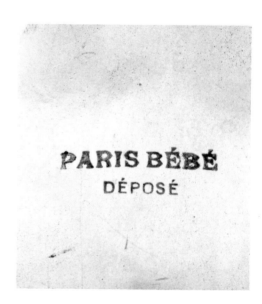

LEFT: Illustration 6. Close-up of the 18in (45.7cm) Paris-Bébé showing the mark on the back of the head.

RIGHT: Illustration 7. Close-up of the 18in (45.7cm) Paris-Bébé showing the stamped mark on the body.

86

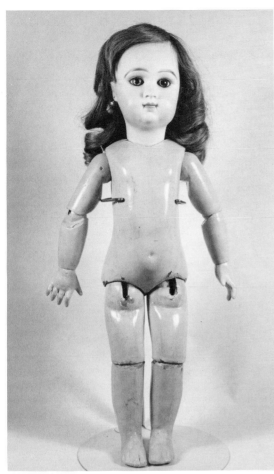

Illustration 8. 18in (45.7cm) Paris-Bébé shown undressed on her jointed composition body.

BELOW LEFT: Illustration 9. 18in (45.7cm) Paris-Bébé, seen in *Illustrations* 5 through 8, shown wearing a beige wool coat dress and bonnet accented by lace and red silk ribbons, black stockings and shoes.

BELOW: Illustration 10. Close-up of the 18in (45.7cm) Paris-Bébé shown in *Illustrations* 5 through 9.

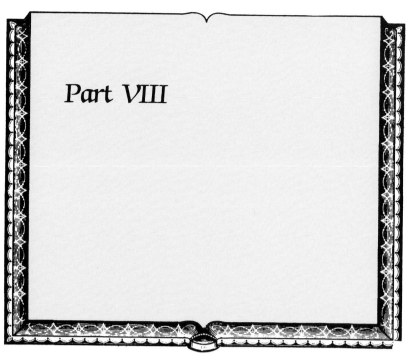

Part VIII

Bru Jne. & Cie., Paris, France, 1866 to 1899.

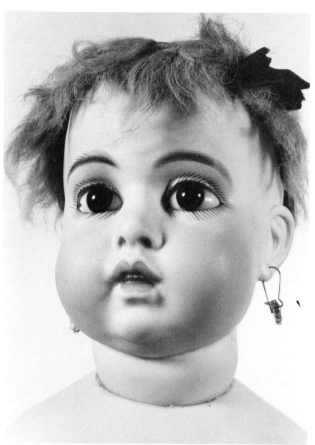

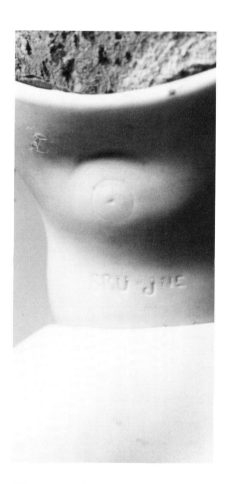

Illustration 1. 18in (45.7cm) Bru. Head marked:

BRU • J^{NE}

Left shoulder marked: **BRU J^{NE}**

Right shoulder marked: **N° 7**

Bisque shoulder head with swivel neck, cork pate and original fur wig; brown paperweight eyes; open/closed mouth; pierced ears; kid body with lower bisque arms; molded bosoms. On this particular doll the little breasts are not tinted pink. *Private Collection.*

Illustration 2. Close-up of the 18in (45.7cm) Bru showing the mark on the back of the head. *Private Collection.*

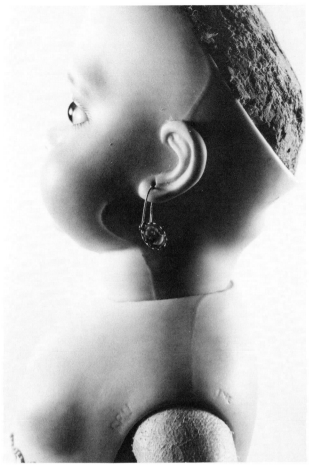

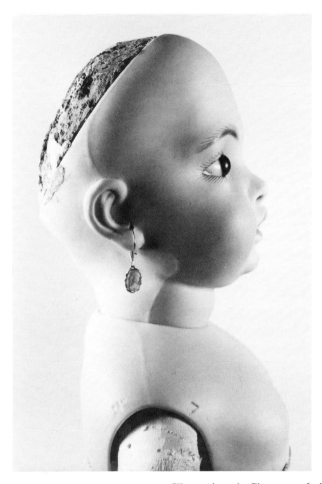

Illustration 3. Close-up of the 18in (45.7cm) Bru showing the mark on her left shoulder as well as the detail of the side of the face and her ear. *Private Collection.*

Illustration 4. Close-up of the 18in (45.7cm) Bru showing the mark on her right shoulder and the detail on the right side of her face. *Private Collection.*

Illustration 5. 18in (45.7cm) Bru, seen in *Illustrations 1* through *4,* shown wearing a green velvet dress with ecru lace and crocheted collar. *Private Collection.*

Pincushion Dolls on Parade

by **Susan Endo**

Photographs by the **Author**

Illustration 1. A 5¼in (13.4cm) Goebel chocolate lady. She is the basic mold from the famous Jenny Lind. She holds a tray with a coffee pot, cup and saucer, and creamer, which are all done in a delft type painting. Her gray hair is adorned with a darker gray ribbon and the sides are done in sausage curls. Her dress has speckled rust and blue-gray dots on the top flounce, which matches the sleeves. The dress itself is a solid blue-gray. Her base has a fancy floral design with her original sticker marked: "Wihelmsfeld Lifelotte Biedermeier 1840." The back of her base is marked with a "4" and the Goebel crown mark: " ♡   ℰ ." She is also marked on the inside of her glazed base with the Goebel crown mark in a royal blue along with the artist's initial "J." The bottom of her tray is incised with the Goebel crown mark along with the numbers "26" and "4¼." What makes her so delightful is that her tray holds three objects, whereas most of the chocolate ladies only have one or two items on their trays.

Pincushion dolls are more than mere porcelain figures with holes in their bases, which at one time might have served as a top to a clothes brush, adorned a lamp shade, helped to pull down a window cover, decorated a trinket box, or were attached to a teapot to catch the drip. The mid 1800s to early 1900s represent the prime period of pincushion dolls.

The more intricate and elaborate dolls are true works of art to be admired for their craftmanship, as well as their esthetic beauty. Well-known names such as Goebel, Dressel & Kister, Schneider, and Rudolstaldt, were but a few of the makers of elegant pincushion dolls. Unfortunately many of the dolls were not marked and their makers remain unknown.

It is interesting to note that many of the finer dolls were designed after famous historical ladies, such as: Mrs. Siddons, a British actress; Princess de Lamballe, of Savoy; La Belle Chocolatiere; Fanny Elssler, an Austrian dancer; Jenny Lind, a Swedish singer; and Marie Antoinette, wife of Louis XVI, to mention just a few. Many other models depict ethnic costumes reflecting conuntries throughout the world.

Since the exuberant interest in antique dolls, the amount of reproductions being made has really escalated. It is important for collectors to be aware that reproductions are not being limited only to the bisque dolls, and that pincushion dolls are also being reproduced. They usually are made from material of lesser quality and lack the finesse that was used

Illustration 2. A 6½in (16.5cm) girl holding a flower pot. Her head is covered with a polka-dotted scarf, tied in a large bow under her chin and another large bow at the base of her neck. Her colors are very muted in blues and coral dots. The "bun" object on top of her head is also of a coral color. She has a fancy floral base and is marked with the number "5" and the Goebel crown mark: " ⌣ ⌣ " on the outside of her base and also on the inside of her base along with the artist's initial "A."

Illustration 4. A 5½in (14cm) model with a green Elizabethan collar, gold crown, orange dress and white lacy sleeves, all trimmed in gold. She holds a purple fan in her right hand. Her brown curls drape her shoulders giving her a very stately appearance. She is marked: "Made In Germany" in front on her base.

Illustration 3. A fully adorned lady, 6¼in (15.9cm), with a fox draped around her shoulders. Her head-dress is yellow, with multi-colored plumes, all trimmed in gold. Her dress is maroon with a green collar. Her look of elegance suggests a real regal quality. She is marked with the numbers: "2649."

Illustration 5. A graceful nude, 9in (22.9cm), from fingertips to base. Her brown hair is decorated with a blue headband and she has an orange line over her eyelids. Her torso is extremely long, exposing her navel. She has a closed recessed base and is marked with the numbers: "9931." The beaded necklace has been added.

LEFT: Illustration 6. Here is an example of a pincushion doll being used as a lamp shade. Her dress is of metal and fits down over a marble base with a bulb, only the base is missing. The doll is 5in (12.7cm) with a blue band and braid in her reddish hair. Her overall height is 10½in (26.7cm). She is a Dressel & Kister and is marked with a blue " C "

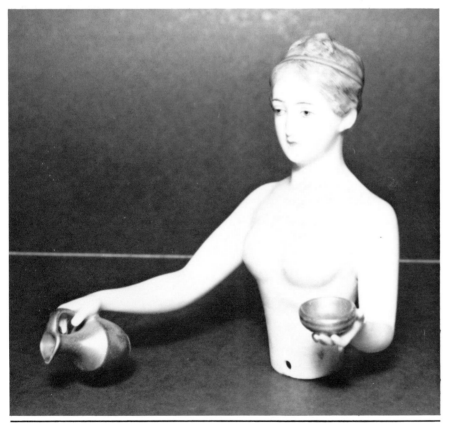

ABOVE: Illustration 8. A lovely example of an unmarked doll. She is 6¼in (15.9cm) wearing a pompadour hair style with long gray curls flowing over her shoulders. Her hair is decorated with lavender flowers and yellow ribbons. Her dress is blue with four orange buttons and a pink collar. She holds a yellow rose in her right hand. Her gold necklace completes her state of dignity.

Illustration 7. A stunning 5½in (14cm) nude with gray hair and a blue band wrapped around the crown of her head. She is holding a gold dish in her left hand and a gold pitcher in her right hand. She is a Dressel & Kister and is marked with a blue " C " inside her base.

Illustration 9. A 7in (17.8cm) nude with a gray pompadour hair style and long curls. Her fingers are extremely long and delicate. Her base has a fancy floral design with the numbers "5½ 320," the Goebel crown mark " " and the letters "R.T."

Illustration 10. A 5in (12.7cm) all-bisque nude, with movable arms and brown glass eyes. She has her original white silk wig and multi-colored silk flowers which decorate her hair in a garland. Her bisque has a pinkish tone with highly rouged cheeks. She is marked with the numbers: "1021."

Illustration 11. A delicate lady of 6in (15.2cm) with applied roses in her gray hair and hand-painted flowers on her dress. Her dress has a white ruffled collar and the bodice is orange and white with gold trim. She holds a pink rose in her right hand. She is marked with the numbers: "9400."

Illustration 12. An elegant lady of 5½in (14cm) admiring herself in the mirror. She wears a purple dress with gold trim and yellow and pink plumes in her brown hair. Her right hand appears to be adjusting one of the plumes in her hair. She is marked with a blue "   "

Illustration 13. A very desirable Oriental figure with a pink kimono, lavender obi and brown fan in her right hand resting on her shoulder. She holds a pink rose in her left hand. She is 3in (7.6cm) and is marked with the numbers: "5978."

in painting the original ones. Most of them are with the arms to the body, as these can be made from a single mold. However, there is one being reproduced that has both arms extended from the body and is made in Taiwan. Reproductions can enhance any collection, as long as they are represented as such, and the collector is aware of what he/she is buying.

As with most pincushion doll collectors, the unusual and rare examples are always sought to highlight their collection. Where have all the extraordinary pieces gone? It is that so few of the finer models were made and those that remain are being housed in museums and private collections? Or do we just have to be more persistent and continue the never-ending search for those breathtaking ladies that are bound to be available to the determined collector? I for one, believe that for those willing to hunt long and hard enough, the exquisite pieces will eventually be uncovered.

How many collectors would have ever dreamed the extent of truly fine pincushion dolls available, at the beginning stage of their collecting? Thank heavens for dedicated collectors who have helped to preserve and cherish the seemingly endless world of pincushion dolls. Here are a few examples of some less common models taken from my book, *A Price Guide To Pincushion Dolls.* □

German Papier-Mâché Dolls

by **Mary Hillier**

Illustration 1. Workroom in Sonneberg, Germany, 1896; "stuffing the skins."

During 1982, when some of my collection was on show at a local school, I went to give the children a few talks on the background of toy making in Victorian times, especially with an explanation of the materials and methods used. Later I had some very nice letters which the youngsters had been urged to write to me and I was amused at one nine-year-old who wrote, "Thank you for coming to show us your DEAD dolls." I realized how "dead" my dolls must seem to them, especially as I had in one case handed round parts of a dismembered "pumpkin head" — the hollow sections, glass eyes, turned wooden limbs and the beautifully hand-stitched clothes. That doll was stuffed with dried moss and was still in her original (rather coffin-shaped) wooden box. What was once a very lively doll industry is also dead.

Papier-mâché dolls must have come in the thousands from that small area around Sonneberg, Germany, where doll making was carried on from the early 19th century. Jo Gerken (*Wonderful Dolls of Papier-Mâché, 1970*) has given a vividly explicit account of the closely inter-related families who were most involved. Her account is invaluable, since she was able to question surviving members of those families and inspect their records. Dressel,

wooden toy making had been carried on there since the Thirty Years War (1618 to 1648) and doll making was largely a cottage industry with a variety that ranged from dolls at 50 pfennig per dozen to 100 Marks each. He was on a visit to acquire new dolls for his three small daughters (Annchen, Lieschen and Miezchen, if anyone needs names for their German dolls!).

molding the heads from the raw papier-mâché. Here the temperature was "like the Sahara" since, after pressing in the molds, the heads had to be slowly dried off on wire racks in the warm atmosphere. This was always considered an unhealthy job. In another studio the heads were sized and painted and almond-shaped openings cut for glass eyes which were brought from

Illustration 2. "Waxing the heads."

Fleischmann, Greiner and Heubach are familiar names to doll collectors. They were born, as it were, with doll making in their blood and inherited traditional methods.

Sonneberg is now behind the Iron Curtain and information is not easily acquired so I was pleased recently to find a German magazine article (1896) in which a writer described the scene when he visited "The Doll Town." He commented that

He gives a lively picture of a family involved in the craft (and there were 12,000 families mostly engaged in the craft at that time). In one room, father and son were swiftly filling up leather bodies from a huge vat of sawdust. It is clear they used a sort of funnel. At a bench next to them his daughter was busy gluing on arms and legs. Their neighboring workman was a "Drucker" or "presser" responsible for

the neighboring town of Lauscha. *Illustration 2* shows a burly workman completing the process by pouring liquid wax from a jug over each head. Finally the eyes were stuck in, hair added made from the pale wool of the angora goat and the dolls taken to the sewing room where a team of women dressed them. Many cheap dolls wore no more than a slight chemise and were later dressed at home. A brightly lit

Illustration 3. An early 12in (30.5cm) wax-over-papier-mâché with natural wool hair.

addition of sulphate of alum or potash was added (about two percent of total). This mixture was first rolled into balls of "dough" which could be rolled out on a table like pastry and cut into squares or strips ready to be forced into the doll head molds.

The finished raw masks would be set out on wire frames to dry, the front mask and back of head being made separate and stuck together when dry. Originally the hand process was performed with great skill and required lengthy training but by the end of the century, metal presses produced the work mechanically.

The whole process became mass organized, especially when papier-mâché limbs and bodies were used for bisque-headed dolls. Often a secret ingredient was used for papier-mâché to prevent the attentions of insects or rats, the commonest deterrents being nicotine dust (snuff), juice from tobacco leaves or from colocynth, the "bitter apple" gourd.

The heads at this stage would have been dull in color and porous, so it was necessary to give them a coating of size and a layer of quickly drying paint before features were added. The size was often made from the gelatinous liquid of stewed parchment shavings (parchment was sheep or goat skin treated for book making). It is interesting how many industries were inter-related and the waste of one used for another in the 19th century.

A special tip for painting cheeks pro-fessionally appeared in one technical book (*Papier-Mâché* by Winzer, 1900). Before

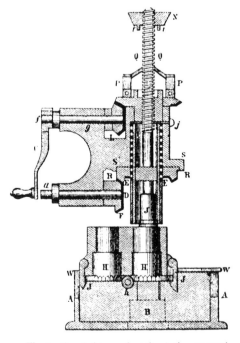

Illustration 4. A type of mechanical press used for making doll masks.

shop on the premises exhibited the finished range of dolls.

What was this material "papier-mâché"? It was certainly not all paper waste and indeed some of the compositions were not paper at all. Recipes were so various and usually preserved with great secrecy. During the 1914 to 1918 war when German dolls were obviously banned by the allies, an English trade magazine (*Toy and Fancy Goods Trader,* 1917) published "German Toy making secrets disclosed" which presumably some refugee had carried off. This was specifically as an aide to British toy makers to imitate.

All the preparations were made from a pulp of soaked and "cooked" paper or sawdust. Paper was prepared by passing through a "devil" or carding machine which

shredded it very fine. White paper waste was used for fine work, brown paper for coarser items. To the prepared pulp was added whiting (ground chalk), plaster of Paris and liquid glue. Variously, according to the waste products easily available, the maker might increase the bulk of fibre by using rye flour, cotton waste (cellulose), linters (mattress flock), combings from woollen mills or kapoc. One recorded maker in Vienna used waste from his Meerschaum pipe factory to make a very refined paste and another recipe used trimmings from a kid glove factory.

The usual proportions were typically: pulp, two parts; whiting, three parts; plaster of Paris, two parts plus glue to mix. To produce a material which would set un-breakably hard and not crumble, a small

Illustration 5. A rosy-cheeked play doll in original condition with molded boots. 1878.

the base complexion paint of the face was quite dry, the workman painted a patch of cinnabar red on the center of cheek and then, taking a dry brush, rubbed it around softly with a circular motion, working away evenly from the center spot. Prussian blue was used for painting eyes and brown umber for eyelashes, eyebrows and hair. Finally a clear varnish could be painted over or the head given a wax bath.

It is hardly surprising with so much individual enterprise that there is enormous variety among the papier-mâché dolls which have come down to us and there was an increasing demand for novelty through the 19th century. The term "milliner's model" has often been used to describe the earliest types of small papier-mâché-headed doll with rigid leather body and wooden arms and legs. It was a fitting name since many must have been used in a shop window to demonstrate fashion or materials and they were convenient to travel as ambassadresses of fashion.

For a display of modeling at its finest, it is only necessary to look at some of the splendid doll heads photographed for the

February/March 1983 issue of **DOLL READER** from the collection of Estelle Johnston. They date from the first half of the 19th century when work was at its finest. The detail of coiffure and features is often so clear one almost imagines the dolls are carved from wood. I am sure that the original models for molds were often carved wood. The lines of the hair and plaits and curls especially seem to reproduce knife cuts and there existed in southern Germany a really outstanding craft of wooden figure carving from the medieval period, as may be witnessed in the religious statuary of their Baroque churches.

Illustration 7, a large 36in (91.4cm) doll with leather body and wooden limbs from Sonneberg is in the collection of Gertrud Rosemann, who has recently opened the Hessisches Puppen Museum, at Hanau/Wilhelmsbad in Germany. (Hanau was the birthplace of the brothers Grimm so it is a very suitable location and easily reached from Frankfurt.) This doll is serenely beautiful, half smiling, almost Madonna-like. She could be the portrait of a local girl, albeit idealized with her loose plaits and plump cheeks. She dates from about 1830 but if some of the coiffure styles were essentially local, others, one must believe, were influenced by more fashionable European styles.

Illustration 8 shows a baby head with open mouth and bamboo teeth but the same model sometimes turns up with a fashionable French body and there are records that Paris, France, enjoyed a high import of German heads.

In the French capital fashions changed swiftly and a fascinating book on coiffure

Illustration 6. Milliners' model resembling wooden carving. *Gertrud Rosemann Collection.*

BELOW: Illustration 7. 36in (91.4cm) doll with Madonna-like face, leather body and wooden limbs.

97

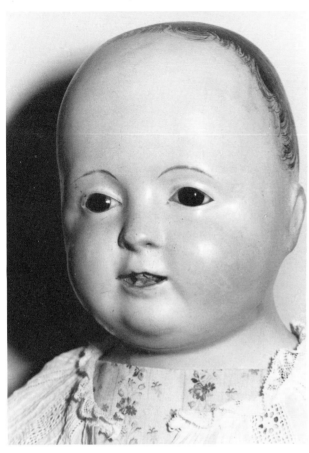

Illustration 8. Baby doll head with glass eyes and bamboo teeth.

BELOW LEFT: Illustration 10. 20in (50.8cm) doll showing Malibran style. 1830. *Courtesy Messrs. Sotheby, London, England.*

(*Coiffure des Femmes en France* by G. d'Eze and A. Marcel, 1886) gives a name to some of the examples copied in doll heads. At the beginning of the century Napoleonic styles favored short hair cut *à la Titus* with curls on the forehead like a Roman Emperor; *à la Galatea* imitated the loose locks of a sea nymph with the wearing of a circlet or bandeau.

At this time mythological subjects were especially popular and portrayed in artists' pictures shown at the Paris Salon. In 1827, when, for the first time, a live giraffe was brought to the Paris menageries there was a fashion for coiffure *à la Giraffe* with hair swept up from the nape to expose a long bare neck and shoulders! In the 1830 period the most popular style was *à la Malibran* imitating the world famous opera star who introduced the curious three section style sometimes called "Queen Adelaide." She had a short, lionized life: born in 1808, she married in 1825, divorced in 1835 and died in 1836 but, at the height of her fame, many dolls were dressed to represent her. In the London Museum there is one carrying a silver skate, memento of an opera performance.

Another very popular style was *à la Berthe* after another actress; the plaits of hair were drawn up below the ears from a central parting. Queen Victoria made this doubly famous as she wore her hair so

Illustration 9. An example of coiffure style *à la Malibran.*

Illustration 11. "Tauflinge," Motschmann type but unmarked.

Illustration 13. The same doll shown in *Illustration 12* but undressed.

Illustration 12. Motschmann type doll, unmarked, with concertina squeak box. 1850s.

styled on her wedding day in 1837. Ringlets *à l'Anglaise* were popular in the 1830s and with them the Pamela bonnet (scuttle shaped) was worn; later on the style encouraged ladies to wear all sorts of flowers, jewels and ribbons in their hair and ornamental combs which often carried an extra hair piece.

By the 1850 period there was a style for loose flowing locks *à la Stewart* and then when Eugenie became the French Empress she led fashion both in hair style and *couture*. One comically named style for hair centrally parted and brought in heavy ringlets to cover the ears was popular for a time and called *"oreilles du chien"* or dog ears. (See *Illustration 17* in Estelle

Johnston's article "A Chronology of Hair Styles of Early Papier-mâché Dolls," February/March 1983 **DOLL READER**.)

After the middle of the century dolls made from papier-mâché had to compete with a luxury output of beautiful china and bisque dolls as well as the poured wax English dolls. Cheaper dolls continued to be produced and unbreakable models must have remained popular as "nursery" dolls, but one must admit a gradual decline in quality. On the other hand, competition produced a lot of variety and novelty. Patents were taken out to combat piracy of clever selling ideas.

After the Paris exhibition of 1855 it seems that some of the dolls introduced

from Japan were copied by German makers and one of them at Sonneberg: Motschmann took out a patent for a baby doll or *gelenktauflinge* (literally "jointed baptismal — or newborn — baby"). Someone commented that they always looked like little boys and of course this would have been true. Japanese dolls depicted boy babies since girls were not especially welcomed. Turned arms and legs imitated Japanese bamboo and a center soft section between the chest and haunch carried a squeaker inside. The method was soon used for other dolls besides babies.

Papier-mâché was well suited to fashioning details of hats, bonnets, snoods

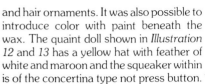

and hair ornaments. It was also possible to introduce color with paint beneath the wax. The quaint doll shown in *Illustration 12* and *13* has a yellow hat with feather of white and maroon and the squeaker within is of the concertina type not press button.

Illustration 14 and *15*, of about 1850, show a pair of cheap wax-over dolls, the smaller one coffee colored and both with lambs wool hair. Another patent for a working doll (German Patent; U.S. Patent

Illustration 16. Patented changeable face bonnet doll.

Illustration 14. A cheap wax-over doll of about 1850. White with pupil-less glass eyes.

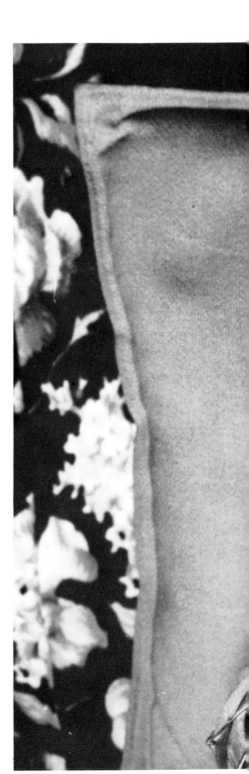

Illustration 15. A cheap wax-over doll of about 1850s. Brown with pupil-less glass eyes.

243752), probably made by Bartenstein, used a hard bonnet to conceal a double changeable expression, smiling and scowling. The head is worked by strings in the side and the arms swing up with a squeak, worked by another string.

Many parts for automata were produced in papier-mâché in Germany for rather simpler models than the luxury automata of Paris and for these it was possible to make character faces of clowns or animals in the same way that a variety of puppet heads and Punch and Judy sets were modeled.

Some years back I stood with a friend on a parking lot in Philadelphia, Pennsylvania, where once the factory of the doll maker Greiner had stood. We tried to imagine the busy scene when they were in full production sending out the fine strong large papier-mâché dolls made there. Greiner and his family came from that same Sonneberg background and introduced German methods successfully. The dolls were made in Philadelphia for over 30 years and I have been shown many fine treasured examples. They too are "dead" just as the many involved in their manufacture but they are not forgotten. More than any other type of doll, papier-mâché seem to retain their character and despite some of the cracks and blows of age, mature. □

BELOW: Illustration 17. Typical Victorian play doll with the Cuno & Otto Dressel mark; well molded arms and legs in hard composition, stuffed body. 1880.

Queen Victoria and Her Dolls

by **Ann Bahar**

The drawings accompanying this article are from *Queen Victoria's Dolls* by Frances Low.

Illustration 1. Mr. Westall was drawing master to the young Princess Victoria during her youth at Kensington Palace. He also painted a masterful portrait of his little student during the years when her life revolved around "Mama," the Princess' governess, Baroness Lehzen, and a fabulous boxful of peg-wooden dolls. *Copyright reserved.*

Queen Victoria was not born a Victorian. Her name evokes a vision of tartan carpets and purple crinolines of stiff ladies staring out of yellowed photographs, of a century bursting with optimism about PROGRESS while the press delivered a flood of morbid tracts and moralizing romances to avid readers. In fact, this is an image of England late in Queen Victoria's reign and hardly resembles the airy, Regency world into which she was born on May 24, 1819.

Princess Victoria's youth was passed at Kensington Palace where she and her mother occupied a suite of rooms on one floor and her maiden Aunt Sophia and eccentric uncle, the Duke of Sussex, lived in apartments on the floor above. Her grandfather, King George III, was mad at Windsor; her Uncle George (later George IV) was the Prince Regent. Jane Austen died two years before Victoria's birth and Thomas Jefferson lived on until she was seven. Clearly, her childhood was closer in spirit to the 18th century than to the bustle of Empire and Industry which characterized the late 19th. The Princess' education was attuned to the age in which she lived. In the palace schoolroom, she was tutored in Latin, religion, dance, voice and drawing. Her drawing master was Mr. Westall, R.A., whose delightful portrait of his young student now hangs in London's National Portrait Gallery.

Victoria's playthings, like her surroundings and daily experience, were one with the age she grew up in. Thus, it is hardly surprising that among her toys there were a number of "Dutch" dolls which cost a mere tuppence apiece in 1825 and which are beyond the means of most collectors today. Eyebrows shoot up, however, when we learn that she possessed *132* of these dolls and that she and her German governess costumed them all.

Princess Victoria adored the artistry and glitter of Regency opera and ballet, and throughout her youth a favorite treat was to be taken to a professional performance. Later, it was grand fun to dress her peg-wooden dolls in outfits which recalled favorite performances. Thus, we meet a tiny Amy Robsart and Robert, Earl of Leicester, from Scott's "Kenilworth," Count Almaviva from "The Barber of Seville" and the celebrated contemporary dancer, Marie Taglioni, each a tuppeny wooden rendering of a full-size flesh-and-blood

performer. Theatrical personalities rub shoulders with titled nobles. There are peg-wooden Duchesses, Countesses and Viscountesses and two sets of noble twins. The little company also includes several peasants, a soldier of fortune and a larger housekeeper with keys at her belt.

Victoria's childhood included few playmates her own age. To compensate for their absence, she created a play world in which her dolls and toys took preeminence. In *Queen Victoria: Born to Succeed* (New York, Harper and Row, 1964), biographer Elizabeth Longford writes that "This silken, feathered, tinselled family with their high-flown names and empty wooden faces turned out to be a substitute for the brothers and sisters the Princess lacked. Her childhood friends were grown-up people or dolls." (Page 31.)

Victoria's 2in (2.5cm) equals 1 ft (30.5cm) scale dolls' house provided a delightful backdrop for doll dramas. The house, now part of the permanent

Illustration 3. Queen Victoria's dolls' house, opened. The entire ground floor is occupied by an enormous kitchen while the larger drawing room upstairs has great potential for imaginative play. The little princess frequently developed games in which her peg-wooden dolls inhabited this toy home. *Copyright reserved.*

QUEEN VICTORIA'S DOLLS

Illustration 4. The title page from Frances Low's *Queen Victoria's Dolls,* published in London in 1894. This Victorian bestseller grew out of Mrs. Low's well-received article in the *Strand Magazine* and remains the best source of information about the young Victoria's dolls to this day.

Illustration 5. Artist Alan Wright's charming drawing of the doll box in which Victoria's dolls were stored when they were not in use. Note Mrs. Martha, the housekeeper, who stands at the left in the sketch. Compare Alan Wright's rendering to the photograph of the actual doll among the illustrations in the article.

collection of the Museum of London, is a simple two-room affair. Downstairs, there is a kitchen; above, is an elegant room that served as a drawing room or ballroom, according to the need of the moment. The Princess also possessed two toy tea services, a peepshow made of cardboard which opened at the top and a toy sofa of painted wood, upholstered in satin and measuring 20in (50.8cm) long. There was a homemade bazaar stall filled with tiny beaded purses and shoes made by the Princess with the assistance of her governess. Any imaginative child would revel in the possibilities for "games" which such a nursery presented.

When Victoria was 14, she packed away her 132 dolls and turned to the grown-up world where, during the years that followed, the Crown, marriage, motherhood and, finally, widowhood, became all-absorbing preoccupations. The Queen's childhood toys might have remained in some dusty storeroom indefinitely if author Frances Low had not discovered them and published an article on the subject in the September 15, 1892, issue of the *Strand Magazine.* Queen Victoria was then at the height of her popularity, midway between the exuberant Golden (1887) and Diamond (1897) Jubilee celebrations. Reader response to the romantic tale of little Victoria and her dolls was so enthusiastic that Mrs. Low hastened to expand the article into a book, *Queen Victoria's Dolls,*

which appeared in 1894. The publicity which that boxful of old tuppeny dolls received in the 1890s created a glow that never faded; the Queen's collection remains the best-known in the world.

Stylistically, Frances Low's book is embarassingly "Victorian." It is thicker with commas than a fruitcake is with raisins, and the sentences are long and contorted. Yet, it retains a strange power to bring alive a fascinating corner of the Queen's life story. Sir Henry Ponsonby, who served the Crown for over 30 years, told Mrs. Low: "Her Majesty was very much devoted to dolls, and indeed played with them till she was nearly fourteen years old. Her favorites were...small wooden dolls, which she could occupy herself with dressing; and they had a house in which they could be placed... Miss Victoria Conroy (later Mrs. Hammer) came to see her once a week, and occasionally others played with her, but with these exceptions she was left alone with the companionship of her dolls....The Queen usually dressed the dolls from some costume that she saw either in the theatre or in private life." Victoria personally dressed 32 of the dolls; the rest were dressed by her governess, Baroness Lehzen. Queen Victoria explained in a footnote to Mrs. Low's text that the Baroness did the fine work which was too difficult for a child to manage. This included the knitting of exquisite doll stockings, worked in gossamer wool on lace

needles.

The author of *Queen Victoria's Dolls* failed to comprehend the rough beauty of the peg-wooden doll. She complained that "they are not aesthetically beautiful, with their Dutch doll — not Dutch — type of face. Occasionally, owing to a chin being a little more pointed, or a nose a little blunter, there is a slight variation of expression; but with the exception of height, which ranges from three to nine inches, they are precisely the same. There is the queerest mixture of infancy and matronliness in their little wooden faces, due to the combination of small sharp noses, and bright vermilion cheeks to the combination of small sharp noses, and bright vermilion cheeks (consisting of a big dab of paint in one spot), with broad, placid brows, over which, neatly parted on each temple, are painted elaborate, elderly, greyish curls. The remainder of the hair is coal black, and is relieved by a tiny yellow comb perched upon the back of the head."

About 120 of the dolls represent women and girls. There is a sprinkling of rag doll infants, and the remaining dolls are seven or eight wooden gentlemen with shiny painted black moustaches. All the costumes are exquisite. "Tiny ruffles are sewn with fairy stitches; wee pockets on aprons (it must be borne in mind for dolls of five or six inches) are delicately finished off with minute bows — little handkerchiefs not more than half-an-inch square are embroidered with red silk initials, and have drawn borders; there are chatelaines of white and gold beads, so small that they almost slip out of one's hands in handling..." There are dolls with crowns, dolls with boas and dolls with velvet hats. The Earl of Leicester sports a white satin tunic slashed with pink and wears the blue ribbon of the Garter on his breast. If we may judge from her dolls, it is quickly apparent that the youthful Queen Victoria was easily amused. Two rag doll babies belong to "the stately Alice, Countess of Rothesay.... The tiny creatures are evidently twins, though one infant is attired in satin with a white satin girdle, whilst the other wears humble lawn. Perhaps...the satin baby is the heir."

Amidst this glitter of Regency theatrical and beribboned court costume, a few dolls stand apart. These include the rag babies, a few cheerful peasants and the housekeeper. Unforgettable among these is Ernestine, whom Mrs. Low calls "the quaintest little doll imaginable which (according to the Princess's handwritten notes made in childhood) 'was brought from Berne.' Unlike the other dolls, it is made of white leather, is about four inches in height, and the same in breadth. She is a little squat, dumpy woman, with a huge waist and a squareness of countenance and figure and frock that is irresistibly humourous. Her short, full, black skirt, edged with red, her green-striped silk apron, muslin chemisette, frilled cape, black velvet stomacher and braces give the buxom little woman an absurd air of reality and familiarity..."

Perhaps because Queen Victoria's reign was so long and spanned the decades of Britain's most sensational expansion, perhaps because she was the first British monarch to commission thousands of royal photographs, we tend to see her life as a series of tableaux rather than as a complex interweaving across time. We shut our eyes and see the family groups "arranged" on stone steps outside

Illustration 6. Frances Low described Mrs. Martha, the housekeeper doll, in the *Strand Magazine* article: "A prince of caps is worn by Mrs. Martha, Housekeeper. She is a bigger and more substantial doll than the rest, with a fat, round, good-humoured face, a broad nose, and an air of prosperous complacency which send your thoughts back to oak chest, lavender-pressed sheets, and the attractive 'family housekeeper' of a certain type of domestic novel." *Museum of London.*

BELOW: Illustration 7. The rag doll infants from the doll box. If the quality of stitching is observed, it seems likely that little Victoria dressed most of these tiny "babies" herself. The baby in the bottom row, center, was one of the children of "the Earl and Countess of Dudley," and somewhere in this nursery are the satin and lawn babies of the Countess of Rothesay. Mrs. Low surmised that the satin baby must be the heir! *Museum of London.*

Illustration 8. Four of the Regency peg-woodens from the collection of 132 which formed the play world of the young Queen Victoria during her childhood at Kensington Palace. Victoria dressed her dolls with the assistance of Baroness Lehzen, selecting outfits which reflected elegant theatrical costumes of the times. *Museum of London.*

Balmoral or at Osborne. There is the view of the Queen, morosely contemplating a white marble bust of the Prince Consort after his tragic death in 1861, grim pictures of a tightlipped, stout little lady in black flanked by stoic betrothed couples or newly-weds, the famous Golden and Diamond Jubilee portrait photographs in which the elderly Queen wears her lace wedding veil over the inevitable black satin dress. However, if we push the clock back to the days before widowhood, before marriage, before the Crown and before photography, we find an unexpected image which wrecks the cliché and improves the historic focus. For the tired Empress to whom Benjamin Disraeli could say: "Madam, I give you India," began life as a tiny Regency child who planted radishes in her vegetable garden and then ran indoors to play with her dolls. ☐

BIBLIOGRPAHY

Fawdry, Kenneth and Marguerite, *Pollock's History of English Dolls and Toys,* London, Ernest Benn, 1979.

Gernsheim, Helmut and Alison, *Victoria R.* New York, G. P. Putnam's Sons, 1959.

H. H. Princess Marie Louise, *My Memories of Six Reigns,* London, Evans Brothers, Limited, 1956.

Jackson, Mrs. F. Neville, *Toys of Other Days,* London, White Lion Publishers Limited, 1975. Reprint of 1908 edition.

Longford, Elizabeth, *Queen Victoria: Born to Succeed,* New York, Harper and Row, Publishers, 1964.

Low, Frances, "Queen Victoria's Dolls," in the *Strand Magazine,* September 1892.

Low, Frances, *Queen Victoria's Dolls,* London, George Newnes, Limited, 1894.

Sitwell, Edith, *Victoria of England,* Boston, Houghton Mifflin Company, 1936.

Illustration 9. Although the Museum of the London notes that this doll was dressed by Queen Victoria at the age of seven, it is more likely that the delicate stitching was managed by the Queen's governess, Baroness Lehzen. Queen Victoria took credit personally for having dressed only 32 of the 132 dolls in the collection. *Museum of London.*

An Olde English "Pedlar" Doll

by FRIEDA MARION

Photographs by Elizabeth Bowden

To own a true Notion Nanny is the dream of many an advanced collector, a dream which was gratified for Lorna Lieberman when she acquired the 9½in (24.2cm) antique doll illustrated here.

Mrs. Lieberman's interest in dolls centers on early types with papier-mâché or composition heads. She designs and makes beautiful original clothes, and although she has given up her designer shop, she enjoys costuming dolls or restoring antique clothing for the dolls in her collection. It was inevitable that she would find irresistible this perfect little Notion Nanny decked out with so many miniature sewing aids!

The 1840-1850 doll has a peg-wooden jointed body. The head has molded hair braided in a chignon coiled over a comb. Similar wooden dolls are shown on page 232 in the Merrill and Perkins *Handbook of Collectible Dolls,* captioned ". . . pegged wooden dolls with modeled plaster heads are rarer than those of all wood." It is often difficult to determine the exact ingredients used for such rare little dolls and Mrs. Lieberman simply calls her doll's head composition.

The face is delicately detailed, with grey lash-lines topped by comely grey eyebrows over the painted blue eyes. Secure on her own wooden stand, the doll displays a gown of lavender and grey striped silk lined

with gauze. Her undergarments include two petticoats, one of linen and one of gauze, but, in keeping with her age, no drawers. In *The Mode in Costume,* page 263, R. Turner Wilcox writes, "Until 1800, only two or three references to them "[drawers]" exist," and goes on to say that even then, drawers were only a decorative part of the costume, showing beneath the skirts, we assume. Since Notion Nannies were dressed in traditional fashion, it is not likely that such garments would have been considered necessary for a doll of this early period.

Over her dress, the little "pedlar" doll wears a red hooded cape bound in narrow black ribbon, and on her head is a fetching lace cap known as a "cornet," bedecked with ribbons, flowers and leaves.

Her pack, suspended by ribbons around her neck, is stuffed with a variety of wares, most of which relate to sewing as befits a true Notion Nanny.

Crammed into her "pedlar's" bag, or attached to it, are laces, buttons and beads, pinholders with tiny pins, canvas needlepoint patterns, doilies, picot-edged ribbons and wee hanks of colored yarns and thread. There are also pretty pieces of dolls' jewelry, dainty silk reticules, miniature song books and a tiny pen-wiper, all commonly sold by the human counterpart of a "pedlar" doll, and many of which are to be found on original antique dolls. A special delight is a little hand-made silk combination sewing-case and needle-book which rolls up neatly, and best of all are the diminutive, wooden peg-jointed dolls' dolls, carefully dressed and ready to rejoice the heart of the most sophisticated doll collector.

The pride and pleasure of preserving a tiny bit of history add greatly to the satisfaction of ownership, and this choice little Olde English "Pedlar" doll deserves the loving place she is accorded in Lorna Lieberman's doll room.

GERMAN DOLLS
and
WORLD WAR I

by **Dorothy S. & Evelyn Jane Coleman**

Usually when dating a German doll it is wise to assume that it was made either prior to World War I or after 1920. The hiatus during the war years and shortly thereafter provided a period when there were very few German dolls being manufactured. Not only were the German doll makers involved with wartime activities but feeling against Germans and their products was also a deterrent.

Some idea of the forcefulness of this anti-German feeling in Britain can be seen by the following quotations from British toy trade journals.

February 1917: "Once upon a time...when commercial travelers from the Fatherland were flooding the world with their eloquence - and their goods - those of us who had good taste feared for a moment that one day the world would be entirely invaded by the hideous products of German rubbish. ... Do you remember the abominable Teutonic ornaments (always adorned with English and French labels)...?

"And the German dolls! - The appalling dolls at Sonneberg, whose ugliness frightened the little children of England and France! ... The German doll will remain an unforgetable example of ridicule. And the awkwardness of the gretchens, with their stiffness and inelegance, which seemed to be symbolised by the heavy clumsy dolls.

"Dolls from Sonneberg were all made after one model, angular and barbarous. If you saw one you saw them all. ...

"The dolls of Sonneberg were al-ways dressed in showy colours, shockingly assorted. ...

"The Great War among other things, has delivered us from the German doll. This alone is something! Babies will never regret it!"

These quotations are from *The Toy and Fancy Goods Trader*; similar sentiments were also expressed by the British periodical *The Toyshop and Fancy Goods Journal* in February 1917:

"Prior to August 1914 we bought all [dolls] the country required...from Germany; Sonneberg, in Saxe-Meiningen, being the chief centre of manufacture. ... The annual report of the Sonneberg Chamber of Commerce sets forth that the German Toy Trade must count on an extremely uphill struggle to regain its prewar position in world markets. ...

"The [British] Committee on Enemy Influence is giving special attention to the matter. ... and will be glad to have any information that is likely to assist in the work of frustrating the wily Hun [German]." The use of the word "all" is questionable as regards dolls from Germany. It is known that Dean and others were making dolls in Britain and that the S.F.B.J. supplied dolls, also. Of course, it was possible that many of the S.F.B.J. dolls were actually made in Germany just prior to World War I.

In January 1918, *The Toy and Fancy Goods Trader* reported:

"German doll manufacturers are experiencing the utmost difficulty in obtaining materials for the dresses of the few dolls which they are producing, and for what is being got exorbitant prices are being paid. This is a striking indication of the great scarcity of textile materials in Hunland. ...

"The German toy manufacturers are keenly alive to the necessity for preparing for after the war trade. They realise that most of their overseas markets are closed against them and that they will need to use every endeavour if they are again to resume commercial relations with their old customers."

The same British magazine in February 1918 stated: "A little over three and a-half years ago, at the time the war broke out, there existed in this country a perfect organisation for the distribution of German and Austrian goods in Great Britain. That organisation consisted of certain importing houses of both British and German nationality...and in some instances of actual English branches of German and Austrian manufacturers. ...

"It is quite true that the actual English branches of German houses have been closed down. ...

"We do not know whether we can rely on a period of total prohibition of certain or all German and Austrian good after the war. ...

"Messrs Heywood [Abel Heywood and Sons Ltd. handled wood toys and dressed dolls]...said that they had decided not to interfere with their business relations with the firms who previous to the war, were looked upon as German houses, but if any of these houses handled a single line of German

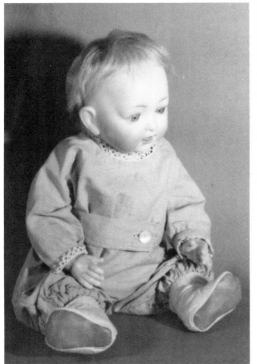

Illustration 1. 14in (35.6cm) excellent quality bisque character head on a bent-limb composition body; wig, sleep eyes, open mouth; original homemade rompers. This doll was bought in Düsseldorf, Germany, only a few weeks prior to World War I. The head bears the mold number 152 which was made by Hertel, Schwab & Co.

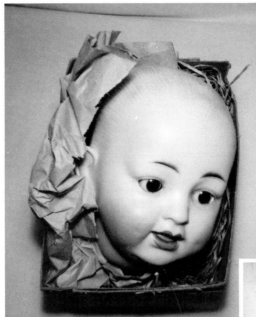

Illustration 2. 5in (12.7cm) excellent quality bisque character head with molded and painted hair, glass eyes and an open mouth. This doll is shown in its original brown cardboard box and is mold number 151 made by Hertel, Schwab & Co. *The late Eleanor Jean Carter Collection.*

BELOW: Illustration 3. Mark on the 5in (12.7cm) socket head shown in *Illustration 2.* The 151 mold number is probably the molded hair version of the wigged mold number 152 shown in *Illustration 1.* Both of these heads were made by Hertel, Schwab & Co. *The late Eleanor Jean Carter Collection.*

goods after the war, their account would be promptly closed, and his firm would refuse to do any further business with them whatever."

Another article in the same February 1918, issue of *The Toy and Fancy Goods Trader*, discussed: "The Toy Trade in Germany, ... the German Toy industry is showing the effects of over three years of war. Simplicity is now the rule in toyshops. Wood which was formerly used only for the cheaper sorts of toys, is now the chief material employed. The manufacture of new dolls is becoming impossible through want of flour, which mixed with cement forms the stuffing for the bodies. Wax, which is used for the heads of the better-class dolls, is almost unobtainable; the same remark applies to the stuffs and lace used for the making of dolls' shoes, hats, dresses, stocking, etc."

In September 1918, *The Toy and Fancy Goods Trader*, painted a very bleak picture of the many substitute materials that had to be used in Germany for dolls and toys. It stated:

"The shortages of countless kinds of raw and subsidiary materials is so great that the manufacture of very many sorts of toys and dolls would have been impossible but for substitutes. For many things, indeed no suitable substitutes have yet been discovered, as for instance, for furs, leather, and plush. ... Sheepskins, goatskins, calfskins, and hareskins are almost out of the question. Nor can the poor quality felts and paper materials take the place of leather and plush; while for dolls' clothing no substitutes will do. The public reject dolls' dresses made of paper or paper stuff, alleging that paper substances are ugly and stiff and soon wear out. ...

"One of the most important subsidiary articles for making dolls is mohair. ... Sonneberg alone worked up several million marks' worth annually. In the meantime, however, a substitute had to be discovered for mohair, and it was found in artificial mohair, which unlike artificial silk, scarcely differs from the real article. But it suffers from the disadvantage of being too expensive, and apart from that has been placed under embargo for Army requirements. There was, therefore, no other course open but to use human hair. Of this, however, the quantities are not large, and as its price is high it came into use only for the very best kind of doll.

"Sewing thread is another subsidiary article for which a substitute had to be found, because the original has become very scarce indeed. It has been replaced to a limited extent by paper thread. Varnish has become so expensive that it is out of the question for the toy industry. ... It is difficult to find glue substitutes, and there is therefore an enormous demand for bone glue. Pasteboard has taken the place of cork."

In January 1919, *Games and Toys* published an article on the "Toy Industry in Germany" from an earlier German periodical. It read:

"Dolls cannot be made any more owing to the lack of the meal and cement used in making the bodies. Also the material for heads for the better kinds of dolls can no longer be obtained, and the same is true of the goods from which the shoes, bonnets, clothes, etc., are made. ...

"The biggest German toy factories have secured large Government contracts to do war work."

The war finally ended in November 1918, but the return to peace was not

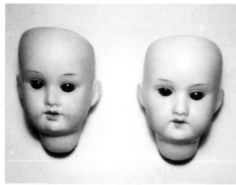

Illustration 4. These two 5in (12.7cm) bisque heads made by Armand Marseille, mold number 390, are very poor quality and were probably made during World War I. Other examples of mold number 390 found with fine quality bisque were probably made before or after the war. These heads are marked: "Armand Marseille//Germany//390//A 11/0 M." *The late Eleanor Jean Carter Collection.*

followed immediately by the full resumption of the German doll making industry. *The Toyshop and Fancy Goods Journal* in July 1919 reported:

"Although Trading with the Enemy restrictions have been somewhat modified, it is hoped that patriotism, common-sense, and good taste will prevent dealers in toys and fancy goods from handling German-made goods for a long time to come. It is amazing, but

true that German bagmen are on the warpath already, beating up for orders." But their presence was most unwelcome in Britain.

The report on the Leipzig Autumn Fair published in *The Toy and Fancy Goods Trader*, October 1919, stated:

"Nearly all branches of German industry are on the verge of bankruptcy, due principally to the shortage of coal and secondly to the loss of export trade, which carries with it the inability to purchase much needed foreign raw materials. ...

"In the doll trade it appears there has been comparatively few actual sales made at the Fair. ...

"The dolls in most cases were poorly clothed and made of cheap material. Better class dolls were four or five times pre-war prices, the reason being of course, the shortage of raw materials (cotton, wool and linen), which the Germans must purchase at the present unfavourable rate of exchange."

In December 1919, *The Toy and Fancy Goods Trader*, reported the following items:

"France has decided to place a big tariff on toys coming into the country from Germany. ...

"During the last few weeks many neutral and also English and American toy buyers have visited Sonneberg. ...

"An association of Sonneberg Doll and Toy Manufacturers is being formed. ...

"A luxury tax of 15 per cent, to be paid by the manufacturers, has been pronounced on...dolls or animals over 50 cm. long. Others not named are to be tax free."

In February 1920, the same magazine reported that "Nearly everything manufactured or sold in Germany is subject to one or more taxes. A tax of 1½ per cent is primarily imposed on all goods sold."

The Toy and Fancy Goods Trader, in May 1920, published an article written by an American which stated; "There are here, as in England, a number of firms showing German toys. These however, it is easy to see, are nearly all either pre-war produced or assembled from old pre-war parts, and I have not yet come across any firm who is taking orders for regular German lines. It is interesting also to know that the two great toy trade journals in this country have adopted the same policy toward this trade which we have taken, and under no circumstance will they accept German advertisements or advertisements for German goods."

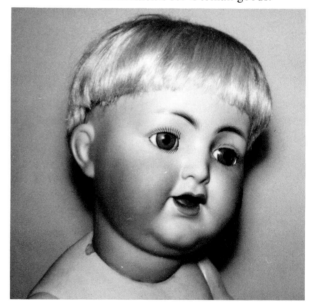

LEFT: Illustration 5. 21½in (54.6cm) bent-limb character baby made by Kämmer & Reinhardt with a bisque head made by Simon & Halbig, mold number 126. This doll was received in America for Christmas 1920. The quality of the bisque is not up to Simon & Halbig's usual standard and the body has metal spring joints rather than rubber elastic which was in short supply during World War I.

ABOVE: Illustration 6. Close-up of 21½in (54.6cm) doll shown in *Illustration 5*. The doll has a wig, sleep eyes and an open mouth. Mark on head is: "K ✡ R//SIMON & HALBIG//126." Circumference of head is 14¾in (37.6cm).

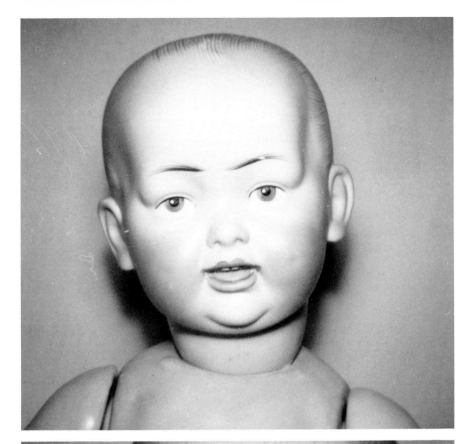

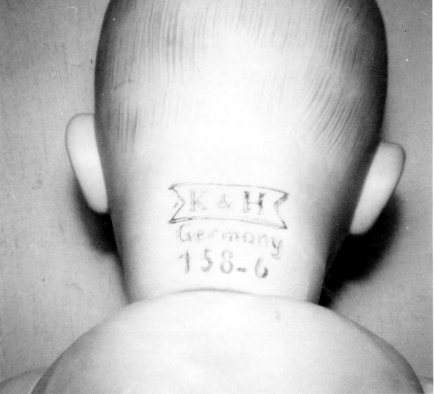

However in April 1921, *The Toy and Fancy Goods Trader*, published an advertisement for Charles W. Baker of London who offered "some of the prettiest and best finished dolls on the market." The accompanying illustration showed a fully-jointed doll dressed in a chemise and having a six-pointed star label with the words "Meine// Einzige//Baby" on it. This label identified the doll as having been made by Kley & Hahn of Germany, but it is not known whether this doll was from old stock or was a recent German post World War I product. A similar advertisement by Charles W. Baker a few months later in the December 1921 issue of the same magazine, showed a bent-limb baby version of the Kley & Hahn Meine Einzige Baby.

The Toyshop and Fancy Goods Journal, in May 1921 reported: "A big shipment of German...dolls reached Swansea on the 12th...German toy manufacturers have branches in France which are not stated to be German and toys are sent there all ready to be assembled."

Martin Raphael & Co. Ltd. of London advertised in *The Toyshop and Fancy Goods Journal* in August 1921 that they "are direct agents for the leading Continental Manufacturers and quote lowest possible prices. Wholesale and Merchants only supplied BABY DOLLS Dressed & Undressed. DOLLS HEADS of China, Celluloid and Steel, Socket, Baby, Shoulder, with and without Wigs." The British used the word "china" for "bisque" and the doll illustrated was named "Melitta." The "Melitta" dolls made by Edmund Edelmann of Sonneberg had bisque heads made by Armand Marseille.

The same magazine in September 1921, reported: "That Germany is recovering rapidly from the economical calamities under which it has suffered is perfectly obvious. ... Wagner & Co., manufacturers and wholesalers of Bayern [Bavaria], Germany and prominent exhibitors of dolls and toys at the Leipsic [sic] Messe." stated "We are too full up with orders from the United States of America to undertake any further orders for your country," meaning England. Wagner & Co. appears to have been D. H. Wagner & Sohn.

By the end of 1921 German dolls were back on the British market and the animosity and problems of the war years appear to have been forgotten. *The Toy and Fancy Goods Trader* in

TOP: Illustration 7. 15in (40.6cm) bent-limb character baby made by Kley & Hahn with a bisque head made by Hertel, Schwab & Co. using mold number 158. Since dolls made by Kley & Hahn were one of the first German dolls to appear in British toy trade journals in 1921 after the war and since mold number 158 could have come after mold numbers 151 and 152, which appear to have been used just prior to World War I, it is possible that this was one of the early dolls made after the German recovery following World War I. *Dorothy Annunziato Collection.*

BOTTOM: Illustration 8. Mark on the bisque head of the 16in (40.6cm) doll produced by Kley & Hahn, seen in *Illustration 7:* "K&H//Germany//158-6." Circumference of head is 10¾in (27.4cm). *Dorothy Annunziato Collection.*

December 1921, published an advertisement of W. Seelig of London. This advertisement included: "Kestner 'Crown' Dolls; Pfeiffer's Viennese Dressed Dolls; Gerlachs Dolls House Articles; Wagner & Zetzsches Kid body Dolls, Shoes, Stockings, Etc.; Sehms Miniature Dressed Dolls; and Sonneberg Dressed and Undressed Dolls." In the same issue there was also an advertisement by Dennis, Malley & Co. with their doll factories in Neustadt, Waltershausen and Catterfeld.

Thus by the end of 1921, after seven years of war and post-war problems the production of German dolls appears to have been resumed. In dating German dolls one must remember that they were probably made before 1915 or after 1920. A few dolls were made in Germany at the beginning of the war and in 1919 some dolls were made for German children but in the Ciesliks' book *Lexikon of the German Doll Industry*, there is a void for the years from 1916 to 1919 in nearly every entry. The German dolls that were made in these years probably can be identified because of the wartime substitutions which had to be used in their manufacture.

Authors' Note: The wartime propaganda against German dolls is pure propaganda and in no way should it reflect on the quality of German dolls. Only the wartime shortages of materials caused inferior German dolls. □

Illustration 9. 12in (30.5cm) bisque head character doll marked: "255//3//0. I. C.," a doll identified by the Ciesliks as made by Kestner about 1921. The bisque in this doll's head is not as good as we usually find in the Kestner dolls, probably because it was made soon after World War I. *Courtesy of Sotheby Parke Bernet, New York, New York.*

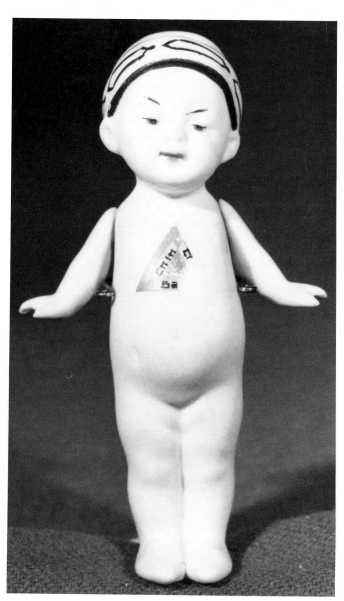

Illustration 10. 4in (10.2cm) all-bisque doll known from its label as *Chin Chin* made by Gebrüder Heubach shortly after World War I. During World War I Japan supplied bisque dolls, among them the all-bisque *Queue San Baby* dolls. *Chin Chin* was the slightly smaller German version made after World War I when Germany was trying to regain its market from Japan and the rest of the world.

Schlopsnies Dolls in...The Extraordinary
STEIFF
Circus
DISPLAY

by **Barbara Spadaccini-Day**

Illustrations by **Gilles de Fayet**

BELOW: Illustration 2. Lady (45cm [17¾in]) and little girl, "Lila Scharpe" (30cm [11⅞in]). Lady dressed in Swiss lawn lace-trimmed dress. Blonde sewn-on mohair wig; beady glass eyes; articulated felt body. Not dated. "Lila Scharpe" dressed in white trimmed, mauve flowered dress with mauve sash. Blonde sewn-on mohair wig; beady glass eyes; painted facial features; felt articulated body. 1921. *Steiff Collection, Giengen, Germany.*

LEFT: Illustration 1. "Erich." Blue cotton suit with white collar, apron, knitted socks and leather shoes; beady glass eyes; sewn-on mohair wig; felt cap. Articulated felt body. No date was given, but this doll appeared in the 1913 New-York catalog issued by Steiff. *Steiff Collection, Giengen, Germany.*

The highlight of an exhibition, "Circus and Toys" held in the Musee des Arts Décoratifs, Paris, France, which ran from the middle of October 1984 to the end of January 1985 was undoubtly a scene of a circus ring. This was no ordinary circus scene. For without being a connoisseur of dolls and animals, many visitors were as spellbound as the most experienced doll collectors.

For the first time in the history of the Steiff firm, some of its treasures had not only been lent, they had traveled much further afield, crossing the boundaries of their country of origin, Germany, arriving in France, to participate in the above named exhibition.

Encased and protected by high glass panels, this huge scene measuring some four meters by four meters (approximately 13 feet square) with its inner circus ring (diameter two meters 75 = 9 feet diameter) and bandstand was part of a temporary exhibition dealing with the general theme of toys inspired by the circus. The toys on display were grouped together either by the material in which they were made — i.e. wood, composition etc., or by subject matter like automata, optical

toys, small mechanical toys; or then again by topic such as clowns or performing animals. The toys on show, as in the other successful exhibition that Monica Burckhardt, curator of the Toy Department, organized during the 1982 winter months, originated from a span of time of approximately a century — from the last quarter of the 19th century to contemporary plastic toys that one can buy in the shops today. As is her custom, present day artisans had been invited to participate as well.

The toys on exhibit were not just limited to those of French manufacture; China, Japan, Czechoslovakia, India, Poland and the U.S.S.R. were represented by items as well as those coming from the other European countries. The United States were well represented with a rare — for France that is — display of a Schoenhut circus, comprising a great number of animals and figures, including a bisque-headed lady equestrian and ring leader.

Although this was not particularly an exhibition for doll lovers, except for the extraordinary Steiff circus, there were several clown dolls and marionettes to be discovered on show in various spots.

Even so, it was a rewarding visit for doll enthusiasts. For never before have they been able to catch a glimpse of so many old Steiff dolls assembled in one place. Steiff dolls, numbering a total of 59, some of which were in pristine condition — "character" and "comic" mainly from the beginning decades of this century.

Some are listed and photographed in the recent reprint of the 1913 Steiff New York catalog. (Reprinted by the Washington Dolls' House and Toy Museum, foreword by Flora Gill Jacobs). Such as "Coloro" and "Caro," two clowns featured on page 24' "Thi" the Indian, the "Mexican cow-boy" and the "Nigger" on page 26; these were listed as Comic dolls. "Erich," a sweet little boy was listed as a "character" doll. This illustrated commercial catalog proves that these were not just one-of-a-kind doll created for display

Illustration 3. "Feuerwehr Kommandant" (Fire Brigade Commanding Officer). Charcoal grey jacket with brass buttons, brown leather shoes. Extraordinary blonde hair treated in two distinctive ways — long disheveled curls on sewn-on short mohair wig; whispy mustache; green glass eyes with black dot for pupil which produces a slightly cross-eyed look, articulated body. This would probably be considered a "comic doll," as compared to a "character doll," according to their 1913 catalog.

Illustration 4. Part of the total Steiff Circus Scene, measuring about 9ft (274.2cm) in diameter. The total scene is made up of almost 80 figures and animals, the majority dating from the beginning of the second decade of the 20th century. *Steiff Collection, Giengen, Germany.*

LEFT: Illustration 5. Man and woman, 55cm and 45cm (about 21¾in and 17¾in) tall. Man dressed in charcoal grey suit with plus-fours type of trousers and out-sized leather shoes; beady glass eyes; greyish-brown mohair wig and grey beard. Articulated body. 1911. Woman dressed in white cotton underskirt, black woolen stockings and black leather heeled shoes; elaborate hat. Beady glass eyes; blonde mohair wig; articulated felt body. Not dated, but probably c.1915. *Steiff Collection, Giengen, Germany.*

ABOVE RIGHT: Illustration 6. Two Steiff Clowns, both 43cm (about 17in) tall. **Left:** Clown with horn dressed in plaid clown suit, white felt cone hat, woolen pompons, black leather slippers with matching pompons; beady glass eyes; articulated body. Horn is gilded painted wood. 1911. **Right:** Identified as "Cloro" in 1913 New-York Steiff catalog. Velvet clown outfit printed with Teddy Bears and fruit, velvet hat, wool neck ruffle and black leather slippers; beady glass eyes and sewn-on mohair wig; articulated body. 1911. *Steiff Collection, Giengen, Germany.*

LEFT: Illustration 7. "Spahi" with kneeling camel. (Spahi were native Algerian horsemen serving under the French government in the 19th and early 20th centuries.) Bright red and blue uniform with white cotton lined red cape, beady glass eyes. c.1914. 43cm (about 17in) tall. Camel made of tan mohair has beady glass eyes. 1914. 40cm (about 15¾in). *Steiff Collection, Giengen, Germany.*

purposes only, they were manufactured in numbers to be sold in shops.

It is interesting for the doll historian to note that in the General Description in this 1913 Catalog, they, Steiff, remark that:

"Our unbreakable Character dolls in felt have brought about a complete reform on the doll-market. We are the originators of the name "Character Dolls," the dolls which, on account of their individual features fascinate the mind of children. The costumes are true to the originals. The clothes take off. The brilliant hair can be combed even if wet and will not come out."

The dolls in this exhibition, representing adults, elegant ladies, well dressed gentlemen, sportsmen, small children, clowns, circus attendants, performers as well as a few humorous caricatures of military men and peasants originated from the talented hand of Albert Schlopsnies who signed and dated (1911) the front cover of the 1913 New York catalog.

Schlopsnies, the artist, created these early Steiff dolls and figures for this circus scene which took its inspiration from the real Sarrasini circus still in existence today. A special tribute should be paid to this form of artistry, and to Schlopsnies who aesthetically captured a certain spirit of humanity and which, combined with the manufacturing skill of the Steiff firm, have together brought into existence some of the finest commercially made dolls, superb and touching, of this 20th century.

Most of the figures and many of the animals displayed in the Musée des Arts Décoratifs come from the period 1911-1920; also included are a few later examples that are not without interest to the doll collector. Schlopsnies probably designed the Sarrasini circus scene at least one or two years previous to the first date given above, because an article appearing in 1911 already shows illustrations of it.

The "Circus and Toys" was well worth a visit for many reasons; but the feature of the greatest interest was without a doubt the splendid Steiff display. □

Editor's note: The unseemly reference to black people quoted from the 1913 Steiff New York catalog is in keeping with our policy of not altering original documentary material. The editors of Hobby House Press, Inc. regret such references, and trust that our readers will understand the necessity for unaltered direct quotes from original documents.

ABOVE: Illustration 8. "Hedy." Kid leather stretched over head form with painted features, brown eyes and mohair wig. Body of light weight composition, rough to the touch, jointed at shoulders and hips. 1952. Height 30cm (about 12in). "Bully" dog. Black and white velvet plush with glass eyes. 1929. Height 9cm (3½in). *Steiff Collection, Giengen, Germany.*

Illustration 9. Tall elegant gentleman in grey suit, dark grey greatcoat, beige "chapeau cintre," two-tone black and tan leather boots, beady glass eyes. 56cm (about 22in) tall. *Steiff Collection, Giengen, Germany.*

The Pierotti Family,

by **Caroline G. Goodfellow**,
Curator of Dolls,
Bethnal Green Museum of Childhood,
London, England

Illustration 1. A child of 18 months or two years of age, with peach wax and titan hair. *Bethnal Green Museum.*

Its History and Dolls

Early in 1982, the Bethnal Green Museum received a letter from Miss Irene Pierotti of Brighton, England. On the advice of Mary Hillier, she had written to ask if the museum would consider accepting her collection of dolls which had been made by members of her own family. The museum accepted her offer with a very definite YES! From Miss Pierotti it was learned that her cousin, Muriel, might also consider the museum a suitable home for her collection of family dolls. This was the simple beginning from which arose the most fascinating set of fully documented wax dolls, complemented by photographs, equipment and related papers which together illustrate the work of one of England's most prestigious doll making families, the Pierottis.

As the name suggests, the family was of Italian origin, and the wax modeling techniques were learned by one Domenico Pierotti, (born about 1760), the son of an Italian wine exporter who had married an English girl about 1750. Domenico spent some of his youth in England with his aunt, a Mrs. Castelli, whose family were modelers and molders. (Their work ranged from plaster ceiling panels to wax-covered papier-mâché milliner's dolls and figures.) Eventually Domenico learned this trade and settled in London, marrying Susanna Sleight in 1790. He had 11 children and the ninth child was Anerico Cephas, born in 1809. This child, known as Henry or Harry, married Jane Gumrell in 1828 and of his 12 children, Charles William, (born in 1841), followed the family trade. After Henry's death in 1871, his business was continued by Charles William, who had married Mary Ann Roach in 1859. His family also numbered 12 children. Charles William died in 1892 from the effects of lead poisoning but his widow continued producing dolls with the help of two of her sons — Charles Ernest (1860 to 1942) and Harry (1872 to 1936) — and three of her daughters — Beatrice (1882 to 1975), possibly Alice (1863 to 1946), Florence (1867 to 1903) or Rose (1875 to !). (Irene Pierotti's father, Augustus Frederick , [1875 to 1940], did not follow the family trade.) Charles Ernest and Harry worked together for some time, and then went their separate ways. They were the last of the family to make dolls and Charles Ernest retired in 1935.

Among the 20 odd documents pertaining to the family which were received, there are the baptismal records of Susanna Sleight and Mary Ann Roach; the marriage certificate of Henry (Anerico Cephas); and the memorial cards of Henry, Charles William and his wife, Mary Ann. It seems all were buried at Hammersmith Cemetery, London, England. Charles Ernest's death certificate has survived. dated September 7, 1942, and it states that he was a retired wax modeler.

Another group of documents relate to Anerico Cephas' application for a passport to visit Paris, France. There are a number of letters and official forms which verify that he was born on April 3, 1809, at 15 Gilbert Street, Bloomsbury, London, and that his father had been naturalized as a British subject.

Among the business documents are several of Henry's advertisements. One states: "H C Pierotti's New Invented Dolls with Human Hair implanted through the Composition to form the wig." It goes on to say: "Young Ladies by sending their own hair can have it implanted through the Composition to form the wig." Another of his advertisements, showing the address "Gallery, London Crystal Palace, Oxford Street," is in the form of a poem listing all the types of dolls and toys sold including kites, balls, games, musical and magnetic toys and even rocking horses. On this advertisement, H. Pierotti is named as the Inventor of the Royal Model Dolls. Henry exhibited at both the 1862 and the 1871 International Ex-

Illustration 2. *Lord Roberts,* dressed as a Field Marshall and made about 1900. This doll's body is the same as the male body shown in *Illustration 4. Bethnal Green Museum.*

119

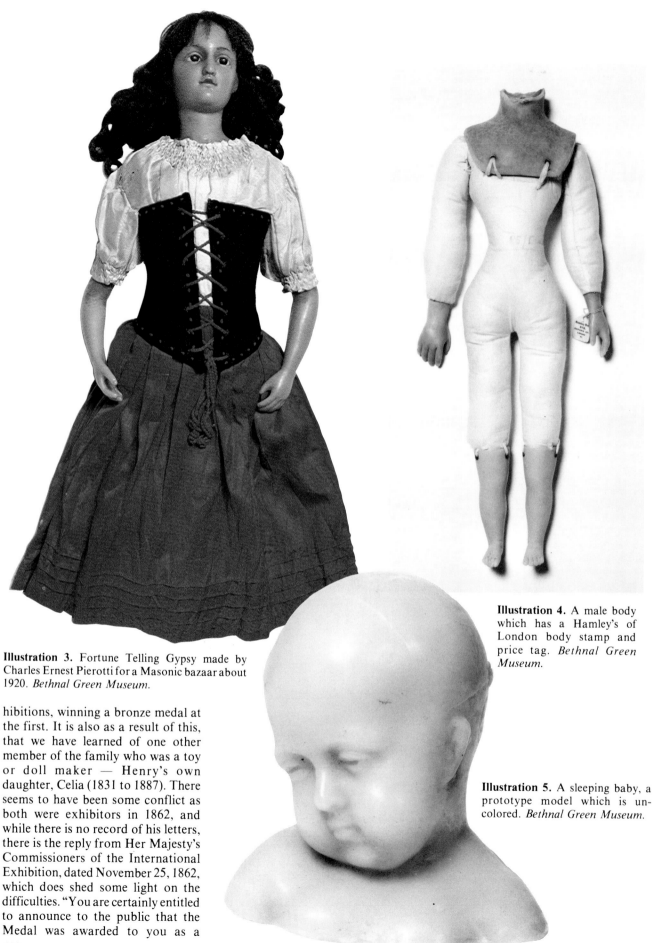

Illustration 3. Fortune Telling Gypsy made by Charles Ernest Pierotti for a Masonic bazaar about 1920. *Bethnal Green Museum.*

Illustration 4. A male body which has a Hamley's of London body stamp and price tag. *Bethnal Green Museum.*

Illustration 5. A sleeping baby, a prototype model which is uncolored. *Bethnal Green Museum.*

hibitions, winning a bronze medal at the first. It is also as a result of this, that we have learned of one other member of the family who was a toy or doll maker — Henry's own daughter, Celia (1831 to 1887). There seems to have been some conflict as both were exhibitors in 1862, and while there is no record of his letters, there is the reply from Her Majesty's Commissioners of the International Exhibition, dated November 25, 1862, which does shed some light on the difficulties. "You are certainly entitled to announce to the public that the Medal was awarded to you as a

120

manufacturer of Dolls; it being obvious that the Jury would not have awarded a Medal for a few toys also exhibited under your name; especially as those Toys were not really exhibited by you, but by your daughter, Miss Celia Pierotti, who, unfortunately, through a misunderstanding of the relation in which you stand to each other, as Exhibitors, was compelled to join with you in exhibiting in one space articles which would better have been kept separate." What a long and complicated statement which really means that the organizers made a mistake!

THE DOLLS

Within the joint collection of the Misses Pierotti, there are nine dolls, nine shoulder heads, 25 assorted limbs and one headless male body. While all the dolls are fascinating, there is one that is unique — the Fortune Telling Gypsy. The wax used for this doll is dark in color and the hair is a mixture of black human and mohair; likewise the glass eyes are very dark brown. Instead of legs, the cloth body is mounted on a wooden pole. Charles Ernest made the doll about 1920 for a Masonic bazaar, and it was dressed by Eleanor Bessie Pierotti, Irene's mother, who had been apprenticed to a court dressmaker. Originally streamers had been attached to the waistline, each with a "fortune" and when the doll was spun around, a person could select his own "fortune." As well as this doll, Charles Ernest is known to have made four others in the collection. One is named "Patrick Enrico" after his own child who died at a very young age. Another is thought to be the last doll he made in 1935.

The most beautiful of the dolls represents a young girl of perhaps 18 months or two years of age. Its wax is of a peach color with the eyes a very dark blue, almost violet. The hair on the head and that used for the lashes is titan. This doll is also large, standing 30in (76.2cm) tall. It is probable that Henry did the modeling and it was made about 1870. There is similarly colored creche baby, only 6½in (16.5cm) long, but this one was pro-

Illustration 6. The only remaining photograph of Charles William Pierotti, who died in 1892. *Miss I. Pierotti Collection.*

Illustration 7. Irene Eleanor Pierotti, aged two years (in 1908) holding a doll. *Miss I. Pierotti Collection.*

Illustration 8. An old man's head of poured wax. *Bethnal Green Museum.*

ABOVE: Illustration 9. A woman's head, a prototype model, showing the row of upper teeth. *Bethnal Green Museum.*

BELOW: Illustration 10. A woman's head, showing the line cut for the insertion of the eyes which would normally be covered by hair. *Bethnal Green Museum.*

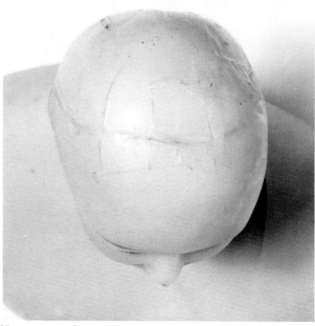

bably made much later by either Charles Ernest or Harry in the 1930s.

While some of the bodies are stamped with the Hamley's of London mark, there is only one doll's head which is signed "C. Pierotti" — a baby made by Charles William about 1885.

The individual heads all appear to be prototypes rather than finished articles. Five represent women and all seem to be portraits. One is molded to show a row of teeth and it is also interesting because it is hairless and has the line where the crown has been cut for the eye insertion. Another head, that of a baby, is quite different in style and is of a sleeping baby with its chin tucked into its right shoulder. As if to prove that not all Pierotti dolls are of pretty children or beautiful ladies, there is one head of an old man who is shown with a sharp nose and chin, a toothless mouth and sagging cheeks. Although it is not possible to attribute all the heads, it is probable that the modeling for most was done by either Henry or Charles William.

The male body, headless from the base of the chin, does confirm that the Pierotti family did make the examples of the *Lord Roberts* doll. A few strands of hair are still attached to the chin and the body is identical. This body has a Hamley's sales ticket and the price was 21/-(shillings) quite an expensive doll in 1900.

One of the dolls gives an insight of one of the family's traditions — the Christmas Fairy. Each Christmas, the youngest child was given a Fairy doll dressed in white and trimmed with tinsel. Irene Pierotti was given hers in 1906 and it was used until 1915. It had been made by her Uncle Harry.

This unique collection of dolls, given so generously by Irene and Muriel Pierotti, form part of the recently redesigned doll display at the museum. They will become the subjects of much research and will form the basis of identification for many people in the future. However, perhaps their most important role will be that as objects of beauty for everyone to enjoy. □

COLLECTIBLE

Celebrity Dolls

by John Axe

Among the most popular dolls with doll collectors and other collectors of nostalgia are celebrity dolls. And of the celebrity dolls the most desirable seem to be those of entertainment personalities. At the end of 1981 a Lenci doll representing Rudolph Valentino set a new record at an auction. The Valentino doll went for a bid of $4,000,00. At a local auction an 18in (45.7cm) *Shirley Temple* doll in the wrong costume brought $375.00. The vinyl *Shirley Temple* doll from the 1970s is now bringing as much as the 1930s composition one did about 10 years ago. Celebrity dolls are expected to rise even more in value.

My recent book published by Hobby House Press, Inc., is THE ENCYCLOPEDIA OF CELEBRITY DOLLS. I have been researching this project for more than three years. It has been my hobby most of my life. There are many hundreds of celebrity dolls, and establishing their identities is often confusing. The dictionary definition for a celebrity is "a renowned or celebrated person." A celebrity doll then would have to be a doll that represents a famous person. I have confined my research to celebrity dolls that were manufactured commercially, as it would be almost impossible to locate all the dolls that were ever made of famous persons, such as artists' original dolls. My interests focus on the dolls that are more available for collectors.

By tracing the trends and developments in celebrity dolls over the years one can see trends and developments in doll design. Cultural changes are also apparent because

of the sort of doll characters that have been produced. Commercially made dolls reflect public taste and interest. Not all of the most admired celebrities during the eras in which dolls were made commercially were rendered in doll form, but of those who were there are reflections of changing standards in customs and social values. The celebrity dolls

themselves are a form of popular history.

Western culture changed immensely during the first decades of the 20th century with the arrival of the movies. The first movies were short films that played in Penny Arcades. The movies gradually became more accepted and moved into places called Kinetoscope Parlors and later into theaters especially built for them. Most of the early films were of a risqué nature and were usually slapstick comedies that appealed to the poor and the young. After the movies began to tell stories they gradually became more accepted as worthy forms of entertainment and also as a form of culture. In 1915 D. W. Griffith's silent classic *The Birth of a Nation* was released. This film was the landmark in motion picture history that caused "respect-

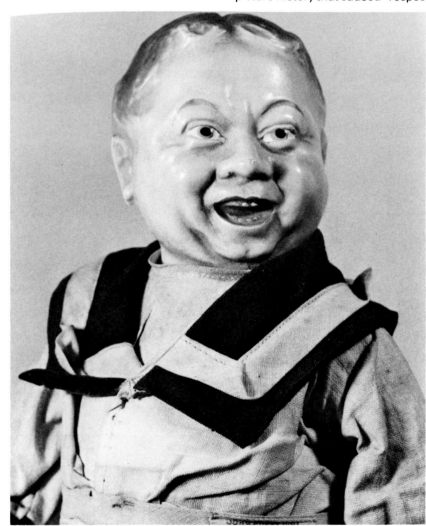

Illustration 1. 13½in (34.3cm) *John Bunny* by Louis Amberg & Son, 1914. Composition head with painted reddish hair and blue eyes; open/closed mouth with painted teeth. The head is marked, but most of the markings are below the wire that holds it on the all-cloth body. Visible is: "© 14." The cloth label on the sailor suit reads:
JOHN BUNNY DOLL
COPYRIGHT L. A. & S. 1914 TRADEMARK REGISTERED
MADE EXCLUSIVELY BY LOUIS AMBERG & SON, N.Y.
WITH CONSENT OF JOHN BUNNY (name in script)
THE FAMOUS MOTION PICTURE HERO OF THE VITAGRAPH CO.
The sailor suit is less common than the soldier suit. *Irene Trittschuh Collection.*

COLOR Illustration 1. 22in (55.9cm) *Shirley Temple as Heidi* by Ideal, 1937. All-composition and fully-jointed. This very rare original, tagged costume is based on the dream sequence in the film *Heidi,* in which Heidi danced and sang as a Dutch girl. The apron is separate. The hat is white organdy. The wig is also seldom seen on an original composition Shirley Temple doll. It is dark blonde mohair in a center part with bangs and long pigtails gathered up in loops. The cotton stockings are also original, as are the hand-carved wood shoes that are rather thin and fit well to the foot. Head marked: "SHIRLEY TEMPLE." Back marked: SHIRLEY TEMPLE (curved pattern) // 22." *Patricia Slabe Collection.*

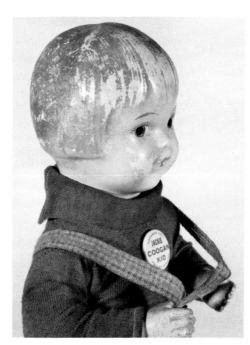

Illustration 2. 13½in (34.3cm) *Jackie Coogan* as *The Kid* by Horsman, 1921. Composition shoulder plate head and arms; cloth body; painted, molded reddish-brown hair; brown painted eyes. The original costume is an aqua shirt and gray pants. Head marked: "E.I.H₅Co.//19 © 21." The pin is original. The pants are labeled: "JACKIE COOGAN KID//LICENSED BY JACKIE COOGAN// PATENT PENDING."

able" persons to patronize the movies.

In 1910 a publicity ploy created the first "movie star." It was realized that a recognizable personality was bringing in the customers and the star system was created. Florence Lawrence had the distinction of being the first performer to see her name advertised as a draw for a film. The first big stars were the slapstick comedians who became as familiar to the public as family members. And doll makers got busy making dolls of movie stars.

Most celebrity dolls, but not all by any means, are dolls of entertainment personalities. Celebrity dolls were also made of baseball, basketball, football and hockey players. They were made of political candidates and office holders. They were made of "heroes" and other people of notable achievement. They were made of military men, patriots, Indian leaders, civic leaders, writers, royalty, personalities from history and famous babies and children who never did anything exceptional.

The greatest majority of celebrity dolls were made during the 20th century. This time period was well into the industrial era when dolls and other playthings could be manufactured on a large scale, and many of these items have survived to become collectible. The following shows some of the trends that celebrity dolls have taken during

each decade of the 20th century. Only a small sample of the dolls from each period is cited.

1900 to 1910. One of the greatest events of the decade was the "discovery" of the North Pole. Robert E. Peary reached the North Pole on April 6, 1909. Frederick A. Cook then insisted that he had done this in 1908, but his trip was later discredited. Peary's little daughter, Marie Ahnightio, was claimed to have been the first white child born north of the Arctic Circle (1893). This certainly is not true, but it made good publicity for Peary. By the fall of 1909 several doll companies began advertising dolls of *Cook*, *Peary* and Peary's daughter, *The Snow Baby*. These were bisque-headed dolls who had jointed composition bodies covered with real fur. The voyages to the north also drew attention to the natives there, so many "Eskimo" dolls were also advertised by various companies, such as Strobel & Wilken.

Illustration 3. 17½in (44.5cm) *Yvonne Dionne* girl by Madame Alexander, circa 1939. Dark brown human hair wig; brown sleep eyes with lashes; closed mouth; composition shoulder plate head, arms and legs; tightly stuffed cloth body with a cryer inside. Head marked: "ALEXANDER." *Rodolfos Collection.*

1910 to 1920. Adult male actors in silent film comedies were easily recognizable persons by this time and became popular in doll form. The first doll of a movie star was of

Illustration 4. 16in (40.6cm) *Prince Edward, the Duke of Kent* by Chad Valley, 1953. Pressed felt head with inset blue glass eyes; blonde mohair wig. The body is fully-jointed of stuffed cotton velvet. The doll is marked with a label attached to the sole of the right foot and was made in England. This doll was originally produced in 1938. The doll shown was manufactured by special request in 1953. *Shirley Buchholz Collection.*

Augustus Carney as *Alkali Ike* in 1913 by the Essanay Film Mfg. Co. Carney played Alkali Ike in a series of rustic comedies and was immensely popular from 1909 to 1913. In 1914 John Bunny, who appeared in more than 200 short comedies between 1910 and 1915, was made as the *John Bunny* doll by Louis Amberg and Son. In 1915 Amberg and other companies began making *Charlie Chaplin* dolls. Charlie Chaplin was the most popular comic of the era and the first to become a millionaire by acting in the movies. These dolls had composition heads and jointed cloth bodies.

1920 to 1930. Child actors in films were sure to appeal to children as dolls. The first child star to be made as a doll was *Jackie Coogan* by Horsman in 1921. Jackie Coogan became an international celebrity after playing a bright-eyed ragamuffin in Chaplin's first feature length film *The Kid* in 1921. The *Jackie Coogan* doll had a durable composition head. Baby Peggy was also a popular child performer in silent films, some of which were remade later in sound with Shirley Temple. Louis Amberg & Son began manufacturing *Baby Peggy* dolls with composition heads and imported bisque heads from Germany by 1923.

The hero of the decade, Charles Lindbergh, flew non-stop from New York to Paris in 1927. The Regal Doll Company commemorated this event with a composition head doll in 1928. The doll was called *Our Lindy*.

1930 to 1940. This was *the* era of celebrated children in doll form. It began with the all-composition *Shirley Temple* doll, the most popular celebrity doll of all time, by Ideal in 1934. Effanbee also brought out composition *Anne Shirley* child dolls that year. This character was based on the lead in the film *Anne of Green Gables* and various Effanbee dolls were used for the earliest *Anne Shirleys,* such as *Mary Lee, Patricia Kin, Patricia* and dolls that were marked "ANNE-SHIRLEY." Madame Alexander presented her child star, *Baby Jane,* in 1935. That same year she introduced the most famous babies in the world, the *Dionne Quintuplets,* as dolls. These are still the largest variety of celebrity dolls of all time. There are 35 different sets of the five dolls, and among the 35 sets there are several different types of costumes. Most of the dolls are made with composition parts but several sets are all-cloth. By the end of the decade other celebrated children were presented as dolls. Among these are *Princess Elizabeth* and *Jane Withers* in 1937 by Alexander and *Baby Sandy* in 1939 by Ralph A.

Illustration 5. 7¾ in (19.8cm) *Laurence Harvey as Romeo* and *Susan Shentall as Juliet* by Madame Alexander, No. 474 and No. 473, 1955. All-hard plastic and fully-jointed; straight-leg walkers. He has a red caracul wig and she has a blonde synthetic wig; both have blue sleep eyes with molded lashes. Backs marked: "ALEX." Costumes tagged "ALEXANDERKINS." *Patricia Gardner Collection.*

Illustration 6. 18in (45.7cm) *Haleloke* by Cast Distributing Corp., early 1950s. All-hard plastic and fully-jointed walker; black Saran wig; blue sleep eyes; open mouth with teeth. The trunk set includes extra Hawaiian costumes. Back marked: "MADE IN U.S.A." *Fran's Dolls.*

Illustration 7. 21in (53.3cm) Bob Keeshan as *Captain Kangaroo* by Baby Barry Toy, late 1950s. Vinyl head and hands; stuffed cloth body; gray painted hair and moustache; blue set-in glass eyes. The black vinyl feet are part of the body construction. Marked on the neck: " © //B.B." Tag on clothing "EXCLUSIVE LICENSEE//BABY BARRY//TOY N.Y.C." Reverse of tag: "CAPTAIN//KANGAROO." *Wanda Lodwick Collection.*

Freundlich, Inc. All of them were in composition.

When George VI was crowned King of England in 1937 the ceremony included the participation of the little princesses, Elizabeth and Margaret Rose. This brought attention to royal children and they became celebrities who were popular figures for doll makers. The most notable of the dolls made of *Princess Elizabeth* and *Princess Margaret Rose* were those in felt by Chad Valley in 1938. There were also dolls of *Prince Edward, the Duke of Kent,* and his sister *Princess Alexandria,* both of whom were cousins of the daughters of George VI.

1940 to 1950. This decade was *the* era of teen and adult movie stars in doll form. During the Depression of the 1930s the movies were doing good business by providing escapist

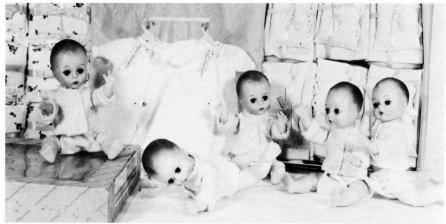

Illustration 8. 7¼in (18.5cm) (Fischer) *Quintuplets* by Madame Alexander, 1964. Hard plastic heads with sprayed brown hair and blue sleep eyes with molded lashes; jointed vinyl bodies. These dolls are never marked. The original sweaters are labeled: "MFR of the//"ORIGINAL QUINTUPLETS"//by MADAME ALEXANDER." The white cotton nightgowns hanging in the center rear have the same labels. The two different pillow and blanket sets in the boxes were also sold for the "Original Quintuplets." They were boxed in sets of six, to be sold individually in retail stores.

fare for those wishing to be entertained. The year 1939 was the greatest of all in the history of Hollywood films. That was the year of such classics as *Gone With the Wind, Stagecoach, Mr. Smith Goes to Washington, Wuthering Heights, Of Mice and Men, Gunga Din, The Hunchback of Notre Dame* and *The Wizard of Oz.*

Ideal had begun producing dolls of *Deanna Durbin,* one of the biggest stars of the late 1930s and the 1940s in 1938. In 1939 Ideal made the Judy Garland as *Dorothy* from *The Wizard of Oz* and Madame Alexander began her dolls of top star *Sonja Henie.* Effanbee was continuing its *Anne Shirley* lady dolls. By August 1940 Madame Alexander was advertising her Vivien Leigh as *Scarlett O'Hara* from *Gone With the Wind* in several sizes. *Sabu* was made by Molly-'es in 1940 and Ideal had a *Judy Garland* teen doll in 1941. These dolls were all-composition.

The most popular child star of the 1940s was Margaret O'Brien. In 1946 Alexander made an all-composition *Margaret O'Brien* doll. This was the last popular celebrity doll in composition. It was also the first celebrity doll in all-hard plastic in 1947. By the end of the 1940s there were very few composition dolls being made, as hard plastic had become the most popular medium for making play dolls.

1950 to 1960. The decade of the 1950s began with celebrity dolls in hard plastic and ended with celebrity dolls in vinyl. Hard plastic permitted more detailing in the faces of the dolls, but very few dolls were produced that were actually "portraits" of the celebrities.

Entertainment personalities continued to be the most popular celebrities in doll form. Alexander made

Mary Martin in 1949 and 1950 from her role on Broadway in *South Pacific.* At about the same time Alexander produced *Piper Laurie,* a starlet in films. Television performers were also made in doll form. An unknown company made *Roxanne* from "Beat the Clock" in 1952; Ideal had *Mary Hartline* from "Super Circus" the same year; The Roberta Doll Company had *Lu Ann Simms* from "Arthur Godfrey and His Friends" in about 1953; the Star Doll Company had *Dorothy Collins* of "Your Hit Parade" in 1954. One of the last dolls in all-hard plastic was *Shari Lewis* from her television

Illustration 9. 36in (91.4cm) *Lori Martin as Velvet Brown* from "National Velvet" by Ideal, 1961. Vinyl head with rooted dark brown hair; the remainder is plastic; fully-jointed with a twist waist and twist ankles; blue sleep eyes with lashes. The original boots are made of vinyl. Head marked: "METRO GOLDWYN MAYER INC.//MFG//IDEAL TOY CORP.// 38." Back marked: "© IDEAL TOY CORP.// G-38." The cloth tag also tells that the character is copyrighted by Metro, Goldwyn Mayer Inc. (Some *Lori Martin* dolls measure 38in (96.5cm). *Barbara DeVault Collection.*

Illustration 10. 12in (30.5cm) *Joe Namath* by Mego, 1970. Soft vinyl head; remainder hard vinyl; painted hair and features; fully-jointed. '""BROADWAY JOE" TM// © MEGO CORP. MCMLXX//MADE IN HONG KONG." In the original package the doll was dressed in a football outfit. This suit is an extra outfit for *Joe Namath* from Mego.

shows for children by Madame Alexander in 1959. This was one of the few dolls for which an attempt at portraiture was made.

The year 1957 brought a change in materials and the return of a great favorite. Ideal made a new series of *Shirley Temple* dolls in vinyl with rooted hair. By the end of the decade there were vinyl-headed dolls of circus clown *Emmett Kelly,* singer *Elvis Presley* and children's entertainer on television *Pinky Lee,* among others.

1960 to 1970. By the 1960s there was a great increase in diversity of types among celebrity dolls. They were no longer mostly child performers and lovely actresses. All of the dolls now had vinyl heads and most of them had rooted hair.

From television there was Donna Douglas as *Elly May* from "The Beverly Hillbillies" from an unknown manufacturer, *Patty Duke* by Horsman, Anne Francis as "Honey West" by Gilbert, Barbara Eden of "I Dream of Jeannie" (as *Jeannie*) by Libby and many other lady dolls. Dolls were also made of male stars. There was Vincent Edwards as *Dr. Ben Casey* from "Ben Casey," Richard Chamberlain as *Dr. Kildare* from "Dr. Kildare," Robert Vaughn as *Napoleon Solo* from "The Man from U.N.C.L.E.," and many others.

From the movies there was Sean Connery as *James Bond* by Gilbert, Julie Andrews from *The Sound of Music* and *Mary Poppins* by different companies in different materials (plastic and vinyl combinations), *Laurel* and *Hardy* from their old films on television, and several other adult characters.

Political figures were made as dolls. There was *President Kennedy*, *Premier Nikita Khurshchev, Lyndon B. Johnson* and *Barry Goldwater*.

Singing groups were presented as small dolls by various companies. Among them were *The Mamas and the Papas, The Beatles, The Dave*

come Back, Kotter;" four dolls from "Happy Days;" and others.

2.   Shindana produced dolls of black performers. Among them were *Rodney Allen Rippy, Flip Wilson, Redd Foxx, Marla Gibbs, O.J. Simpson, Jimmie Walker* and *Julius "Dr. J." Irving.* Unfortunately, Shindana is now out of business.

3.   The Bicentennial year, 1976, saw "The Heroes of the American Revolution," the Hallmark series of famous Americans and the first six *First Ladies* by Madame Alexander. At the present rate of production the entire *First Ladies* set by Alexander will not be complete

Illustration 11. 21in (53.3cm) Jimmie Walker as *Talking J. J.* from "Good Times" by Shindana, 1975. All-printed cloth. The pull ring makes *J. J.* say phrases like his famous reaction, "Dyn-o-mite." Tag: " © 1975//TANDEM// PRODUCTIONS//INC.//SHINDANA TOYS." Sewn skin made in Taiwan; doll made in the United States.

Illustration 12. 6¾in (17.2cm) *P. T. Barnum* by Hallmark, No. 400DT113-9, 1979. All-cloth with printed clothing and features. Copyright by Hallmark Cards, Inc., August 1979. Made in Taiwan.

Clark Five, The Monkees and *The Spencer Davis Group.*

Madame Alexander made several dolls who were not advertised as celebrities, but everyone knew whom the dolls represented. These were *Jacqueline* and *Caroline* (Kennedy), (Fischer) *Quintuplets* and *Leslie* (Uggams).

1970 to 1980. This decade saw the largest diversity of celebrity dolls ever and several new trends in doll making. Most of the dolls continued to be made of vinyl, which will probably become the longest continually produced material for play dolls of all time. There are six definite trends:

1.   Television star dolls produced in sets. There were Penny Marshall and Cindy Williams as *Laverne* and *Shirley; Charlie's Angels,* four dolls from three companies (Hasbro, Mego and Mattel); *KISS*--four bizarre male musicians in Kabuki makeup; six dolls from "The Waltons;" five dolls from "Wel-

until almost the end of the 20th century.

4.   Nostalgia. There were dolls of *The Wizard of Oz* stars from the 1939 movie; *Our Gang* child stars from the 1930s; *Shirley Temple,* for the third time; and *Charlie Chaplin* again.

5.   Dolls made for boys. There were *Shaun Cassidy* and *Parker Stevenson* as *The Hardy Boys.* There were large sets of dolls from science fiction movies and television shows. Among them are *Star Wars, Star Trek, Buck Rogers in the 25th Century, The Black Hole,* and *Battlestar Galactica.* These dolls came in sets of two different sizes, about 12in (30.5cm) and about 3 3/4in

Illustration 13. 7¾in (19.8cm) *Charlie Chaplin* by Peggy Nisbet, No. P755, 1970s. All-plastic with jointed arms; black painted hair and blue painted eyes; wood cane and cloth rose. Made in England.

(9.6cm). There are so many different sets of the smaller dolls, or "action figures," that they will certainly become hot collectibles in the future.

6. Dolls made especially for collectors. Peggy Nisbet dolls include all the types of celebrity dolls mentioned, featuring dolls of royal persons. These are made in England, as are Ann Parker dolls. The Ann Parker dolls concentrate on "English characters and costumes." Many of the American commercial companies began producing dolls especially for collectors, with Effanbee taking the lead with its Limited Edition Doll Club, which presented the Dewees Cochran self-portrait doll.

1980 and Beyond. The trends from the 1970s are continuing. Ideal is making 12 different Shirley Temple dolls. New companies are making dolls especially for collectors. Effanbee is in the lead with the most artistic and realistic celebrity dolls ever produced by a commercial company. The *W.C. Fields, John Wayne* and *Mae West* dolls were collectible even before they were available for sale.

Celebrity dolls will always be collected and they will always be desirable dolls. They are "someone," not just a doll with an ambiguous name and identity.

Illustration 14. 12in (30.5cm) Harrison Ford as *Indiana Jones* from *Raiders of the Lost Ark* by Kenner, No. 46000, 1981. All-vinyl and fully-jointed; brown painted hair; blue painted eyes. Head marked: " © G.M.F.G.I. 1979." Back marked: "©G.M.F.G.I. 1978 KENNER PROD.//CINCINNATI, OHIO 44512//MADE IN HONG KONG." This is the same doll as Harrison Ford as *Han Solo* from *Star Wars* in 1979 except that the *Han Solo* has brown painted eyes.

Illustration 15. 3¾in (9.6cm) Gavin MacLeod as *Captain Stubing* from "The Love Boat" by Mego, No. 23005/1, 1982. All-vinyl and fully-jointed; painted fringe of gray hair; painted features; molded clothing. Copyright by Aaron Spelling Productions, Inc. Made in Hong Kong.

This is probably the first movie star doll. Augustus Carney as *Alkali Ike* from a *Playthings* advertisement, November 1913. These dolls were supposed to have sold in great quantities during 1914.

CELEBRITY DOLLS IN COMPOSITION

by **John Axe**

The celebrity dolls with heads made of composition have always been very popular with collectors. Some attempts at portraiture are not accurate with these dolls. Many molds, such as the ones used for Ideal's *Shirley Temple* and Madame Alexander's *Princess Elizabeth* and *Margaret O'Brien*, were also used for other dolls. Often the facial features are not as well delineated as are dolls of porcelain, plastic or vinyl. But composition as a doll medium has a charm and a feeling that is difficult to describe. Unlike dolls of porcelain, plastic or vinyl, commercially made dolls of composition, which were produced from about 1910 to about 1950, will probably never again be made like they were during that time period. Composition dolls require more care and good sense to maintain than dolls of other mediums, but this vulnerability of their nature is also part of their appeal. Celebrity dolls of composition in good condition will maintain their value because they are truly artifacts of a past era that would be very difficult to reproduce in the same way again.

ABOVE: 14½in (36.9cm) *Charlie Chaplin* by Louis Amberg & Son, 1915. Composition head and hands; straw-filled cloth body with pin and disk joints. Deeply molded hair and painted features. The jacket is labeled. *Coleman Collection. Photograph by Ann Coleman.*

ABOVE: *Our Gang Dancing Comedy Dolls* by Sayco from a *Playthings* ad, April 1926. The dolls have composition heads with painted features and composition lower arms. The bodies have a key-wind mechanism to make the legs of the dolls move. The dolls are, from left to right: Allen Clayton Hoskins as *Farina*, Jackie David as *Jackie*, Mary Kornman as *Mary*, Mickey Daniels as *Freckles* and Joe Cobb as *Fatty.*

LEFT: 15½in (39.4cm) *Judy Garland* as *Dorothy* from *The Wizard of Oz* by Ideal, circa 1939. All-composition and fully-jointed; dark brown human hair wig; brown sleep eyes with lashes; open mouth with teeth and a tongue. Head marked: "IDEAL DOLL // MADE IN U.S.A." Back marked: "USA // 16." *Emilie Marie Reynolds Collection.*

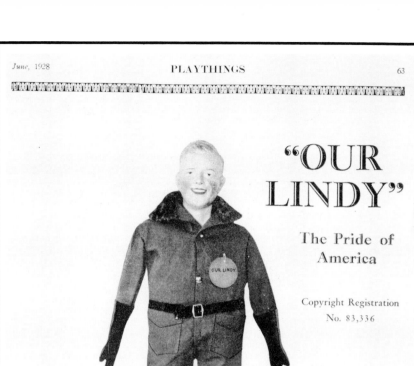

ABOVE: 33in (83.8cm) Charles A. Lindbergh, Jr., *"Our Lindy,"* by the Regal Doll Mfg. Co., Inc., 1928. *Playthings,* June 1928. The composition shoulder plate head is marked: " © REGAL DOLL CO. // "SCULP" E. PERRUGI // 1928."

RIGHT: 10in (25.4cm) *Dionne Quintuplet Annette* baby by Madame Alexander, circa 1935. All-composition and fully-jointed; painted brown hair; brown sleep eyes with lashes; closed mouth. Head marked: ""DIONNE" // ALEXANDER." Back marked: "MADAME // ALEX-ANDER." The bib is embroidered with Annette's name and the white dress is labeled. The white wooden high chair is 14½in (36.9cm) high and came with the doll in the original box. *Rodolfos Collection.*

LEFT: 11½in (29.2cm) *Dionne Quintuplet Yvonne* by Madame Alexander, 1936 to 1938. All-composition and fully-jointed; painted brown "curly" hair; brown sleep eyes with lashes; closed mouth. Head marked: "ALEXANDER." Back marked: "MADAME // ALEXANDER." The doll's original box has stock number 1506 printed on the label. The dress tag is printed in red: ""DIONNE QUINTUPLETS" (in script) // MADAME ALEXANDER // NEW YORK." The "locket," incised "YVONNE," is more rare than the pin attached to a bar.

RIGHT: 12in (30.5cm) Fanny Brice as *Baby Snooks* by Ideal, 1939. Composition head and hands; wooden turso and feet; "flexy" wire arms and legs. Designed by Joseph Kallus. Painted light brown hair; painted blue eyes; open/closed mouth with painted lower teeth. The original costumes came in various shades and patterns but were the same basic style. Head marked: "IDEAL DOLL."

OPPOSITE PAGE: 16in (40.6cm) *Shirley Temple Baby* by Ideal, 1935. Composition head, arms and lower legs; cloth stuffed body; blonde mohair wig; green flirty eyes; two upper teeth and three lower teeth. Head marked: "SHIRLEY TEMPLE." The original outfit is a pink organdy dress under a pink rayon coat and hat; white leather booties. The pin is also original. *Betty Shriver Collection.*

BELOW LEFT: 15in (38.1cm) *Sabu* by Molly-'es, circa 1940. All-composition and fully-jointed with brown skin tones; painted black eyes. The doll is not marked. The cardboard tag attached to a hand tells that he was inspired by Alexander Korda's film *The Thief of Bagdad.*

BELOW: 21in (53.3cm) *Deanna Durbin* by Ideal, circa 1939. All-composition and fully-jointed; dark brown human hair wig; green sleep eyes with lashes and eye shadow; open mouth with teeth and a tongue; red painted fingernails. Head marked: "DEANNA DURBIN // IDEAL DOLL." Back marked: "IDEAL DOLL." The gown is labeled.

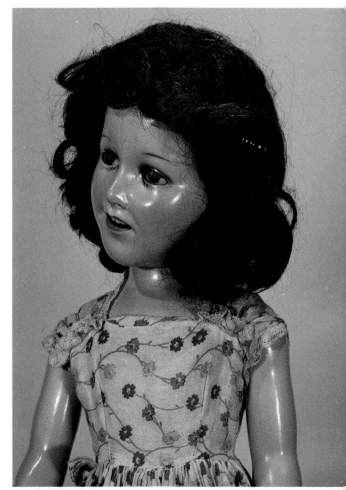

LEFT: 18in (45.7cm) *General Douglas MacArthur* by Freundlich Novelty Corporation, 1940s. All-composition with jointed arms and legs only. The hat is molded with the head; painted features with black eyes. No markings, except for the paper tag attached to the jacket. *Jean Pritchard Collection.*

BELOW LEFT: 14in (35.6cm) Vivien Leigh as *Scarlett O'Hara* by Madame Alexander, circa 1940. All-composition and fully-jointed; black human hair wig; green sleep eyes with lashes. The doll is not marked. The labeled gown is yellow taffeta and the bonnet matches. The jacket is black velvet. The petticoat has a wire hoop in the hem to make it stand out.

BELOW: Wigged *Baby Sandy* (Henville) by Ralph A. Freundlich from an advertisement in *Playthings*, April 1940.

Bring the Sensational "Ba

A DOLL

plus **A PERSONA**

Sandra Henville (*Baby Sa*
lovable two-year-old screen
who, literally over night, mad
tion picture history by capti
the hearts of millions of ch
and grown-ups in the screen cl
"East Side of Heaven," "Unexp
Father" and "Little Accident

Next Picture
"Sandy Is A Lady"
to be released
latter part of April, 1940

A NATURAL

Obviously a natural, this irre
infant now reproduced in am
realistic doll form and back
powerful screen, radio and ma
publicity is a precedent sm
Freundlich value that will in
start your doll sales soaring
record highs.

COPYRIGHT NOTICE
We have been granted exclusive pe
to manufacture the Baby Sandy
will vigorously protect our rights
infringers.
Licensed by
MITCHELL J. HAMILBU
for UNIVERSAL PICTU

RALPH
The World's Larg
Sales Rooms 200 5T
NEW Y

Every doll collector dreams of finding "that special doll" in a box. This dream came true at a recent doll show with the find of *Miss Dolly Schoenhut* with her stand and her box.

The December 1915 *Ladies' Home Journal* Schoenhut ad states in part:

"An Invitation to Meet Miss Dolly Schoenhut. Who Can Do Almost Everything But Talk."

The ad shows *Miss Dolly Schoenhut* dressed holding a large scroll with information about the Schoenhut dolls and a picture of the doll in a union suit and two undressed carved head dolls in posed positions.

M. Elaine and Dan Buser's *Guide to Schoenhut's Dolls, Toys and Circus* on page 64 has a picture of a page from the 1915 Schoenhut Doll Catalog. The page reads in part:

"New for 1915. Conventional 'Doll Face' Dolls. All-Wood. These four Special Dolls have faces to imitate the finest Bisque Head Dolls. One number in each size, viz: 14 - 16 - 19 - 21 inches. Imitation Glass Eyes (not movable). Real Mohair Wig."

The page shows three dolls: two in union suits and one dressed. Under the dolls are the size in inches followed by "/316." The bottom line of the page states: "In ordering goods, always give number."

The *Miss Dolly Schoenhut* found with her box is 21in (53.3cm) tall. She has her original long blonde mohair

Illustration 1. *Miss Dolly Schoenhut.*

Miss Dolly Schoenhut and Her Box

by **Pidd Miller**

Illustration 2. Lid of the Schoenhut doll box.

wig. Her carved eyes (imitation glass eyes) are light blue and she has painted eyebrows and upper and lower eyelashes. Her mouth is open/closed with four teeth. Her cheeks are rosy pink and her face paint is in excellent condition. Her body is all wood with steel spring joints. She wears her original knit union suit with lace around the neck, arms and legs and buttoned in the back. She wears her original long light blue cotton sockings with a hole in the sole and white shoes with two holes in the sole. Her blue and white dress was "made at home" and was sewed on the doll. (The label on the end of the box states: "Not Dressed.") She is marked with a Schoenhut incised mark on her back. The metal Schoenhut stand measures 4⅝in (11.8cm) in diameter and the rod which fits in the

hole in the doll's foot is 3/4in (2cm) tall and 3/32in (.2cm) in diameter.

The box is in poor condition; however, the lid is in one piece as is the end with the label. The box measures 22in (55.9cm) long, 7¾in (19.8cm) wide and 4¾in (12.2cm) deep and is made of heavy tan cardboard. The inside of the box is faded blue. The one remaining intact box corner is reinforced by a metal corner. The lid has two white paper labels printed with black ink. The smaller label on the lid measures 5in (12.7cm) by 3in (7.6cm) and reads: "NOTICE! Before tieing on the lid, place a wad of tissue paper over the face to prevent scratching."

The other label on the lid measures 8⅛in (20.6cm) by 5in (12.7cm) and shows a picture of three Schoenhut dolls — a wigged girl doll dressed, a

wigged boy doll dressed and a carved head boy doll undressed holding a Schoenhut label.

On the inside of the box lid is a large label yellowed from age printed in red ink which measures 15½in (39.4cm) by 5¼in (13.4cm) with information about the care of the Schoenhut doll. The left one-third of this label shows ten different poses of Schoenhut dolls. These dolls are undressed with carved heads — two girl dolls and three boy dolls — each in two different poses. This same set of pictures were used in the December 1914 *Ladies' Home Journal* Schoenhut ad. One end of the box has a label with the information for this doll.

The box lid and box end has been framed with glass on both sides to preserve them for future doll collectors. □

Illustration 3. A close-up view of the right side of the lid. Across the top of the label: "THE 'SCHOENHUT' ALL WOOD PERFECTION ART DOLL." To the left of the picture of the three Schoenhut dolls: "AMERICAN//INGENUITY//and//PRODUCTION//A Real Manikin.//A fully jointed figure,//entirely made of wood.//Painted in Enamel Oil//Colors.//No Loose Joints.//No Re-stringing.//No Broken Heads." To the right of the picture: "Real Character Faces as//you see Pretty Children//every day on the street.//Modeled by Famous//Artists.//The Joints are Steel Spring and Swivel//Action. Can't Break.//No rubber used." Below the picture: "Copyright 1912 by the A. Schoenhut Company//THE QUALITY AND SUPERIOR FINISH MAKE IT//THE CHEAPEST DOLL ON THE MARKET//IT OUTLASTS FIFTY OF ANY OTHER JOINTED DOLL. Patented January 17, 1911."

Illustration 4. On the inside of the lid box the following information is printed: "NOTICE TO PURCHASERS OF THE 'SCHOENHUT DOLL'//UNDRESS THE DOLL AND STUDY THE JOINTS, YOU WILL FIND IT VERY INTERESTING." In very large letters: "DIRECTIONS: Always turn the arms or legs around to such//a position that the groove in the ball joint runs//same direction you want to bend the limb."

"Before posing the Doll, study carefully the way the various joints of the arms and legs are made, and see in what position the limbs move freely, and in what position they will not move. The joints all have swivel connections so that any part can be turned clear around. In order to bend a limb at an angle, a groove is cut in the ball end of each joint of the arms and legs to allow a passage for the springed hinge. You will readily observe that the limbs should always be moved in the direction of the groove; for instance, to sit the Doll down, have the groove on the upper legs face the front, and you can readily bend the upper legs up; then, to bend the lower legs down, have the grooves at the knee face the back and then bend the legs down, and you have the Doll in a sitting position. To extend the legs sidewise, first turn the whole leg around and get the grooves in the position you want to make the bend.

"In dressed Dolls where you can not see the above mentioned grooves, you can feel them so that you know in which way they are turned. By following the above directions you will have no trouble at all to pose the Dolls in any conceivable position.

"The construction and possibilities of the various joints of the 'SCHOENHUT DOLLS' are simply wonderful, and in order to have them made so that the Doll can be posed in any natural position, the limbs have to be made so that they have **a limit** to their movements, and **to force** the **limbs beyond the limit** means to break the joints, but with a very little study this cannot happen, and you will have a Doll that will last for a generation.

"The heads on the 'SCHOENHUT DOLLS' are cut out of solid wood and are painted with fine oil paints, so that they can be washed when soiled. We guarantee that the heads will not break and that the paint will not wash off. Of course, with rough usage it is possible to knock or chip the paint off, the same as on any other kind of painted wood work, no matter how fine it may be, and against such usage we cannot give a guarantee." Stamped in ink: "Do not soak the doll in water."

Illustration 5. A close-up view of the posed Schoenhut Dolls on the inside lid label. Above the picture: "Illustrating a few poses to show the Flexible Movements of the Joints." Below the picture: "Patented July 17, 1911." In larger lettering: "The newest Invention in Dolls - The 'SCHOENHUT DOLL' - All Wood."

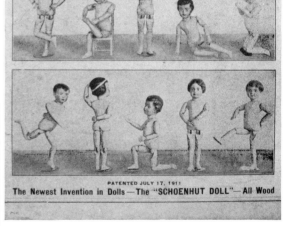

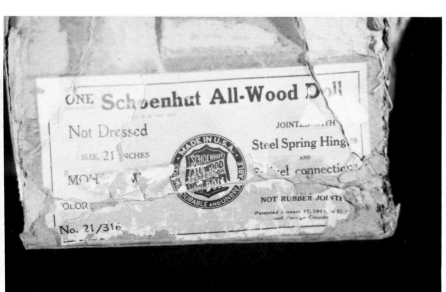

Illustration 6. Box end. "ONE Schoenhut All-Wood Doll." In the center is a picture of the Schoenhut doll metal button. To the left: "Not Dressed//SIZE 21 INCHES//MOH (unable to read, however, must be mohair wig)//COLOR (unable to read)//No. 21/316." On the right: "JOINTED WITH//Steel Spring Hinges//AND //Swivel connections//NOT RUBBER JOINT-ED//Patented January 17, 1911 USA//and Foreign Countries."

A Baker's Dozen from Lenci

by Barbara Whitton Jendrick

ever possible. Such is the case with the Lencis shown here.

Some of the dolls have been seen before but the majority have not. Finding all of these in one collection seemed too good of an opportunity to miss. After photographing the dolls in groups for the Richard W. Withington, Inc., October 1981 Auction Catalog, I reshot them individually for this article.

My thanks to the Margaret Woodbury Strong Museum in Rochester, New York, for allowing me to use their 1927/1928 original Lenci catalog for purposes of identification as the previous owner cut most of the Lenci labels off the dolls. The catalog enabled me to state definitely that the dolls were Lenci even though they were not so marked.

An additional point of interest is that the doll in *Illustration 2* brought a world record price for a Lenci of $4600.00 at auction.

Illustration 3. This 11½in (29.2cm) charmer is marked with her original Lenci tag and is dressed and ready to travel with her hatbox in hand.

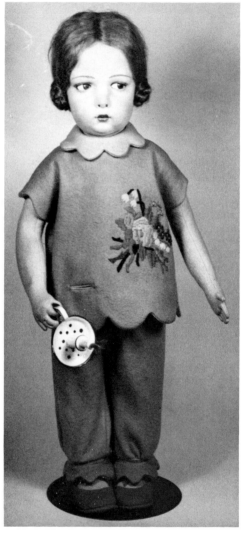

Illustration 1. 22in (55.9cm) girl dressed in felt pajamas ready to go to bed with candlestick in hand. With eyes to the left, she almost looks a little afraid to go upstairs alone. The label reads "Lenci Made in Italy 109-73."

Illustration 2. 26in (66.0cm) lovely blonde lady in pink organdy and felt is unmarked but is shown in the original 1927/1928 Lenci catalog in the Margaret Woodbury Strong Museum Collection. Her half-closed eyes and open smiling mouth with teeth only add to her charm.

One of the benefits of handling doll auctions is the fact that you get the opportunity to handle many, many dolls that you might otherwise not see in your lifetime. Along with this benefit goes the responsibility to share unusual items with others when-

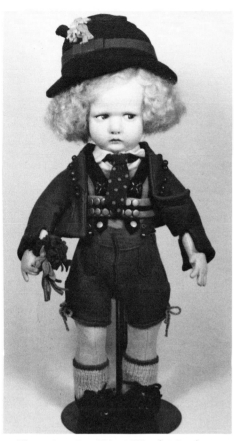

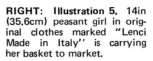

RIGHT: Illustration 5. 14in (35.6cm) peasant girl in original clothes marked "Lenci Made in Italy" is carrying her basket to market.

BELOW LEFT: Illustration 6. 19in (48.3cm) marked Lenci girl in original clothes also has a tag that reads "LOMBARDIA LUCIA."

BELOW RIGHT: Illustration 7. 29in (73.7cm) unmarked Lenci lady in yellow organdy with orange felt trim. Again we see the half-closed eyes and open mouth with teeth.

Illustration 4. This 18½in (47.0cm) unmarked blonde curly haired boy is all original and is definitely a Lenci.

Illustration 8. This 29in (73.7cm) unmarked Lenci Spanish lady is all original in her lovely felt gown. She is also shown in the 1927/1928 Lenci catalog.

Illustration 10. A 16in (40.6cm) all original unmarked Lenci matador dressed in red and black.

Illustration 9. An all original 11in (27.9cm) marked Lenci peasant who also has a tag that reads: "SARDA."

Illustration 11. This 12½in (31.8cm) Lenci peasant girl is marked "Lenci" and also has a tag marked "SARDA."

Illustration 12. Marked on her foot, this 12in (30.5cm) Lenci girl in pink organdy and felt is all original.

Illustration 13. This 9in (22.9cm) blonde girl on a wheeled cart is marked "Lenci" on her foot. She is wearing her original felt and rayon costume. The flowers on the cart are felt.

The "Body Twist" Dolls

A Photographic Essay by Patricia N. Schoonmaker
Photographs by John Schoonmaker

Advertising in 1929 declared the Body-Twist Dolls to be Amberg's 50th Anniversary Achievement. The copy read: "Have you seen the doll with the BODY TWIST. 'IT' is altogether different! And 'IT' is the loveliest dolly. Ask your dealer to show you 'IT' with its cute little pup on a leash. 14 inches fully dressed. Durable, all-composition, with one extra natural motion no doll ever had before. 'IT' can turn or bend like any little girl. Beautiful organdy or print dress. Ball jointed head, arms, legs, and center of body. With dog $3.00.

"TINY TOTS, Brother and Sister in Combination Box. With extra dress, romper and fine extra coat and hat for each doll. Tiny Tots also have the famous patented Body Twist. 8 inches tall. $2.00." (The advertisement appears to have been clipped from *Child Life* magazine.)

Playthings magazine of February 1929 showed line drawings or sketches of three different body-twist dolls: *Sue* with side part, *Peter Pan,* and a definite *Patsy*-type with bangs. All three were called "IT" even though they had separate identities. In June of 1929 Amberg declared in *Playthings,* "We have not caught up yet on deliveries. Double sets of dies now going on presses!" The patent pending serial number was given as 320018. "Remember 1929 is an Amberg Year."

This writer has no information on the designer of these dolls, but the heads are marvelously detailed sculpture very unlike the average doll. The Amberg torso was in two sections only, the bottom half of which had the appearance of a ball joint.

Madame Hendren and Horsman brought out competitive dolls. These would contain an actual separate wooden ball in the mid-torso. A larger 24in (61.0cm) Horsman example had a separate hip section which allowed the doll to sit very naturally. Later, Madame Alexander's *Wendy-Ann* would have a body-twist torso, as well as one version of the Mary Hoyer doll. None of these dolls are commonly found and all are outstanding collector's items.

Illustration 1A. 14in (35.6cm) Peter Pan, wearing green costume and cap with feather. Original box end. Marked on back: "AMBERG//PAT. PEND// L.A.&S. © 1928." Mary Elizabeth Poole Collection.

Illustration 1B. Front view of undressed Peter Pan.

Illustrations 1C, 1D and 1E. Rear views of rare Peter Pan doll showing unusual windswept sculptured hair. Marked: "AMBERG//PAT. PEND//L.A.&S. © 1928." Mary Elizabeth Poole Collection.

Illustration 2A. 14in (35.6cm) Sue, the "IT" girl by Amberg. Original clothes.

Illustration 2B. Side view of head of Sue. Shows "body-twist" torso. Marked: "AMBERG//PAT. PEND//L.A.&S. © 1928."

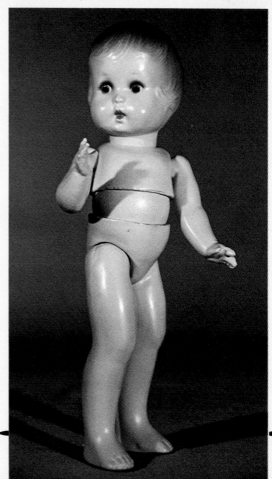

ABOVE: Illustration 3. Story: "The Dolls With The Body-Twist." The "It" Doll by Amberg. 14in (35.6cm) all-composition with two-piece torso. All original clothing. 1928. Photograph by John Schoonmaker.

ABOVE RIGHT: Illustration 4. Close-up of Brother "It" doll by Amberg.

RIGHT: Illustration 5. 14½in (36.9cm) Dimmie doll by Madame Hendren. Composition with hollow wooden ball in middle torso.

Illustration 6. Original advertising for Dimmie and Jimmie, dolls by Madame Hendren. **Toys and Novelties,** April 1929.

Illustration 7. 14½in (36.9cm) **Boots** by Horsman with body-twist feature. Wears old hand-knit beret and sweater along with blue wool pleated skirt.

Illustration 8. 14½in (36.9cm) **Dimmie doll** by Madame Hendren

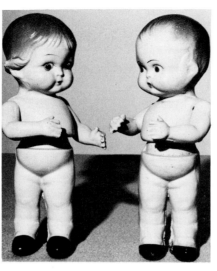

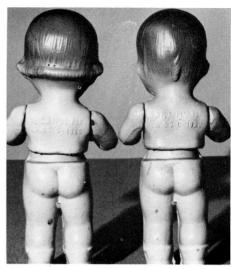

Illustration 9. Peter Pan, undressed, with **Sue,** the "IT" doll, obviously both the work of the same artist. Mary Elizabeth Poole Collection.

Illustrations 10A, 10B and 10C. 8in (20.3cm) **Tiny Tots,** body-twist dolls by Louis Amberg & Son; all composition; molded painted yellow hair; amber side-glancing painted eyes, painted upper eyelashes; closed mouth. Boy is wearing blue overalls and the girl is wearing a blue dress with red trim. They are marked on the shoulders: "PAT APPL'D FOR//L.A.&S © 1928." The label on the clothing reads: "AN AMBERG DOLL with//BODY TWIST//all its own//PAT. PEND. SER. NO. 32018."

Illustration 11A. Horsman's **Boots** shown with Madame Hendren's **Dimmie. Boots** is unmarked.

Illustration 11B. Dimmie is ink stamped on her back: "MADAME HENDREN DOLL//Patent Pending."

Illustration 11C. Choice dressed **Dimmie.**

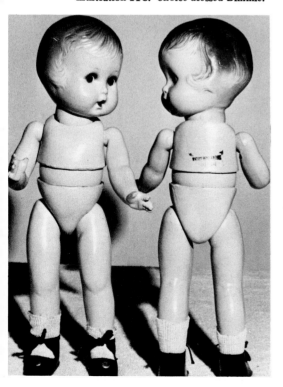

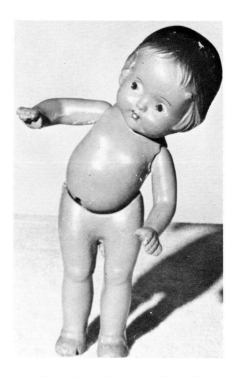

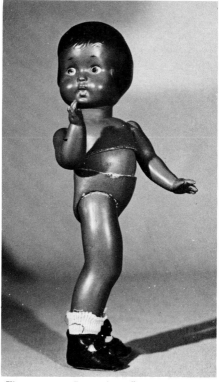

Illustrations 12A and 12B. 10in (25.4cm) black "body-twist" doll by Horsman; also came as a white doll. Marked on back at waist: "PAT. APPLD." Frances James Collection.

Illustration 13A. 14in (35.6cm) black Boots by Horsman with three-piece body-twist torso. Frances James Collection.

Illustration 13B. 14in (35.6cm) black Boots as a boy with body-twist torso; wearing original gold and blue cotton suit with pearl buttons. Frances James Collection.

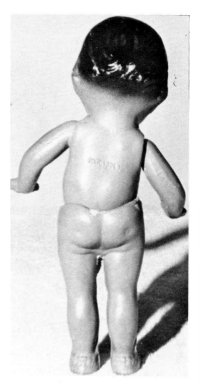

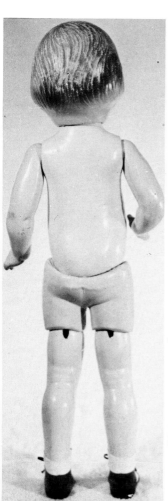

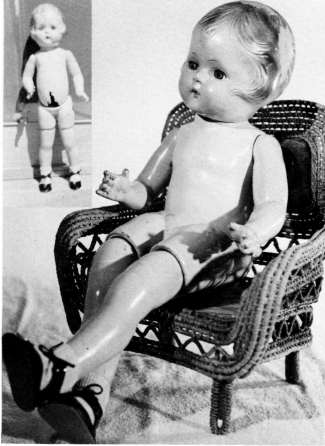

Illustrations 14A, 14B and 14C. 24in (61.0cm) Horsman version of a "body-twist" doll. No advertising has been located for this model; hence, her name is unknown. Sonni Hemi Collection.

148

Käthe Kruse
& Her World Famous Dolls
by Lydia Richter

Close-up of Käthe Kruse *Doll I.*

PREVIOUS PAGE: Käthe Kruse *Doll I;* cloth head, painted hair; circa 1935.

In 1910, Käthe Kruse's biggest success began at the exhibition for handmade toys at Hermann Tietz (Hertie) Department Store in Leipziger Street, Berlin, Germany. It was the first time that her unbreakable cloth dolls were introduced to the public and words of approval and admiration were voiced for these sweet little artistic dolls. Her first large order came from America, the country with unlimited possibilities. She also received a lot of praise in America, and many more orders were to follow.

How did this Käthe Kruse doll, this very popular, beloved and famous German play doll come to be developed and wherein was her secret of success? Käthe Kruse

said: "The combination of primitiveness and simplicity is the secret of my dolls."

This sounds rather simple. But was it?

First of all, one has to mention the fact that the production of these dolls was not a commercially thought of idea, but arose from the loving feeling of a mother, who wanted to give her child a warm and cuddly doll as a present, to hold and to love.

It all began in the year 1905. Käthe Kruse was then living in Ascona, Switzerland, with her two daughters Maria (Mimerle) and Sofie (Fifi). The three year old Mimerle stood with empty arms and hands, while her mother was taking care of the baby sister, and so it was natural that she expressed a wish: "I would also like to have such a baby." What mother would not fulfill such a request? And so the first Käthe Kruse doll was produced.

The first Käthe Kruse doll was a potato doll. Its head consisted of a covered potato, and its body was made out of a towel filled with sand. Käthe Kruse noticed that Mimerle was especially fond of the

doll's weight. Thus this idea was later used for the doll *Träumerchen* which became famous under the name of *Sandbaby.* But first of all, many versions were made before any success was achieved.

One day in Munich, Käthe Kruse found a beautiful Fiamingo head, which resembled her own children very strongly. She had mentioned this many years later to her daughter Sofie (Fifi). These Fiamingo heads were produced by Dutch and French artists, who were working in Italy. One of these was a model for the first Käthe Kruse doll, which appeared, from 1913 onwards, in the first Käthe Kruse doll catalog as *Doll I.* It never received another name and is still called *Doll I* to this day. All other names, for example *Karlchen, Fritzchen, Rotkäppchen* and *Margretchen* are so named due to their clothing in the catalog, so that they are kept apart when ordering.

Doll I was produced for many years with the standard size of 43cm (approx. 17in). Only in the 1940s did its size change to 45cm (approx. 17¾in); production ceased in 1958. Until 1930, this doll had wide hips and separately sewn on thumbs. On the left foot sole there was Käthe Kruse's signature as well as a serial number.

The production of doll head I was as follows: From the Fiamingo head, metal molds were made; these molds were then filled with dipped (glue) gauze, pressed by hand, and after this had dried and the shell was hard, it was stuffed with wood wool. For the body, Käthe Kruse made a pattern from a plaster cast of a Christ child. This pattern was then used to produce a body of a chubby child with wide hips. The body was made of muslin and was stuffed with reindeer hair. This Käthe Kruse *Doll I* was the only one produced until 1922; in that same year *Schlenkerchen*, the only smiling Käthe Kruse doll, with a size of 33cm (13cm) came onto the doll market.

This doll today is a rarity and is desperately sought by many doll collectors, because without *Schlenkerchen*, a Käthe Kruse doll collection is incomplete.

In 1925, *Träumerchen* appeared at the Leipziger Fair as the newest creation from the Käthe Kruse workshop in Bad Kösen in central Germany. Everyone was of the opinion that this little doll was a small

NEXT PAGE: 50cm (approx 19⅝in) Käthe Kruse *Sandbaby, Träumerchen*; magnesit head with a 35cm (13¾in) circumference; 5 lbs in weight; wearing old silk dress; from the 1940s. 50cm (approx 19⅝in) Käthe Kruse *Sandbaby, Träumerchen*; cloth head with a 36cm (approx 14¼in) circumference; 5 lbs in weight; wearing old hand-sewn baby jacket with pearls; circa 1930. 50cm (approx 19⅝in) Käthe Kruse *Sandbaby, Träumerchen*; plastic head with a 37cm (approx 14½in) circumference; 5 lbs in weight; wearing original cap and shirt; from the 1980s. 50cm (approx 19⅝in) Käthe Kruse *Sandbaby, Du Mein*; cloth head with a 37cm (approx 14½in) circumference; 5 lbs in weight; wearing old baby clothing; 1928.

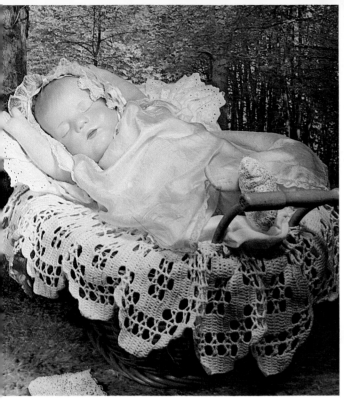

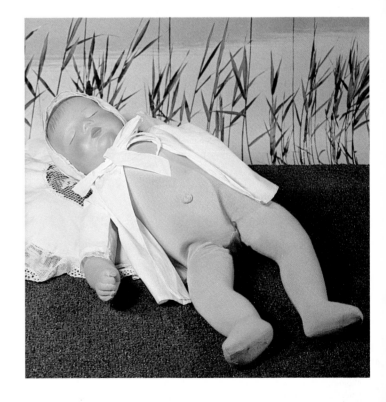

wonder and a perfect artwork. It was a 5 lb, 50cm (approx. 19⅝in) tall, heavy baby, produced carefully by hand, and was similar in size to that of a real baby. The head hung helplessly downwards, if one did not support it; the body felt soft and warm, due to the stockinette material which gave it a realistic feeling.

The idea for this doll came from Dr. Wagner, Käthe Kruse's family doctor. It was when the son Max came into the world, and he was standing at the crib admiring this beautiful baby. He encouraged Käthe Kruse to produce a sweet little baby doll for teaching purposes in baby care. The son Max was the inspiration for *Traumerchen*, but was not the model. The model for this head was a plaster cast of a baby's head. One could buy these plaster cast heads in any particular shop. It is suspected that this plaster cast head was a death mask. The cloth head of *Träumerchen* was produced in a similar way as that of *Doll I*. The eyes of *Träumerchen* are always closed and have painted on eyelashes. The body consisted of a wire skeleton, cotton and small bags of sand as ballast and was wrapped tightly with gauze. The body's covering was made from stockinette, so that naked it was nice to look at. The arms are always sewn on, while the legs are cut together with the stockinette material. On the bulging stomach a lifelike navel is sewn on, and on its bottom there is an opening for placing a thermometer.

In the beginning the baby came mainly with a layette and bonnet, but also as a baby in swaddling clothes, in a baby basket with a handmade pink cape, pink feather pillow and feather bed as well as on a checkered or white baby's pillow. Later on lovely clothing was designed for it.

It is important for collectors to know that to this day *Träumerchen* is available in different sizes and different weights as well as materials. It will be unknown to many, that *Träumerchen* (the same doll) is available with open eyes as well, and is called *Du Mein*. The *Du Mein* is also available as a *Sandbaby* as well as a play doll without sand. Since it is impossible to describe all the important criteria in one article, the buyer of a Käthe Kruse doll should be in a position to check its authenticity (there are copies). Therefore I would like to refer them to my book, *The Beloved Käthe Kruse Dolls*. This book will help further in difficult situations.

Träumerchen and *Du Mein*, just like all other Kathe Kruse dolls, had Kathe

Kruse's signature and a serial number on the left foot sole, as well as a patent tag attached to the hand.

Since the production of cloth heads was very tedious and thus expensive, they started to produce, in the 1930s, a head made out of magnesit (a cement-like substance), and from circa 1965 onwards the heads were made out of plastic. Due to this, these Käthe Kruse dolls lost a lot of their charm and radiance.

Not many of these dolls were sold in America, because the shipping costs were too high for these heavy dolls.

With the appearance of *Doll VIII*, the *Deutsche Kind*, whose name was translated into *Graceful Child* for American and English catalogs, Käthe Kruse once again had great success. *Friedebald* and *Ilsebill* (the first catalog names) were the first Käthe Kruse play dolls, which had expensive hand-knotted real hair wigs with lovely stylings. Their bodies were not small and chubby, like *Doll I*, but were large and slim; their thumbs were not separately sewn on, but were cut together with the material. The model for this *Deutsche Kind*, as well as for the earlier window manikin dolls was a bust made by the father of Max Kruse's son-in-law, Igor von Jakimow, of Käthe

Kruse's second oldest son, Friedebald. Käthe Kruse said that with this doll, she was able to capture the child's charm. Friedebald died young and today he is a legendary figure.

Another bust made by Igor von Jakimow, which portrays a lovely child's head, was used as a model for the head of *Doll VII*, *Hampelchen*. This *Hampelchen*, (its name was given due to its loosely attached legs) came out at the beginning of the 1930s and had very little success because it could not stand. Its body was sometimes attached to the heads of either *Doll I* or with the *Deutsche Kind*, *Doll VIII*. It is unknown to this day who modelled for Jakimow's bust, but one thing is certain, it was no child of Käthe Kruse's.

From 1929 until 1958, the charming window manikin dolls whose heads were produced by the talented Kruse daughter, Sofie (Fifi), also belonged to the production series of Kruse workshops. It is a great pity that there are not many window manikin dolls left; they were used as working dolls, and therefore when they were not of any use or damaged they were thrown out.

Since 1958, nearly all Käthe Kruse dolls are produced from synthetics. Except for *Träumerchen* and *Du Mein*, which

LEFT: 35cm (approx 12¾in) Käthe Kruse *Rumpumpels*; modeled by Hanne Kruse; plastic heads; original clothes.

BELOW LEFT: Käthe Kruse *Deutsches Kinds*; cloth heads, original real hair wigs; original clothes as seen in old catalog; from the 1930s.

were exceptions until 1965, whose heads were made from magnesit. The production series of the Käthe Kruse workshop in Donauwörth, Bavaria, received an additional enrichment through two dolls, *Däumlinchen* and *Rumpumpel* produced by Mrs. Hanne Adler-Kruse, the youngest Käthe Kruse daughter. As in the past, all doll heads are painted by hand, the wigs are hand-knotted and the bodies are partly hand-stuffed.

The old Käthe Kruse dolls are important collectors' items in the world today. Several years ago, they were seldom found in antique and doll shops, because they were not recognized as antiques and today they are difficult to find. Due to our books, which, for the first time, revealed fundamental in-depth knowledge about Käthe Kruse dolls, the demand for these dolls has increased tremendously. One should not forget that these handmade dolls were not produced in large quantities such as porcelain dolls were. And many owners cannot part with these lovely dolls, because too many memories are attached to their childhood. Just the name Käthe Kruse has a magical touch for many people.

Also the interest and demand for window manikin dolls and for the new Käthe Kruse play dolls from Donauwörth has increased tremendously. □

50 Years —
Shirley Temple Dolls

by Patricia N. Schoonmaker

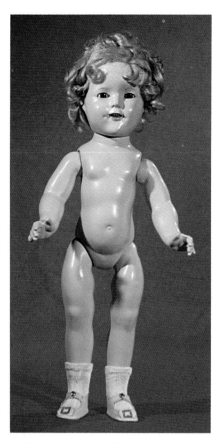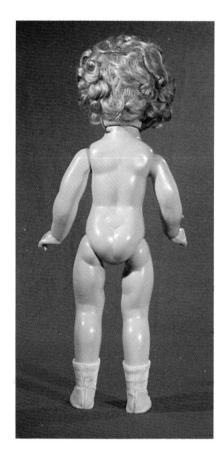

Illustrations 2 and 3. Left: Front view of a *Shirley Temple* doll showing the perfectly formed human body, first used on Ideal's *Ginger* doll but intended for an eventual *Shirley Temple* portrait doll. **Right:** Back view of a *Shirley Temple* doll. Note the dimples in the derriere and rounded calf of leg.

PREVIOUS PAGE:
Illustration 1. Three early *Shirley* dolls in a Shirley Temple trunk. Left to right: 11in (27.9cm), 18in (45.7cm) and 15in (38.1cm) verisons. The last two are from the *Stand Up and Cheer* movie.

Christmas 1984 will be the 50th anniversary of the original composition *Shirley Temple* doll's first appearance under America's Christmas tree! The earliest mention in toy trade publications is found in *Playthings*, September 1934:

"The Ideal Novelty & Toy Co. have added a new doll called 'Shirley' to their extensive line of Ideal dolls. Shirley has the same well shaped body, legs and arms as 'Ginger' the Ideal innovation that has met with such favorable response in the trade. Shirley's pert, animated expression is also enhanced by the new Ideal double action glance eyes and lashes, and her head is crowned with a beautiful wig in a choice of three colors: brunette, blonde or auburn. A variety of charming costumes is also available, the outstanding color schemes being pink, blue, maize, green or white. Little Shirley will, of course, be on display in the Ideal showrooms in the Fifth Avenue Building."

Ginger was introduced to the trade in the preceeding June 1934. The body, arms and legs were said to be molded with absolute fidelity to the human body as well as having new style ball and socket joints that enabled arms and legs to assume natural and graceful poses.

Advertising claimed that due to the perfect body, dresses, for the first time, really fit the doll. It now appears the *Ginger* body was designed for a Shirley Temple creation, should Ideal be successful in receiving permission to market them.

The competition to be the firm who received this contract was intense. Announcing the "Shirley" doll (not Shirley Temple) with blonde, brunette or auburn wigs may have been a type of smoke screen while Ideal perfected the celebrity doll.

In *The Shirley Temple Story* by Lester and Irene David, G. P. Putnam's Sons, New York, Mr. Abe Katz gave an interview on getting the doll ready for the Christmas season, 1934. Mr. Ben Michtom of Ideal Toy & Novelty Co. had a brother-in-law who worked for the William Morris Agency in California who obtained for him an introduction to Mrs. Gertrude Temple, Shirley's mother. Apparently no approval or contract was given until the completed

doll was presented. Mr. Katz, Ideal's Production Manager, stated that negotiations went on for months. He recalled they had the body but needed the head, and supposedly 20 molds were made by designer Bernard Lipfert before Mr. Katz was satisified. (One wonders if any of the other molds found their way onto the market as "look-alikes.") The first costumed doll portrayed Shirley as she sang and danced "Baby Take a Bow" in the movie *Stand Up and Cheer*. The doll was shipped to Mrs. Temple who approved it and the doll went into production. Special hazel eyes had to be ordered from the supplier. The curls were not as profuse at this time as later dolls would be as Shirley's own coiffure was a bit softer and more casual at this early date.

The prototype doll had peaches and cream shades of paint, a light blonde wig of mohair, light brown eyebrows and a line outlining the upper eye with painted eyelashes beneath the eye. Lips were a soft shade of red with orangey tones. The mouth had six teeth with felt behind them and the dimples were prominent.

The wig on the protype doll is bound in tape at the inside hairline edge, a nicety that was later omitted. This doll is slightly broader in the face than was accurate when Shirley appeared in *Stand Up and*

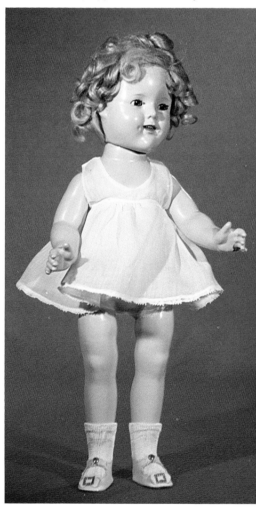

Illustration 4. 18in (45.7cm) prototype doll in original lace-trimmed undergarment and slip.

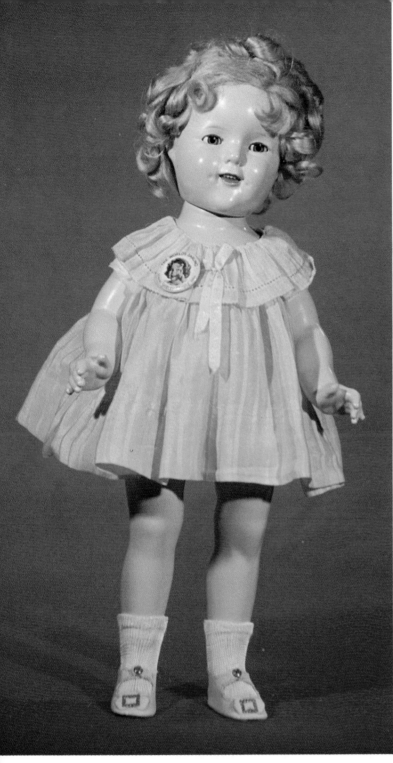

Cheer. (Possibly at Mrs. Temple's request, the following dolls were ever so slightly slimmer in the face.) A second clue to the prototype doll is that it is marked: G_P //IDEAL//N. & T Co." on the head with no mark on the torso at all. The company thought the celluloid trademark button and the woven label at the back of the dress, both with Shirley's name, was sufficient.

They quickly changed their minds. By September *Ginger,* the doll with the so-called anatomically perfect body (after introduction in June) had been copied by two firms, causing Ideal to file complaints with the Code Compliance Director. These firms agreed to discontinue manufacturing such dolls. Ideal stated in *Playthings* that the imitation referred to the body only of the dolls. (Later the entire doll would be copied many times over.)

The first four sizes were 15in (38.1cm), 18in (45.7cm), 20in (50.8cm) and 22in (55.9cm) at $3.00, $5.00, $6.00 and $7.00. These were expensive dolls at this time and not every child who wanted one was able to have it. *Playthings* magazine, October 1934, announced that Ideal Novelty & Toy Co., Fox Films Corporation

Illustration 5. *Shirley Temple* doll wearing a yellow silk-type deluxe pleated party dress with white organdy collar which is hemstitched, white silk cuffs on sleeves, double row of yellow stitching at hem top, woven design silk ribbon on collar. The button has a pink edge with black printing: "THE WORLD'S DARLING// GENUINE SHIRLEY TEMPLE DOLL."

RIGHT: Illustration 6. Back view of the dress on the prototype doll showing the label which reads: "SHIRLEY TEMPLE (in red print)//DOLL DRESS// REG. U. S. PAT. OFF//IDEAL NOV. & TOY CO.//NRA (eagle symbol) CODE//MADE IN U.S.A."

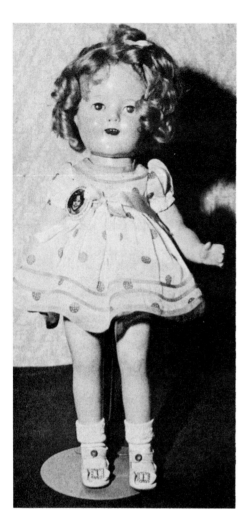

Illustration 7. 18in (45.7cm) prototype doll in rare green version of the dotted dress from *Stand Up and Cheer. Marge Meisinger Collection.*

and Shirley Temple's parents united in cautioning against the use of this name in any way other than on the Ideal *Shirley Temple* doll.

Under "New Toys on Parade, Just On The Market," *Toy World* magazine, November 1934, stated:

"Everyone who has seen fascinating and adorable little Shirley Temple — and who by this time has not? — will realize the scoop which Ideal Novelty & Toy Co. has staged in securing the exclusive rights to manufacture the Shirley Temple doll — an exact replica of America's new sweetheart.

"The hair is matched and the dresses are similar to the ones that little Shirley has actually worn in various movie plays. All of the dolls will have a celluloid button with Shirley Temple's picture and a facsimile of her signature.

"As indicated before, the Ideal Co. right is exclusive, and no other company or individual will be able to produce Shirley Temple dolls.

"By the way of promoting the sale of these dolls, arrangement has been made by which the Fox motion picture theatres all over the country have lifesize cut-outs of Shirley Temple, which will be loaned for advertising purposes, as will be mats for printing reproductions.

"Leading department stores are already planning store-wide promotions.

"There is no doubt that there will be a tremendous demand — which is already being felt. The manufacturers state that production is necessarily limited, no samples can be sent out, and orders will have to be filled in rotation." ☐

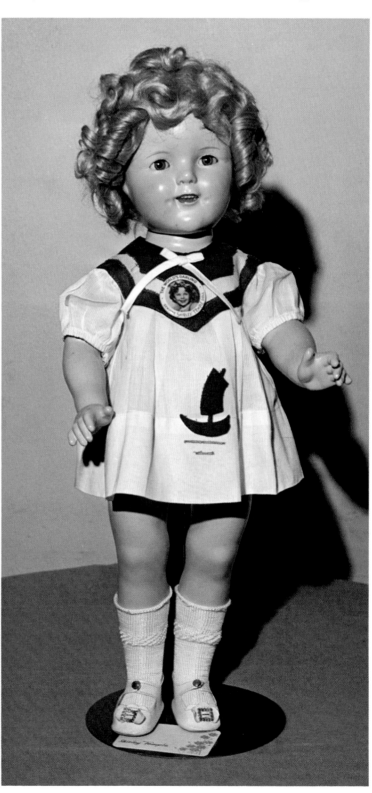

Illustration 8
Shirley doll seen in the sailboat dress, one of the first four styles created.

RIGHT: Illustration 11. The portrait of Shirley Temple which was chosen for the original trademark.

Illustration 10. Shirley poses with a 22in (55.9cm) prototype doll with a human hair wig, modeling a blue and white sailboat dress from her personal wardrobe.

RIGHT: Illustration 12. Shirley in a still from *Baby Take a Bow.* Ideal Toy & Novelty Co. never did copy this elaborate costume. Some look-alike manufacturers did attempt a version but the proportions were not correct.

ABOVE LEFT: Illustration 13. Unretouched photograph of Shirley posing with a 22in (55.9cm) prototype doll. This may have been one doll only in four different costumes.

ABOVE: Illustration 14. Shirley in a very early Fox Studios' publicity photograph in 1934 in a dress which was one of the first four costumes reproduced for the *Shirley* doll.

LEFT: Illustration 15. Unretouched photograph showing Shirley with a prototype doll in a matching party dress. Shirley's collar is all lace while the doll's dress collar is organdy with cotton machine embroidery. A later *Curly Top* dancing dress would have a similar appearance.

UNITED STATES PATENT OFFICE

Ideal Novelty & Toy Company, Brooklyn, N. Y.

Act of February 20, 1905

Application October 24, 1934, Serial No. 357,464

STATEMENT

To all whom it may concern:

Be it known that Ideal Novelty & Toy Company, a corporation duly organized under the laws of the State of New York, located and doing business at 273 Van Sinderen Avenue, in the county of Kings, Borough of Brooklyn, city and State of New York, has adopted for its use the trade-mark shown in the accompanying drawing.

The trade-mark has been continuously used in its business in interstate commerce since October 10, 1934. The portrait shown is that of Shirley Temple.

The particular description of goods to which the trade-mark is appropriated, is DOLLS, COSTUMES FOR DOLLS, PARTS OF COSTUMES FOR DOLLS, AND DOLLS' WIGS, comprised in Class 22, Games, toys, and sporting goods.

The trade-mark is usually displayed by printing same on labels which are attached to packages containing the goods.

IDEAL NOVELTY & TOY COMPANY,
By MORRIS MICHTOM,
President.

Illustration 16. Trade-Mark 328,814 which was first used October 10, 1934. This portrait was used to mark the boxes for dolls, costumes and wigs.

First Showing

in Oakland and San Francisco

Only at BREUNER'S

(Unretouched Photograph of Shirley Temple Doll)

GENUINE
"SHIRLEY TEMPLE"
DOLLS

Shirley Temple herself . . . not in movies—but in a doll so real, so lifelike that every little admirer of Shirley Temple will want one for her very own. Real blonde curls, eyes that sleep and have real eyelashes . . . exquisitely dressed with copyrighted clothes that are patterned after Shirley Temple's own dresses. Too adorable

18-Inch Doll	20-Inch Doll
$5.50	$6.95

IMPORTANT —Only a limited number of the Shirley Temple dolls can be made before Christmas. Stores in the East are selling them by thousands. We don't expect to be able to get enough to supply the entire demand later. Therefore, we suggest you place your order at once and have a "Shirley Temple" laid away for Christmas.

BREUNER'S

HI gate 4343   Broadway at 21st   Oakland

Illustration 18. Rare early advertisement showing the *Shirley Temple* doll in the party dress from Shirley's personal wardrobe that she wore when posing with the first doll. 15in (38.1cm) and 22in (55.9cm) dolls were also available. *San Francisco (California) Chronicle*, November 11, 1934. *Rita Dubas Collection.*

LEFT: Illustration 17. Actual trademark label and box end label showing the two types used.

Illustration 19. An operator curls wigs at the Ideal factory in the 1930s. *Rita Dubas Collection.*

Illustration 20. A worker assembles the bodies at the Ideal factory in the 1930s. *Rita Dubas Collection.*

Illustration 21. Workers paint the eyebrows, eyelashes and lips at the Ideal factory in the 1930s. *Rita Dubas Collection.*

Illustration 22. To avoid mussing, the wigs were not attached until after the dolls were dressed. The Ideal factory in the 1930s. *Rita Dubas Collection.*

DOLLS IN
"FOREIGN COSTUMES"
AT
TOY FAIR
IN THE 1940s

by **John Axe**

Photographs by the **Author**.

Illustration 1. Dolls dressed in various "foreign costumes" from the 1940s. They are all 11in (27.9cm) tall; all-composition and fully-jointed with mohair wigs. These dolls were made by either Dream World Dolls or the National Costume Doll Company.

163

Over the years many dolls have been produced by domestic and foreign doll companies that represent the costumes worn in other lands. These dolls are called "dolls in foreign costumes," "dolls in folk costumes," "dolls in national costumes," "dolls in regional costumes," "dolls in international costumes" and other terms. The most correct term is "dolls in regional costumes," as the costumes usually represent a certain region of a nation. An example of this are the dolls that represent Germany. Doll companies usually dress such dolls in an outfit with red pompons on the hat. This represents a folk costume from the Black Forest *region* of Germany, and was never a "national" costume for Germany. The same applies to all the doll señoritas which represent Spain and are most often found in flouncy dresses that are typical of Andalucia, a region of southern Spain.

The "foreign" costumes on dolls are usually not authentic; but they do show the flavor of folk dress of a part of a country, however simplified the representation may be. The worst offender among "international dolls" is *Africa*. Africa is a continent, *not* a country, and from Africa there are hundreds of regional costumes, none of which is typical of all Africa. Some collectors dislike dolls dressed in "foreign" costumes because the costumes are not "authentic" dress of any kind or any time period, yet they are typical of the era in which they were made and have many elements of the proper costume or time period.

Dolls can be, and should be, enjoyed for themselves. It does not matter if the costumes, particularly of dolls representing other lands, are "authentic." The preservation of folk or regional costumes never depended on the maintenance of dolls to keep a record of these traditions. Many original costumes from the past are preserved; paintings, drawings and photographs of them exist; families save them from generation to generation. Most of all, dolls dressed in "foreign" costumes make nice collections. These dolls were primarily sold for little girls to play with and to collect, and indirectly they taught the child something about other peoples of the earth.

Many collectors are familiar with the 11in (27.9cm) all-composition dolls from the 1940s that are dressed in "foreign costumes" and are usually referred to as "Dream World Dolls." Actually, these dolls were distributed by (as opposed to "made by") several doll companies. Dolls with cardboard hang tags with the "Dream World Dolls" logo can still be found in nearly mint condition. Dolls from the other companies are more difficult to identify.

All of these dolls were made by a single source, as they are identical. It was just as common in the 1940s for one molding company to make composition dolls from identical molds for various firms to market as it is today with vinyl dolls that are from the same molds, but are finished differently for distribution and marketing by several different companies. (Today, though, none of the larger American doll companies permit another company to utilize the same molds, as was done in the past. A good example of this is that during the early

Illustration 2. *Colonial*, probably by Dream World. The wig is pure white. The gown has a pale green top over a dark green skirt, and both are satin and are stapled to the doll, as are all the costumes for these dolls. The feathers in the hat are black and this is stapled to the doll's head.

Illustration 4. Only the National Costume Doll Company advertised the *Chinese Girl*, so it is safe to assume that these three dolls are from that company.

Illustration 3. *Little Miss Muffet* from the National Costume Doll Company. Like all other dolls from this type she is 11in (27.9cm) tall, all-composition, has blue painted side-glancing eyes and the wig is a strip of waved mohair. The hair is black. This doll is only jointed at the arms and legs, but otherwise the molding is the same as the dolls in "foreign costumes." The clothing is cotton and is stapled to the doll, including the white mobcap.

BELOW: Illustration 5. The dolls with the Dream World hang tag are called *Dancer (La Conga Queen);* the other one with the long gown is either the same or *Carmen* by the National Costume Doll Company. The one in the short dress is by one of these sources, or perhaps another doll company who used the same basic dolls. (These are the Carmen Miranda-types.)

1950s Madame Alexander, Arranbee and American Character all used the same mold for hard plastic girl dolls, which were wigged and dressed differently by each of the three companies.)

The 11in (27.9cm) all-composition dolls called "Dream World Dolls" all have great similarities:

*They are all-composition and fully-jointed.

*The head has slightly molded hair and usually has a mohair "wig" over it. This is not actually a wig, but a strip of waved mohair of various shades that is glued over the head and sometimes styled differently.

*The dolls almost always have blue painted side-glancing eyes.

*None of the dolls are marked.

*Most of the dolls have the clothing stapled in place, and staples were used generously.

*The underclothing is usually stiffened white cheesecloth. The underpants have braid trim that is white or various colors that have no relation to costume color.

*The shoes are white leatherette and have a shoestring tie across the instep.

*The clothing is almost always satin (with some taffeta used), trimmed with floss braid. Tops of gowns are often braid trim that is stapled to the doll to form bodices.

Two distributors used the exact same dolls, dressed them in a similar way, and even used the same names for the dolls. These are "Dream World Dolls," distributed by Herbert H. Krause & Associates of Chicago, Illinois, and "Dolls of All Nations" and "Fairy Land Series," distributed by the National Costume Doll Company of New York, New York. Dolls from these two sources can not be identified accurately as to which company they belong to if they do not have the "Dream World Dolls" hang tag. The dolls are so much alike it seems fair to suppose that these dolls were even dressed and processed by the same source.

Dream World Dolls

The "Dream World Dolls" were advertised in *Playthings* from February 1944 to June 1947. In the earlier advertisements for the dolls the copy stated: "Merchandised and distributed nationally by Herbert H. Krause & Associates, Chicago, Illinois." By early 1945 Herbert H. Krause & Associates also had a New York office in the Empire State Building. In 1946 the dolls were advertised as "manufactured by" the Krause company; in 1947 advertising copy gave a Chicago address for the "plant" where the dolls were made.

The "Dream World Dolls" are cute and worth collecting, but if one studied only advertising a different idea would develop than would if one studied only the dolls.

Illustration 6. This is the first advertisement for "Dream World Dolls" in *Playthings* (February 1944). Note the logo at the top left under "1944." This is the cardboard hang tag that is attached to the arm of the dolls.

Illustration 7. The first advertisement by the National Costume Doll Company appeared in *Playthings* in March 1945. Note that the doll in the top row, second from the right, is dressed in a crocheted costume. The dolls from Mary Ryan are dressed in a similar outfit.

166

Illustration 8. Undressed doll to show the construction of the Dream World/National Costume dolls. She is 11in (27.9cm) tall, all-composition and fully-jointed. The wig is blonde mohair that is glued to the head in a strip without a cloth foundation. The side-glancing painted eyes are blue. Note the holes in the torso. These are from the costume having been stapled to the doll.

See Illustration 6. Note the wording, such as "lustrous lifelike hair" and "the finest American workmanship." One must be suspicious of all pictures from doll advertising (especially in the past). The dolls that were photographed for ads were painted better than dolls in regular production and have more carefully delineated eyes and mouths. The pictures were also "doctored" and touched up so that the lines of bodices and waists and the draping of skirts showed up better than these simple costumes would have otherwise. The doll business has always been highly competitive and all sales tactics were mastered in the early years of the industry.

Another advertisement for "Dream World Dolls" stated:

"Undoubtedly the last word in doll artistry. Beautiful costumes in brilliant satins. Character portrayals are authentic. American workmanship. Superb characters are now available—each more beautiful than the other. All are irresistible! All *genuine* Dream World Dolls sell well *all* year 'round!" (*Playthings*, February 1945).

The "Dream World Dolls" were said to be "styled by Armand," and this gentle-man's picture was included in the early ads. Later Armand did not get credit for the dolls, but of their hair it was said, "Salon coiffured life-like wigs."

By late 1944 other companies were marketing the same dolls and, as stated earlier, the ones from the National Costume Doll Company were identical. Doll companies always copied a good selling product from each other, which has led to many court actions, but in the situation of Herbert H. Krause & Associates and the National Costume Doll Company it was more than just copying. The Krause ads of 1945 stated, "Imitation is the sincerest form of flattery but...it is not a genuine DREAM WORLD DOLL unless it carries this trade mark tag." (A picture of the hang tag was shown.)

In 1945 there was also a line of "Dream World Doll Furniture." It appears to have been constructed of a heavy cardboard and wood and was covered with satin materials. There was a "Fairyland Bed" for 6in (15.2cm) and 7in (17.8cm) dolls; a "Deluxe Hollywood Bed" for the larger dolls; a "Jewel Chair," whose seat was a "secret compartment" and an "Americana Cradle." The beds had removable quilts and spreads.

By 1947 "Dream World Dolls" were called "America's Most Exquisite Dolls!" They were measured more accurately, as ads said that they were in sizes ranging from 11in (27.9cm) to 18in (45.7cm).

National Costume Doll Company Dolls

The National Costume Doll Company began its advertising in *Playthings* in March of 1945; the only other ads were in February of 1946 and February of 1947. (This coincides with the annual Toy Fair promotions.) These dolls looked just like the Dream World Dolls in costume presentation and the basic doll was identical to the Dream World Dolls. The National Costume Doll Company had its offices in New York, with showrooms also in San Francisco, California, and Dallas, Texas.

The first selection was 12 dolls (see *Illustration 7*) that were "outstanding in value—charm—and authenticity." Two sizes were advertised—8in (20.3cm) and 12in (30.5cm). In 1946 the dolls were in two series. This was the "Dolls of All Nations" and "Fairy Land Series" and they were advertised as 7in (17.8cm) to 15in (38.1cm) and were "all dressed in beautiful Satin Gowns."

In the February 1947 issue of *Playthings* the dolls were called "National Costume Dolls" and the information in the advertisement told about them:

"Each of the 18 Characters is the result of long, careful research to assure absolute authenticity, plus unmatched skill to produce the Nation's most beautiful dolls out of the finest materials procurable.

"Whether you are interested in 11" Dolls with painted eyes or 15" and 18" Dolls with sleeping eyes, they all have movable arms, heads and legs. Each is packed individually in a handsome box.

"*At the Toy Fair*—See the National Costume Dolls and you'll see America's finest! Always imitated—never equalled!"

The National Costume Doll Company also complained about its dolls being copied, and by 1947 they were also listed at 11in (27.9cm), as the Dream World Dolls were by this time.

Other Dolls like the Dream World and National Costume Dolls

Several other doll companies were also using the same molds as Dream World Dolls and National Costume Dolls during the 1940s. The best examples of the other 11in (27.9cm) dolls that were made with these composition parts are the Madame Alexander *Scarlett O'Hara* (unmarked, wears a tagged gown) and the Arranbee *Nancy Lee* (identified by a cardboard hang tag). The molding is the same as the Dream World and National Costume dolls, except that the painting and finishing was more carefully done and more detailed. Also the dolls of Alexander and Arranbee had sleep eyes in these 11in (27.9cm) sizes.

The dolls that were the closest to the Dream World Dolls and the National Costume Dolls were from a company called Mary Ryan. This firm advertised in *Playthings* in September of 1944. Mary Ryan was located at 225 Fifth Avenue, New York, and also had another showroom

Illustration 9. The boxes that the dolls came in when new. At the top is the box for the "Dolls of All Nations" from the National Costume Doll Company. It is resting on a box that has a white background with blue stars over it. This is from *Swedish* by Dream World Dolls, with the name stamped on the end. Other boxes for Dream World Dolls are plain white with the name of the doll stamped on one end.

in the Merchandise Mart in Chicago. The dolls were called "La Madelon Dolls" and they were "by Madeleine Frazier." (They were not advertised as "made by" or "designed by" Madeleine Frazier.) The description of the Mary Ryan Dolls by Madeleine Frazier read:

"These American-made dolls are costumed with a French touch that gives them elegant chic. The dolls can be disrobed and the costumes are exquisitely made for tubbing or dry cleaning. The dolls are of composition with movable limbs. Their wigs are carefully selected for quality and color, and each is beautifully coiffured."

Of special note is the fact that the costumes were not stapled to the bodies of these dolls. Three of the dolls were costumed in "hand-made crocheted wool" and were dressed as little girls; another was a "Skating Doll" which wore a crocheted wool dress with a felt jacket and hat. There were also six "Character Dolls," of which four were dressed in "foreign costumes." There dolls retailed for $5.00 and $6.00 each, which was relatively expensive in 1944. A way to identify Mary Ryan dolls and separate them from Dream World Dolls and National Costume dolls, besides having no staples to hold the costumes in place, is that all of the costumes were "little girl" length and skirts were either to the knees or to the ankles.

It is not known who made the composition component parts for the dolls, but all of them surely came from the same supplier, where they were also painted, finished and wigged. The dolls of Alexander and Arranbee had better wigs, with a foundation to which they were sewn, unlike the others which were all pieces of mohair glued to the doll's head in a wig form. One thing worthy of note on all of these dolls is the condition in which the composition has remained. Most of them that are found today in original costumes are not cracked or crazed and the paint surface has not flaked or peeled off the dolls. Because of the practice of stapling the clothing to the dolls from Dream World and National Costume, the dolls are still found with their original costumes intact. Even hats and ribbons were securely stapled to the dolls. The only items of the costumes that were removable were the socks and shoes. □

The following is a list of all the advertised dolls from Dream World Dolls, National Costume Dolls and Mary Ryan Dolls for comparison purposes.

ABOVE: Illustration 10. Two *Brides* and two *Bridesmaids*. All four dolls have reddish-brown hair. The *Bridesmaids'* gowns are two different shades of lavender. There is no way to determine which company issued these dolls, but they are either from Dream World or National Costume.

RIGHT: Illustration 11. *Nun* by either Dream World or National Costume. There is no hair under the wimple. The costume is black and white and the crucifix and rope belt are original to the doll.

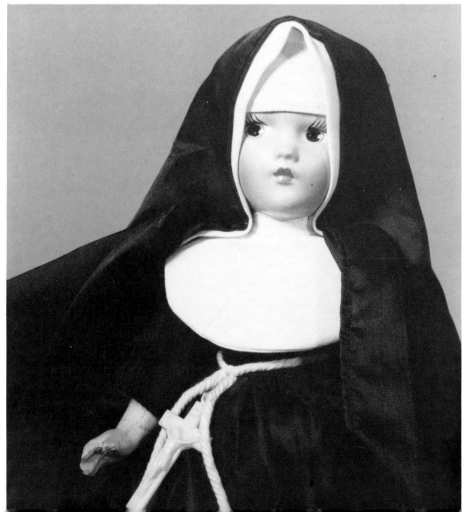

National Costume Doll Company
DOLLS OF ALL NATIONS

Spanish Girl
Colonial
The Bride
Dutch Girl
Carmen
Alsatian Girl
Casa Blanca
Nurse
Bridesmaid
Swedish Girl
Nun
Italian Girl
Chinese Girl
Sweetheart Girl
French Girl
Russian Girl
The Queen
Tyrolean Girl
Cowgirl

FAIRY LAND SERIES

Little Emily
Mary and Her Little Lamb
Tom Sawyer
Becky Thatcher
Alice in Wonderland
Mother Goose
Margery Daw
Jill
Queen Isabella of Spain
Little Bo Peep
Old Mother Hubbard
Mary, Mary, Quite Contrary
Beauty and the Beast
Little Miss Muffet
Heidi
Goldilocks and the Three Bears
Polly Put the Kettle On
Cinderella
Little Red Riding Hood
Martha Washington
Gretel
The Poor Little Match Girl
The Sleeping Beauty
Meg, of "Little Women"
Jo, of "Little Women"
Beth, of "Little Women"
Amy, of "Little Women"

Herbert H. Krause & Associates
DREAM WORLD DOLLS

Senorita
Colonial
Bride
Dutch
Dancer (La Conga Queen)
Alsace-Lorraine
Casablanca
Nurse
Bridesmaid
Swedish
Nun
Italian

Flower Girl
Norwegian
Peasant
Mrs. America
Scotch
Czech

Mary Ryan Dolls

Mimi, Suzette, Madeleine
Skating Doll

CHARACTER DOLLS

English
Dutch
French
American
Italian
Red Cross Nurse

Illustration 12. The costume represents Spain. The skirt is bright red taffeta. The top of the gown is representative of the simple construction of the garments of these dolls. It is a green strip of trim that is stapled to the waist with two strips of white lace stapled under it to form straps for the gown. The mantilla is black lace with a cloth rose in it. If this doll is from Dream World she is *Senorita;* if from National Costume she is *Spanish Girl.*

RIGHT: Illustration 13. The original box for this doll is stamped "Cowboy." The modeling and construction are identical to that of the Dream World and National Costume dolls, with the head having painted brown hair. Neither company listed a Cowboy in its advertising and the unmarked box is different than the boxes from either company, so his manufacture remains a mystery.

Illustration 14. Skating doll by Arranbee, 1940s. Her modeling and construction are identical to that of the Dream World/National Costume dolls: All-composition and fully-jointed; 11in (27.9cm) tall. The head even has the same slight hair molding as the other dolls. The difference is in the painting, which is neater and includes eye shadow and pink blush on the knees, and the fact that she has blue sleep eyes with eyelashes. The composition is also smoother and shinier. The dark blonde mohair wig is glued to a cloth foundation and is sewn and has a side part. The costume is also removable and better finished. It is a white velvet skirt and jacket lined with red flannel with a matching bonnet. The trim is a braid of flowers of different shades. This is the doll that is erroneously described as "an unmarked Sonja Henie" and it came in several different sizes.

Hedwig Dolls

by Z. Frances Walker

Illustration 1. *Suzanne* from *Petite Suzanne.*

Do you have in your possession a doll with a tag that reads "Hedwig Dolls Registered — Authorized Characters from the books of Marguerite de Angeli?" This is on one side of the round paper tag fastened to the doll's wrist. The other side of the tag has a picture of four girls with the names below them of *Lydia, Suzanne, Hannah* and *Elin.* The tag is yellow, printed in black.

The doll will be nicely dressed in some unusual dress. The Hedwig whose name appears on this tag is Hedwig M. Ryglewicz — a person of Polish ancestry. Hedwig made the costumes on the dolls, but where did she get her models?

On March 14, 1889, in Lapeer, Michigan, a baby girl was born to Shadrack George Lofft and his wife, Rubby Tuttle Lofft. The baby was their second child and was called Marguerite.

Marguerite married John Dailey de Angeli in 1910. Marguerite had a beautiful

voice and had thought of a career in opera, but decided on marriage instead. Dai came from a musical family and at one time played first violin with the Philadelphia (Pennsylvania) Symphony, the forerunner of the Philadelphia Orchestra.

Marguerite had not only musical talent, but also artistic talent. She became an illustrator. Through her illustrating she met Margaret Lesser, an editor with Doubleday. It was Margaret Lesser who suggested Mrs. de Angeli not only illustrate, but also write books for children.

The first of her well-researched historical children's books was *Henner's Lydia,* a book about a little Pennsylvania Amish girl who lived on a farm, attended a one room school and wore the plain clothes of her sect. In 1936 the book was published and Marguerite de Angeli was a children's author.

In 1941 (several books later) *Elin's Americka* came out. It was at this time that Marguerite's friend, Hedwig Ryglewicz, asked permission to dress dolls to represent the characters in the books. Hedwig, her husband, Edward, and the de Angelis were long time friends brought together by their love of music. They all played and sang together.

Since Marguerite had dolls to illustrate her books on her mind, she was delighted. A doll collector friend had suggested them to her when she visited a children's library to talk about her books.

Now that dolls were a real possibility, the two friends visited manufacturers of dolls. They finally decided on a glass-eyed, composition doll 15in (38.1cm) tall. The neck is in one piece with the body. The head sits rather high on it and swivels freely. The doll's arms and legs are straight with joints only at the shoulders and hips. There is no mark on the dolls, but Mrs. Ryglewicz told me they were bought from the Ideal Doll Company. Some of the later dolls were bought from other companies.

Marguerite and Hedwig were interested in getting a suitable doll to represent the character, not in who manufactured it. Hedwig dolls represent characters from books; the dolls are secondary to the costume.

Marguerite de Angeli had done her own art work to illustrate her books and it was very important to her that the dolls be recognizable as the children of her stories.

The four dolls illustrated on the tag were the first group made. Later others were to join them.

After acquiring the dolls, the next step was to make them look like the characters; the wig was the most important feature to change. It was a project of taking a modern composition doll and giving it the appearance of a little girl of a different era or culture. *Henner's Lydia* needed long brown hair, braided and arranged in a

Illustration 2. *Hannah,* the doll on the left, shows the first type of doll dressed by Hedwig; glass eyes; swivel neck composition body. The one on the right was dressed at least 15 years later. She has painted eyes, swivel neck; her dress material is different, but the style is the same, also a Hedwig doll.

knot. *Petite Suzanne* was a blue-eyed blonde with her hair arranged in a long bob. *Thee Hannah* was a Philadelphia Quaker girl who parted her red-brown hair in the center and drew it into a bun on the back of her head. *Elin*, of *Elin's Americka*, being a Swedish girl of 1650, wore her blonde hair in long braids tied with ribbons.

It was easy to decide on the costume for the illustrations in the various books determined style and material. Acquiring the material was more difficult. It was not easy to find duplicates of the materials Marguerite had used in the colored illustrations in the books. However, if you compare the dolls to the illustrations you will find Hedwig did very well.

The clothes were made on a sewing machine. They fit well. They can be removed for they are fastened with small buttons and buttonholes. The dress decorations match the designs of the illustrations.

The books are considered children's classics and are used by many teachers as required reading when studying about the group of people represented by them. Mrs. de Angeli won the Newberry Award for the outstanding children's book of the year in 1949 with her book entitled *Door in the Wall*. In 1971 a new de Angeli book was on

Illustration 3. *Lydia* and *Hannah* from *Henner's Lydia* and *Thee, Hannah*.

Illustration 4. *Elin* from *Elin's Americka*.

the market — *Butter at the Old Price*. It was an autobiography.

Mrs. de Angeli is no longer writing, but is living a quiet life in a retirement home on the outskirts of Philadelphia, Pennsylvania. Hedwig Ryglewicz is not dressing dolls for her eyesight is failing. There will be no more of these attractive contributions to the doll world made by two talented and active ladies — Marguerite de Angeli and Hedwig Ryglewicz.

Dolls I have seen include *Lydia*, a brown-haired girl dressed in Amish rose cotton dress made with a tucked bodice and full skirt. Her shoes and long cotton stockings are black. She has a black apron and black Amish bonnet. She has untrimmed white cotton underwear. *Lydia* is not yet a church member so does not wear the plain white cap which is worn indoors by the Amish women.

Suzanne is a French Canadian little girl whose home is in a small village on the Gaspe' Peninsula. Her clothing consists of a one-piece cotton undergarment with the panties and petticoat attached to the bodice. It is trimmed with lace. Her dress is made of pink rosebud cotton print. It has a plain bodice with high round neck and full skirt just to her knees. She wears long black stockings and black shoes. Her coat

is red wool made with a double cape collar. *Suzanne* wears a red stocking cap.

Our Quaker girl, *Hannah*, has not yet joined Meeting so she is not wearing typical Quaker dress. Her underwear is from the same pattern as *Suzanne's*, only trimmed with very fine rickrack. Her dress is yellow sprigged calico made with a drop shoulder to which long sleeves, gathered into a cuff, are attached with a plain yellow cording. The same cording is used where the gathered skirt is attached to the plain bodice. The neck is finished with a white lawn collar. Her stockings are white, her shoes black. She has a brown taffeta typical Quaker bonnet which ties under her chin.

Elin is the little Swedish girl who started Hedwig dressing dolls. She is a blue-eyed blonde with long braids tied with red bows. Her blouse is white with long sleeves. Her skirt is red with red and white around the bottom. Her felt vest is laced with red ribbons. *Elin* wears a flowered white shawl around her neck; her apron is an attractive multi-colored stripe. She has a close-fitting red cap made with gold cording around the edges. She is quite colorful — a Swedish girl of 1650.

The next two characters are the ones I imagine Hedwig enjoyed dressing most,

Illustration 5. *Cecilia* and *Aniela* from *Up the Hill.*

leather shoes. *April* is obviously a much later doll.

Mrs. de Angeli wrote and illustrated several books with boys as the main characters. Hedwig did not enjoy dressing boys. She did make one, *Yonie,* from the book *Yonie Wondernose.* He is in Mrs. de Angeli's possession. *Yonie* is her one and only Hedwig doll and she has no intention of parting with him.

Hedwig Ryglewicz dressed dolls to illustrate only six or seven of Marguerite de Angeli's books. However, they are a contribution to the American doll world, even though a small one. They show the work of two persons interested in music, literature and illustrations. Their work has made these books for children come alive in the three-dimensional form of dolls. □

Illustration 6. *April* from *Bright April.*

for they were two little girls from two different provinces of Poland. *Aniela* was from the province of Lowicz, the home of Chopin. *Aniela* wears two full petticoats, the under petticoat trimmed with embroidery, the outer one very full trimmed with lace. She wears a white organdy blouse, a full two-tiered striped cotton skirt trimmed with braid and a row of lace. Her jacket is sleeveless, made of green felt and trimmed up the front with braid to match that on the skirt. She wears several strings of small beads. On her head she wears a kerchief of flowered cotton. She has long white stockings and black shoes.

Her friend, *Cecilia,* comes from the province of Krakow. Her underwear is the same as *Aniela's.* Her dress is of white organdy trimmed with rows of brightly colored ribbons. She wears a dainty white organdy apron trimmed with lace and ribbons. Her vest is made of red velvet cut long and shaped below the waist. The vest has gold sequin trimming around the edges. The front is laced with red ribbons. On her head *Cecilia* wears a wreath of flowers, tied with ribbons hanging down her back.

She has long braids that hang down while *Aniela's* braids are gathered in a knot on the back of her head. Both of the Polish girls have painted eyes while the first four dolls had glass sleep eyes. The two Polish dolls from *Up the Hill* were bought in 1972; the first four were purchased in 1951.

It is extremely likely that they came from two different purchases, perhaps even different manufacturers. They are the same size and have the same body construction.

Bright April is the title of a book about a little black girl — the color of coffee with cream in it. April is the character's name. *April* is an entirely different doll from the others. She is 13in (33cm) tall, jointed at shoulders and hips; the right arm is slightly bent at the elbow. She has brown sleep eyes and black bobbed hair. Her underwear is like that of the other girls. She has a short-sleeved white blouse with a lace-trimmed collar. Her blouse fastens down the front with small white buttons. Her skirt is blue cotton, above the knees and circular. She wears no stockings and has brown plastic shoes; the other dolls had

173

Life-sized Dolls by Käthe Kruse

by **Magdalena Byfield**

ABOVE: Illustration 1. 19in (48.3cm) sleeping infant doll made of stockinette with the head only painted in oils and weighted with sand. Weight: seven pounds.

BELOW: Illustration 2. 19in (48.3cm) wide-awake version of the stockinette infant with slight variation in the head mold. Weight: seven pounds.

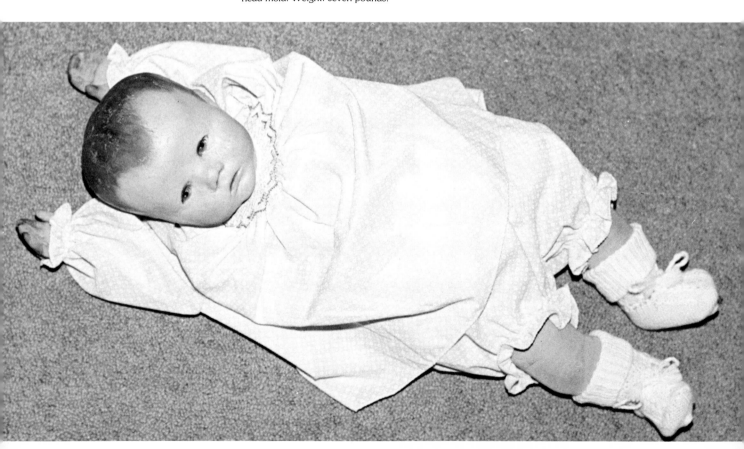

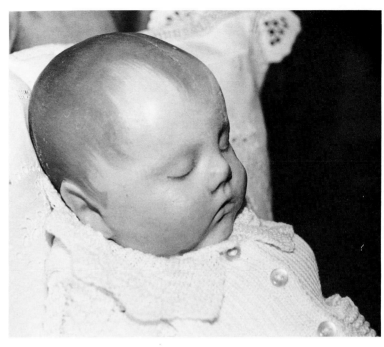

Illustration 3. *Katie.* Note the slightly frowning expression created by a pressure crease between the right eye and the nose.

Illustration 4. *Mandy.* In this head the press mold has gone exceptionally deep in the mouth area creating an open/closed appearance to the lips.

If you have the inclination and space to collect life-sized dolls, you should be aware of the many and varied types made by Käthe Kruse. Collectors not knowing of the many Kruse variants with different faces and unusual body construction think of her dolls in terms of the solemn-faced and now familiar small dolls made as boys, girls and toddlers. While these stock heads and body designs were mass-produced over a long period in an unchanging pattern, others were made concurrently in smaller numbers; many with specific character faces and several not intended as toys at all but as store window mannequins, while others served the double purpose of toy and model.

The best known of these must now surely be the *Sand Babies*. These baby dolls are renowned for their realism of movement; in whichever pose they are arranged or carelessly laid, they appear completely relaxed and alive. Made entirely of stockinette, the mask only (including the ears) was made in a press mold, laid over a sand-filled molded foundation (probably carton) and the whole hand-painted in oil colors which did not, however, extend down the neck. The head thus has a naturalistic lolling motion and gives the doll an overall weight of seven pounds. The stockinette of the cotton wool padded body was peach-colored and was left unpainted. A charming final touch was the application of a coiled rosetta navel to the belly. One version was produced with the eyes painted asleep (*Illustration 1*) and this mold differs from that in which the eyes are

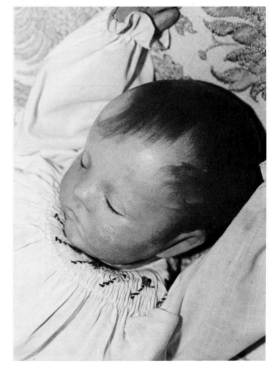

Illustration 5. *Antonia.* Dark swirling hair, a tight-lipped mouth and extra long eyelashes are the individual points of this doll.

painted open (*Illustration 2*). The latter appears to represent a baby aged some weeks while the "Sleeper" shows a baby only days old. Both, however, are 19in (48.3cm) in length.

It is said that the dolls were advertised as indestructible and washable but they are, in fact, neither, being in many ways extremely vulnerable. Because only a very thin layer of primer was used between the stockinette and the oil paint (which was

also applied very thinly), there is a tendency for the paint to flake, particularly at the back of the head. In early specimens the stiffened painted stockinette stands away from the carton foundation at the top and back of the head so these areas are, in effect, quite soft and the paint work here can suffer the most in consequence. The faces also dent very easily and should never be stored lying on or against a hard surface. Stockinette is subject to laddering

175

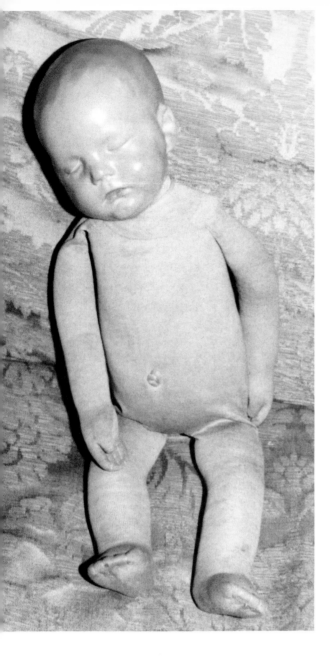

LEFT: Illustration 6. 19in (48.3cm) painted rubber-headed *Sleeping Baby* on a stockinette body. Note crisper delineation of features in this medium. Weight: seven pounds.

BELOW: Illustration 7. A rubber-headed specimen shown with the paint work stripped to reveal five separate sections bonded together. These are *solid* white rubber to give the same weight as the sand-filled stockinette head.

angles, this was done to emphasize rather than create each doll's unique qualities.

It is thought that those with painted dark brown hair and little swirling curls (showing a mastery of brush work on the part of the decorator) are the earlier specimens. The lighter hair is said to denote a doll of the 1930s but this is purely conjecture. My own feeling is that as the dark coloration effectively concealed the otherwise obtrusive stitch work on the head while the light brown color leaves the seams highly visible; the dark was therefore a later design improvement if anything. It is most probable, however, that both dark and fair babies were run concurrently.

A variant of the *Sleeping Baby* that had no stitch seam problems is the rubber-headed specimen (*Illustration 6*). Note how much crisper the delineation of the features is using this material; even a dimpled chin becomes apparent. This head is solid white rubber made in five separate sections bonded together with red rubber (*Illustration 7*). The head was painted in oil in the traditional manner and the doll also weighs the statutory seven pounds and is 19in (48.3cm) long. Another has been seen with a composition head but I have been unable to locate one for illustration here.

The open-eyed babies display equally unique qualities embued by the individual artist -- indeed more so as the eye color

when a fibre snaps and has to be rewoven with a crochet hook and fastened off with matching thread where this happens. So it must be appreciated that these heavy and wholly enchanting fabric dolls require very careful handling and thoughtful storage. They were used extensively in hospitals for midwifery training purposes and some of the best preserved specimens have come from this source. They were also used as display models in baby wear shops but in the main, of course, they were marketed as toys for children.

To the collector one of the most interesting aspects of the *Sand Babies* is that no two are exactly alike due to the hand-painted finish which embues each single doll with its own personal characteristics. Note the distinctive variations in three different heads (*Illustrations 3, 4, and 5*) out of the same press mold. Deliberately photographed from different

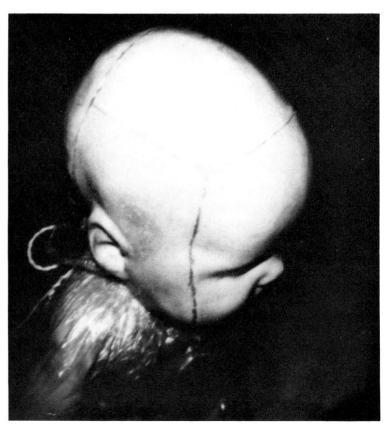

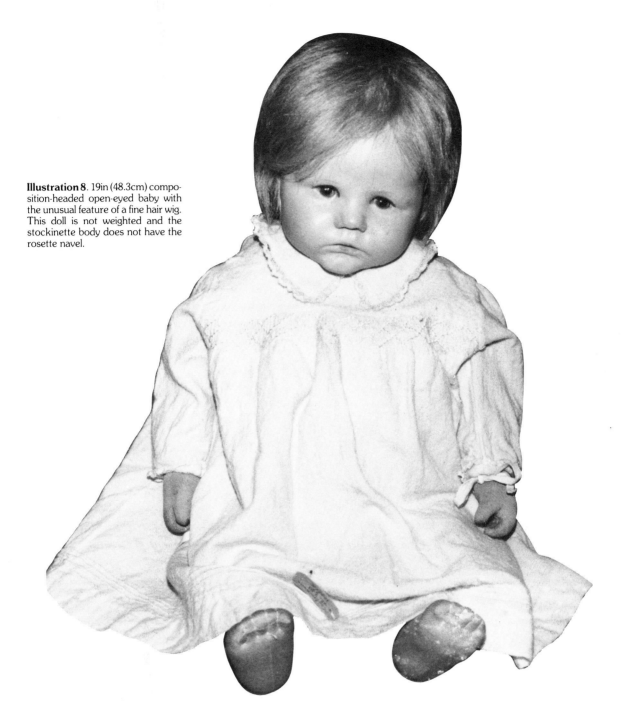

Illustration 8. 19in (48.3cm) composition-headed open-eyed baby with the unusual feature of a fine hair wig. This doll is not weighted and the stockinette body does not have the rosette navel.

varies greatly. The doll in *Illustration 8* is exceptional in that it has a composition head and an exquisitely constructed fine baby-hair wig while still being the usual 19in (48.3cm) though *not* the seven pound weight. It also does not have the rosette navel. Similar to the open-eyed baby with painted hair, it does, however, have a somewhat older appearance and on close inspection it can be seen that the mold used for this doll was, in fact, slightly different. Most notably the nose and ears are more pronounced.

The 28in (71.1cm) doll in *Illustration 9* can only be posed in a seated position testifying that this was a display mannequin. Her unusual feature is a swivel neck

whereas most mannequins have lift-off heads. Her head is composition with an enchanting plump face *(Illustration 10)*. The features are painted in oil with grey-green eyes and applied hair eyelashes. The stockinette body, arms and bent legs are rigidly padded except for an area at the leg tops which has been left hollow, thus giving swing-leg articulation. The arms have wire armatures and some movement can be achieved with effort. The fine brown hair wig is intricately knotted in small groups through a muslin cap glued to the head.

A much earlier display model head was made in a two-piece press mold of papier-mâché lined with muslin and most artistically painted in oils *(Illustration 11.)*

Note the pouting mouth and funnel neck which seats down on the stockinette body over a padded cone. This model has dark brown painted hair beneath a black wig which is undoubtedly a later addition. He is a 40in (101.8cm) standing figure with fully-jointed wooden stockinette covered arms and hands, of which each stockinette bound finger can be separately articulated.

The 37in (94.1cm) pair of mannequins *(Illustration 12)* are of a similar design to the little girl in *Illustration 9* but their composition heads lift off to reveal at the base of their necks a squared metal bar that seats down into a square opening in the neck socket cup, enabling the heads to be set in three different positions -- facing

177

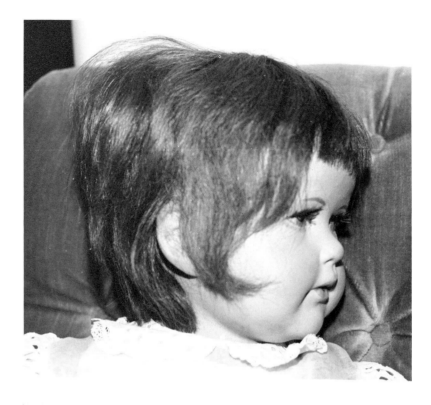

RIGHT: Illustration 10. Close-up of the mannequin in *Illustration 9* to show unusual plump character face.

BELOW: Illustration 9. 28in (71.1cm) composition-headed girl mannequin with swivel neck. This figure can be posed in a variety of seated positions only.

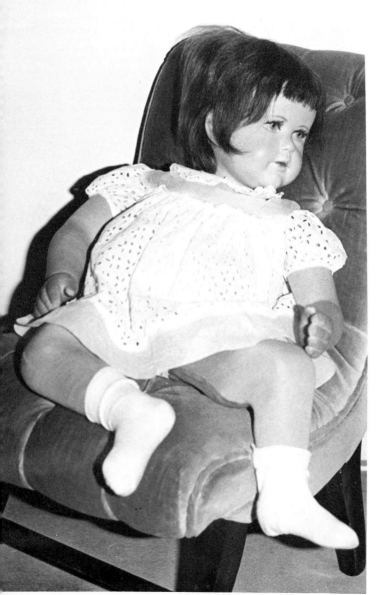

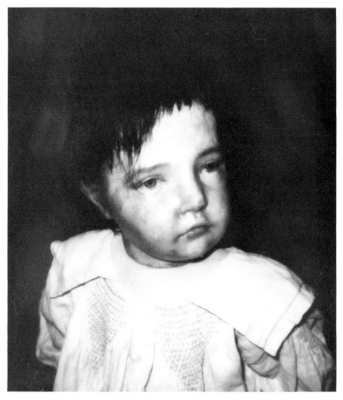

Illustration 11. 40in (101.8cm) early papier-mâché character head with funnel neck that seats down over a padded stockinette cone extending up from an articulated stockinette covered body.

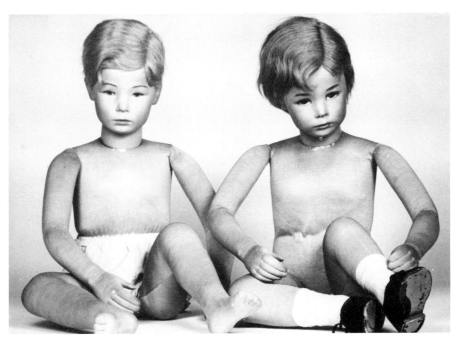

Illustration 12. A pair of 37in (94.1cm) store mannequins with composition lift-off heads on seated stockinette bodies.

(Illustration 13) dressed and undressed to show body construction.

The advantages of collecting the life-size work of one exceptionally versatile doll artist are manifold. In the case of Käthe Kruse there are no bisque heads to spring hairline cracks, no glass eyes to fall in and no fabric used that is attractive to moths. Also, if the worst comes to the worst, oil painted heads (like oil paintings on canvas) can be restored by an expert. Life-sized dolls are relatively easy to dress in clothes of their own era as old children's clothes are cheaper and easier to come by than the miniature garments of small dolls. My own Kruse collection has been dressed by my childhood dresses of the 1930s and some worn by my children between 1958 and 1964. The dolls and mannequins being in scale to one another can be grouped in charming attitudes and a comparatively small number can make a dramatic display in a large glazed showcase that would take very many small dolls to fill equally. Children of even the recent past do not look at all like those of the present, so a delightful unity is achieved by grouping these dolls together with each an individual yet belonging in dress and facial style to one whole nostalgic scene.

Last, but not least, one has the enduring pleasure of looking upon the creations of one of the most sensitive and talented doll makers of the 20th century.

forwards or in profile to the left or right. They, too, have swing-leg articulation and armatures in the arms, and they, too, can only be posed in a variety of *seated* positions. They have the typical Kruse wigs of fine hair knotted into muslin caps, but these have four press studs underneath to correspond with four stud cups set in the head -- thus making the wigs interchangeable. Life-sized *adult* mannequins were also made by the Käthe Kruse factory and one lady figure is illustrated here

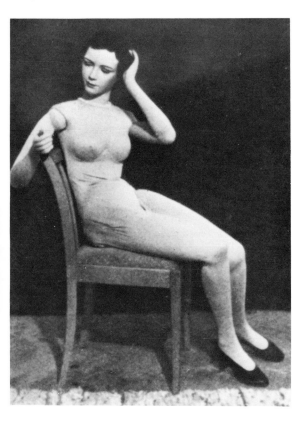

Illustration 13. Two views of an adult mannequin with composition head on a stockinette body. This figure, too, can only be arranged in seated positions.

More Fashionable Fifties-- Revlon Dolls!

by Margaret Groninger
Photographs by Jane Rishel

Illustration 1. Box top found on all larger (15in [38.1cm] on up) *Revlon* dolls. "So beautiful her name just had to be Revlon."

The ten years of the 1950 to 1960 era were loaded with what could be termed fashion dolls - - dolls that wore adult attire; dolls, in fact, on which the clothing was the most important part of the doll in many cases.

Two distinct types of 1950s fashion dolls existed. The first, in the early part of this period, was an older child type which, however, often wore very grown-up clothing. The *Sweet Sues* (by American Character), *Honeys* (by Effanbee) and *Tonis* (by Ideal) lacked busts and high heels. The second wave brought dolls with more adult bodies (as if the pre-teens had simply grown up a year or two). It remained for the 1960s to streamline the lady doll into one in which the head was actually too small. The late 1950s ladies were better proportioned - - except for a slight leaning toward chunkiness (in contrast to the live models they represented), perhaps with good reason. The idea of an adult female body on a doll was a trifle shocking for the times; the chunkier torsos made the bustline a little less obvious.

Madame Alexander's *Cissy,* who arrived around 1955, is widely accept-

ed as the original adult doll in the modern era, on whom all later versions were based. Probably the real originator was Valentine's *Aida* ballerina doll, sold in 1954. While *Aida* had only a hint of a bust, she did feature longer, more adult legs than the stolid young girl dolls popular then. Still, *Cissy* made the biggest splash, causing even the sophisticated *New Yorker* to exclaim that she wore a bra "for heaven's sake!" and high heeled shoes.

Cissy was definitely an upper class lass, featured in F.A.O. Schwarz catalogs and sold in the more exclusive stores. Many similar dolls followed in her wake, some of them quite cheap, but a number in what might be termed the "middle class" bracket. Probably the best known of the middle classers was Ideal's *Revlon,* the darling of Macy, *Good Housekeeping* and the Sear's Christmas catalog set. She was a good quality doll for those who could not afford, or did not have access to, the more expensive Madame Alexander offering.

The August 1956 issue of *Toys and Novelties* magazine announced her arrival. "Ideal Toy's new Revlon doll - - available in September - - has the 'full formed figure of a teenage girl.'" Promised the article, she would be sold in sizes from 18in (45.7cm) to 23in (58.4cm), in prices ranging from $12.00 to $25.00, and wearing three styles inspired by Revlon's best-selling cosmetics. Before returning to rave about *Cissy,* the *New Yorker* did give *Revlon* at least passing notice in its December 1st issue that year, remarking that the $11.98 version sold at Macy had "a wealth of hair long enough for all sorts of elaborate hairdos."

Another year had to elapse before the trend toward adult dolls solidified. In 1957, *Look* magazine noted (November 26, 1957), "the fashion in dolls this year is high fashion" (from there the article went on to highlight a bevy of lady dolls photographed just like adult models against New York settings), while the magazine section of the November 3rd *New York Times* sighed, "this season,

every major manufacturer introduced his own version" of what the *Times* was careful to call the "full-figured" doll (as opposed to "teen-age"). Most popular, advised this last article, were the 10½in (26.7cm) versions.

Indeed, the smaller editions were everywhere. Vogue (*Jill*), Madame Alexander (*Cissette*), Nancy Ann Storybook Dolls (*Miss Nancy Ann*) and others had them. Ideal's contribution was called *Little Miss Revlon.* She was special to Ideal because her debut coincided with the firm's 50th anniversary, a fact mentioned in a two page 1957 *Toys and Novelties* advertisement for her. "Introducing Little Revlon," it heralded, praising her as an exciting new miniature version of Ideal's Best-Seller . . . the *Revlon* doll. She had all the features of her bigger sister: "Magic Touch" skin (hard plastic body, softer head), adult figure with bust and high heeled feet, twist waist, pierced ears and sleep eyes. In addition, those with sufficient funds could buy 30 outfits for her at that time (more were added later), which was right in line with the times - - the *Look* treatment already mentioned announced that some of the smaller fashion dolls had as many as 40 different costumes, adding that such dolls had started a style revolution in doll clothes. (The *New York Times Magazine* had been amazed at the tiny extras like sunglasses, hats and roller skates available for such creatures.)

Illustration 2. 10½in (26.7cm) *Little Miss Revlons* in original clothes, with box. Left to right: Redingote outfit ("Visiting Outfit Series"); regular bridal gown; Jeans and Shirt ("Playtime Series"), the last lacking her straw hat.

The year 1958 was one of complete acceptance. Then the Sears Christmas catalog featured three 20in (50.8cm) *Revlon* dolls (mentioning the same could be had in 15in (38.1cm) and 18in (45.7cm) versions as well), plus the *Little Miss Revlon* in her quaint two-piece lacy white bra/panty girdle ensemble - - and seven extra outfits to be bought separately, including a blue ballerina tutu, fleecy red coat and beige raincoat with clear plastic boots. No mention was made of the largest doll in this series, the 23in (58.4cm) *Revlon,* who might thus be considered the rarest of the quintet (personally, I think the 15in [38.1cm] *Revlon,* is the hardest to find these days). No matter what the size, the doll had either ponytail with bangs or curly bob with bangs also, in either very light blonde or reddish brown. What is curious about the advertisement for the larger *Revlons* is the caption for one describing its outfit as "Kissing Pink," although the outfit is definitely blue (the real "Kissing Pink" dress was either striped pink and white or pink with red hearts). Also shown in the same ad is a Revlon look-a-like called "Happi-Time Modiste," which might have fooled some. She was several dollars cheaper than *Revlon,* even though she was wearing a "fur" (plush, actually) coat, so was apparently a cheaper copy by another firm. Shown at the bottom of the listing sketches of clothes for the lady dolls; however, nothing suggests that these dresses were by Ideal. Unlike *Little Miss Revlon,* the 15in (38.1cm), 18in (45.7cm) and 20in (50.8cm) *Revlons* came fully clothed. Besides the mislabeled "Kissing Pink," the two choices shown were "Queen of Diamonds" ("luxuriously dressed for the evening in dress with lame bodice, lined velvet coat and lame scarf" the coat being a brilliant red) and "5th Avenue" ("casual lounging ensemble of cotton blouse, slacks and high heel shoes" plus long champagne colored cotton fleece jacket - - the slacks in navy and the sleeveless shell top a light blue).

By 1959, the craze was slacking off. Traditionalists could cling to Madame Alexander's *Cissy,* who would be around in more or less same form for a few years to come; but the masses hankered for something new. It

showed, in the Sears Christmas catalog of 1959. *Little Miss Revlon,* always the most popular of the set, still hung on to her half page spread, but the larger *Revlon,* again in three sizes minus the 23in (58.4cm), only warranted one shot, that in her lacy one-piece black underwear. In short,

the big dolls no longer had extra outfits, though *Little Miss Revlon* did: six of them, including a black lace full-length formal and stole, and a white bridal gown. The day of the bigger *Revlon* was over.

Never shown in any of the ads examined is the *Revlon* mystery doll, the one collectors call *Mrs. Revlon* (because some examples have graying hair). Marked simply "14R" rather than with the usual *Revlon* mark, "VT," the mystery miss is not so attractive as the regular *Revlon.* Since examples have turned up wearing official *Revlon* dresses, it may indeed have been by Ideal, perhaps using parts bought from another company rather than their own, a procedure not common to that firm, however. I hesitate to call this doll a true *Revlon.*

Summing up, though the *Revlon* doll in all her forms was an attractive and well-made doll, her clothes were what counted most. And she had many. A folder that came with *Little Miss Revlon* one year showed 46, grouped under headings like "Night Time Series" (six outfits, including a television lounging ensemble with harlequin glasses); "School Series" (eight, many with handbags); "Playtime Series" (six, one of which was a beach costume with cute coolie hat and sunglasses while another featured pedal pushers); "Junior Miss Series" (four, all frilly daytime dresses);

Illustration 3. 18in (45.7cm) *Revlons.* Left to right: "Cherries a La Mode" (red flocked cherries on navy organza), "Kissing Pink," unnamed blue velvet dress with white fur stole.

"Novelty Series" (ballerina, sailor girl, nurse, calypso, artist); "Visiting Outfits" (seven, all with hats and some with coats); "Formal Series" (four, all floor-length); "Bridal Series" (one regular bride, one deluxe or debutante bride and one bridesmaid, the last with large straw picture hat); and "Coats" (three, including a spotted, hooded raincoat and a herringbone tweed item).

The *Revlon* doll has one claim to fame not found with most of her rivals - - her connection with a real (and very adult) product, Revlon cosmetics. That, plus her manufacture

by a major toy company, Ideal, assured her instant notice. However, it was the fact that she was a good quality doll, well attuned with the trends of her age, that made her accepted. And accepted still by today's collectors.

Illustration 4. 20in (50.8cm) *Revlons.* Left: pink floral organza party dress, natural straw hat. Right: light turquoise satin dress. Both outfits have large cloth tags at waist that read "Revlon Doll by Ideal."

Illustration 5. A quartet of *Revlons,* from 10½in (26.7cm) to 20in (50.8cm), minus only the largest 23in (58.4cm) version. 15in (38.1cm) doll wears floral cotton gown in orange and gold tones and has a paper tag on her waist.

Anili Dolls--
How They Came to America

by Shirley Buchholz

Photographs, including copies of old photographs, by John Axe

Illustration 1. Three little girls dressed in costumes. The one in the center is Anili Scavini as a child. *Courtesy of Carla Caso.*

An article in the June/July 1979 issue of **DOLL READER** by Bill and Carol Boyd piqued the imaginations of American doll collectors.[1] The Boyds tantalized us with descriptions of lovely dolls being made in Italy. These dolls bore tags that read *ANILI.* They first discovered Anili (pronounced Ahneeli) dolls in Rome in 1976 and learned that they were being produced by the daughter of Elena Scavini, the woman the doll world has always known as Madame Lenci. Two years later, in 1978, they visited Anili Scavini in Turin and were told some of the history of the dolls.

It came as a surprise to most American collectors reading the Boyd article that at some time following her departure from the Lenci factory Madame Lenci had sculpted a variety of faces in the manner of those that she had done when she and her husband, Enrico, had founded the

1 This informative article also may be found in the new publication by Hobby House Press, Inc., *The Best of the Doll Reader.*

famous doll factory. These are the masks that Anili now uses to make her dolls.

This was exiting information. Dorothy S. Coleman's recent book, *Lenci Dolls, Fabulous Figures of Felt,* had revived interest in those enchanting creations that captured the fancy of the world in the 1920s and early 1930s. Indeed, the information that Madame Lenci was alive until 1976 was news to the American doll collectors, for much speculation and nothing definitive had been written in the doll books that were available to us because the authors had no real knowledge of her during and after World War II. (Later information from Lenci's granddaughter gives the date of Elena Scavini's death as February 1974.)

We read the article avidly, but were frustrated because there were no pictures of the dolls. What were they like?

One of those strange quirks of fate answered our questions. A casual conversation with a noncollector revealed that she had a friend here in Pittsburgh, Pennsylvania, who came from Italy and that her friend's mother and grandmother

both made dolls. "Have you ever heard of a doll maker called 'Lenci'?" she asked.

The question was directed to Joyce Kintner, a fellow doll collector. Joyce could hardly wait to call me with her news. The granddaughter of the famous Madame Lenci lived right here in our home town!

We hastened to make an appointment and met and became friends with Carla Caso. We learned that her mother, Anili Scavini, is indeed the daughter of Elena Scavini and that she, Carla, had been reared in her grandmother's home. She was very familiar with the Anili dolls. They had been a part of her life since childhood. Carla had watched her grandmother work on designs in the small studio that Madame Lenci had in their home and her grandmother had taught her how to cut the felt flowers "with a large cookie-cutter thing." Then, too, she had often worked in their shop where the dolls and other boutique items produced in the small factory were sold.

We were bursting with curiosity. Did she have any of the dolls to show us? She brought out a well-loved *Red Ridinghood* doll that belongs to her own daughter and a clown, *Wolfango,* made for Carla when she left Italy for America. Inside his coat a loving grandmother had embroidered "Nonna Lenci" (Grandmother Lenci).

Mrs. Caso seemed pleased with our enthusiasm for the dolls, but also a bit puzzled. She had never been around doll collectors before and, as you well know, they are a bit different from the ordinary population!

As we bombarded her with questions, she brought out other lovely things that came from Anili's shop for us to see and then showed us several works of art that had been created by her grandparents and a painting by Gigi Chessa (born, Turin 1898; died 1935) and a sculpture by Giovanni Riva (born, Turin 1898; ?). These two were among the famous artists of Italy in the years just before and between the two great wars.

Although we admired the painting, the most interesting piece to us was the bronze plaque that shows the head of Carla's grandmother in bas relief. It is almost Art Nouveau in style with flowing hair and her name "Lenci" along with a little bee, the symbol of industry. It is dated 1915, the year after her marriage, and is signed *RIVA*.

This first meeting led to further interviews for I was interested in writing about her grandmother. As we became more at ease with each other, Poma, as Carla is known to her family and friends, told me that she had in her possession three books that had been written by Madame Lenci detailing much of her life and other family history.

In response to questions that I felt would be of interest to the doll collecting community, she graciously translated portions of these books into English and provided me with family photographs to be used in a series of articles that were eventually published in *Doll News*, the official publication of The United Federation of Doll Clubs, Inc. [2]

Some facts that particularly interested me were that Elena Scavini's parents were of German and Austrian birth and that she had lived and worked in Germany for many years prior to her marriage; that her pet name, "Lenci" was the diminutive of the German form of her name, "Helenchen". Another surprise was that she had worked on and off as a photographer for about ten of the years she had spent in Germany. One of the lovely art photographs in Poma's possession is of a gracefully posed nude woman. It is signed "Lenci" and dated 1914.

The series of articles were one result of our meeting. Another was to get photographs of some of the Anili dolls so we could see the variety for ourselves. We were delighted with them and asked Poma if she thought her mother would send us some dolls for our collections. When the answer was in the affirmative, we selected dolls and made arrangements for them to be shipped from Italy.

2"Lenci--Her Story," *Doll News*, Summer, Fall and Winter 1980 issues.

Illustration 2. The woman who started it all, Madame Lenci, with the woman who made this article possible, Carla Caso. This photograph was taken on one of their last visits together in Italy in July 1972. Madame Lenci was 86 years old. With them are the Caso children, Enrico and Elena. Elena is wearing a dress designed by Anili. *Courtesy of Carla Caso.*

After their arrival, naturally our new acquisitions went to doll club with us for "show and tell." Just as predictably, some of the other members also wanted Anili dolls for their collections. Word travels fast in the doll world. Other requests arrived and suddenly Joyce and I found ourselves in business. It was the only suitable way we could handle it.

Anili dolls are made in a small factory in Turin. It is here that Anili also produces the charming boutique items such as purses, tote bags, pillows, baby and children's clothing, toys and the like. Here she also designs and makes the expensive costumes for Carnival (we call it

Illustration 3. 36in (91.4cm) *Wolfango*, the clown that Madame Lenci sent to America with her granddaughter. Anili still makes a wide selection of clowns of all sizes. *Carla Caso Collection.*

Mardi Gras) that both she and her mother are noted for. The considerable talent that Anili Scavini inherited from her parents is quite recognizable.

All of the dolls are individually made to order after selections are made from photographs. It is incredible that she is able to achieve such a variety of different dolls just using the five masks designed by her mother. The individuality comes from the hand-painted features. Basic coloring is done by one of the four or five women who work on the dolls, but Anili, herself, does the finishing painting of the faces. The slant of the eye, the turn of the lip, the arch of the brow -- these are all the little artistic touches that give each doll its personality.

various models are made in slightly different manners which may be seen in the illustrations.

Their wigs are usually of synthetic material styled in a variety of ways and occasionally there will be one with mohair braids. It depends upon what she has on hand at the time. A few of the earlier dolls had wigs designed from felt (*Fioraia* and *Monello*, for example) but this does not appeal to most American collectors.

Anili dolls and their costumes are meticulously made of the finest fabrics. Since the operation is a cottage industry type, there is careful supervision by Anili herself of all that is made under her name.

At our request, the dolls she ships to us in America are all signed

Fioraia are this type. These dolls have stiff legs, but do not sit. *Liz* is a slim 17in (43.2cm) doll with a mature face. The *Midinette* is the 23in (58.4cm) version of *Liz*. They both use the same mask and have the softer arms and legs. Smallest of the dolls is the 12in (30.5cm) *Miniatura*. These dolls are made in the same manner as *Liz* but have a more childish face, the fifth mask. The heads all turn even though the body construction is different.

Illustration 5. The face of the 17in (43.2cm) *Caricatura*. It is more of a toddler type.

Because of their method of manufacture, there will never be a great number of Anili dolls made. They are not as limited as those that are entirely made by a single artist, but rather are like those made by the British doll artist, Ann Parker, who also has a cottage industry but finishes the faces of the dolls herself. They do not roll off an assembly line, but of course, they are not priced like the dolls that do, either.

I had a call the other day from a person in our area. She said that she had seen a photograph of one of my Heubach dolls and that one of her neighbors who recently moved away told her that his mother's family made dolls in Germany. Their name was Heubach. I had better follow that lead, too. One never knows.

Illustration 4. The two faces found on the 23in (58.4cm) *Grugnetto* style Anili doll.

Over the many years that the dolls have been in production there have been about 80 or 90 different outfits designed for them. They run the gamut from frothy bed doll types to children and characters from storybooks. There are dolls in nationality costume, clowns, pretty ladies and all kinds of youngsters, but to date, no infants. Some of the outfits were designed by the mother, some by the daughter. At this writing there is no way of determining who designed the earlier costumes other than those of the dolls called *Monello* and *Fioraia* which were designed by Madame Lenci. All of the later ones have been designed by Anili, who still holds to the family tradition of quality and beauty.

The dolls are constructed with pressed felt faces, felt arms and legs and firmly stuffed cloth bodies. The

and dated on the foot. There were perhaps a dozen or so that were shipped to the United States before her arrangement with us that are not signed. Of course, any that are purchased in shops in Europe are not signed, either, according to our information. The dolls are dated in the European manner of day/month/year instead of our American system of month/day/year.

There are six different types of dolls that use the five masks. *Grugnetto* is 23in (58.4cm) with firmly stuffed, disc-jointed legs and can sit and stand alone. Two different masks are used for this doll. One is smiling and one is pouty. The same masks are used for the *Cenerentola* which is a 27in (68.6cm) version with soft arms and legs. *Caricatura* is 17in (43.2cm) and uses one mask that is a pudgy child. *Monello* and

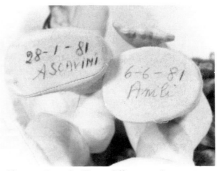

Illustration 6. Two different signatures found on Anili dolls. They are generally signed on a foot.

Illustration 8. The 1⅜in (3.4cm) label presently used by Anili is a gold cardboard circle with colorful flowers and her signature over a red heart. An earlier tag was smaller and simply a gold circle with the signature over a red heart. The tags are usually found sewn to the back of the dolls' clothes.

Illustration 7. Left: The more adult face of the 17in (43.2cm) *Liz* model. Right: The childish face of the 12in (30.5cm) *Miniatura*.

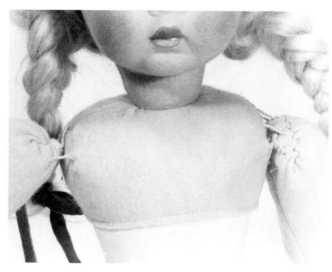

Illustration 10. Close-up of the method of attaching the arms of the Anili dolls.

Illustration 9. Front view of the 23in (58.4cm) *Grugnetto* without her clothing. This is the model with the disc-jointed legs.

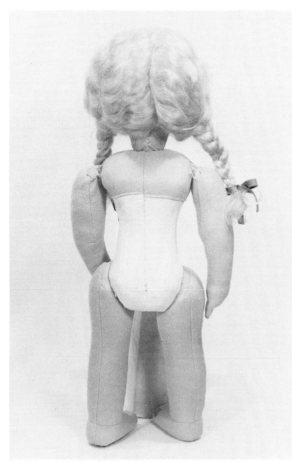

Illustration 11. Back view of the *Grugnetto* shows its construction.

Illustration 12. Front view of the undressed *Miniatura* (left) which has swinging, soft legs and the *Caricatura* (right) which has stiff legs.

Illustration 13. Back view of the *Miniatura* and *Caricatura*. All the long and soft legged dolls are made in the same manner as the *Miniatura* (*Liz, Midinette* and *Cenerentola*).

Illustration 16. The bronze sculpture of the head of Lenci by Riva. *Carla Caso Collection.*

Illustration 14. Boxes for Anili dolls are white with toys and dolls outlined in black and colored a dusty rose shade. The dolls are tied with a ribbon that has Anili's name and address woven into it.

Illustration 15. A sampling of the great variety of costumes that may be found on the Anili dolls. Felt and organdy are the two materials that are used most. A few dolls are dressed in taffeta or cotton. The toddler in the left rear is *Fioraia,* one of the dolls whose costume is known to have been designed by Madame Lenci. Next to her is *Manon* dressed mainly in colorful felt. The other large doll, *Lencina*, is clad primarily in organdy with felt trim, as is *Blanche,* the *Miniatura* in front. *Liz Harlequin* wears felt and cotton.

TOY FAIR

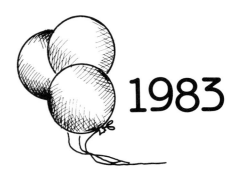

1983

TOP: *Dolls from the Opera* by Madame Alexander are "Mimi" (left) and "Carmen" (right). *Photograph courtesy Alexander Company Catalog.*

ABOVE: Madame Alexander's *Dolls from Storyland* include *Little Women* characters "Laurie," "Jo," "Amy," "Meg," "Marme" and "Beth." *Photograph courtesy Alexander Doll Company.*

LEFT: Eugenia Dukas has designed doll fashions for the Effanbee Doll Corporation for over 35 years. *Photograph courtesy Effanbee Doll Corporation.*

Snow, collector dolls, Teddy Bears and other soft animals were topics of intense discussion during the 1983 American Toy Fair in New York City, February 7-15. An international array of commercial firms representing such countries as Germany, France, England, the United States, Japan, and other far east countries presented thousands of doll designs to an army of buyers who will be showing these dolls later this year. The beautiful weather early in the week made the struggle through the massive snow storm bearable. The professional toy buyers had a difficult time picking products from the astounding array of dolls commercially manufactured for doll collectors. Be patient in your wait for the dealer to get inventory. If these outlets provide means for registering your interests, why not take advantage of this opportunity. You, the collector, will have to do research as to what designs appeal to you and then stretch your pocketbook for acquisition for your collection. We hereby present this detailed report to make your doll collecting more enjoyable!

Alexander Doll Co.

At the Alexander Doll Company there were some new dolls that should be of interest to collectors. This year they have added a new category — the *Opera Series.* In this group there are two dolls, "Carmen," the leading character in Bizet's opera *Carmen,* and "Mimi," from Puccini's opera *La Boheme.*

In the girl doll category they introduced the "Fairy Godmother." There have been many costume changes on existing dolls as well. The "Little Huggums" baby dolls now only come with molded hair, and wear pink or blue sleepers. The Alexander Doll Company has discontinued their "Sweet Tears" and replaced her with "Sweet Baby." The face of the doll is the same, but she no longer is a drink-and-wet baby doll. In the "Pussy Cat" category all of the dolls have costume changes. Their 14in (35.6cm) doll is dressed in pink dotted swiss; the 20in (50.8cm) doll is dressed in solid blue; and the 24in (61.0cm) doll is dressed in pink candy stripe with a white apron. The "Puddin" dolls are now attired in checks to match their size. The 12in (30.5cm) *Little Women* dolls have all new costumes.

"Beth" is wearing pink with a pink checked pinafore; "Marme" is now wearing brown with white apron and mob cap; "Meg" is attired in purple with purple printed pinafore; "Amy" is dressed in blue with blue printed pinafore; "Jo" is attired in red with blue checked pinafore; and "Laurie" is now dressed in pastel blue instead of silver metalic. "Lucinda's" costume is now pale pink with blue accents. The best news may be the first-time introduction of a *color* company catalog, 1983 Alexander Dolls. This catalog is available now as long as the limited supply lasts ($5.00).

Effanbee Dolls

The Effanbee Doll Corporation continues what has propelled them into being a leading collector-oriented doll company. The original costume designs, augmented by the originality in doll face molds, point towards another successful introduction of dolls for collectors in 1983.

The Great Moments In Literature Series will feature the Mark Twain Collection in 1983 and 1984. "Mark Twain" 16in (40.6cm) is dramatic in the southern white suit and molded features such as bushy white hair, mustache and heavy eyebrows. The character he helped to create, "Huck Finn," 13in (34.3cm), stands in an unusual molded stance with one leg angled. He has an unruly mop of red molded hair, a freckled face with a mischevious grin and a front tooth missing.

Effanbee's *Legend Series* features a 17in (43.2cm) "Groucho Marx." Groucho is reproduced with all of his famous trademarks: a wide mustache (executed in grease paint), a black swallow-tail coat, spectacles, and a cigar.

The Presidents, a new series of character dolls inaugurated by Effanbee, will be added to annually. Each doll will be made for only two years. The 1983 dolls are 16in (40.6cm) "George Washington" and 18in (45.7cm) "Abraham Lincoln." "George Washington" has molded snow-white hair in a 18th century pony tail style. His clothes are made from a felt-like fabric, complete with cape and three-cornered hat. "Abraham Lincoln" wears a black suit, white shirt, black tie and a stove-pipe hat.

Craftsmen's Corner includes several new designs. Joyce Stafford of NIADA has designed "Little Tiger" to accompany "Lotus Blossom" (last year called "Orange Blossom"). "Little Tiger" is dressed in a blue mandarin top, blue loose pants, wears black sandals, and is holding a red kite. Jan Hagara, known for her doll art and plates, has created a child doll, "Cristina," exclusively for Effanbee. "Cristina," 15in (38.1cm), is dressed in a beige lawn dress and a hat trimmed with lace; she wears black shoes. Faith Wick introduces an 18in (45.7cm) "Scarecrow," a reproduction of her porcelain edition. Astri Campbell adds an *Astri's Lisa Grows Up* Collection. This 11in (27.9cm) doll is available in PJ's with robe, a sailor suit outfit, a crocheted sweater and dress outfit, and a pink dress. One can purchase the doll and her outfits in a trunk ensemble. Other collections to note are the *Grandes Dames Collection, Bobbsey Twins Collection* (outfits of the 20's, 30's and 40's), the *Madame Butterfly Collection* (an 11in [27.9cm], 15in [38.1cm], and 18in [45.7cm] oriental-dressed costumes) plus many more.

World Dolls

One of the outstanding and popular celebrity dolls issued in 1983 will prove to be "Marilyn Monroe" by World Doll Co., Inc. There are to be three different versions: an 18in (45.7cm) vinyl with red dress and red boa (see color picture for drawing that doll was modeled after); a 16in (40.6cm) porcelain doll with glass eyes, white sequin full-length dress; and a third version limited to 300 porcelain dolls with the same full-length white sequin outfit enhanced by a full length white mink coat and removable diamond earrings. This special edition porcelain doll is expected to retail in the $6,000 range and will come with a special presentation case.

World Dolls Co., Inc. also features for 1983 the *Louis Nichole Collection,* a collection of vinyl and porcelain dolls that marries a romantic combination of special French crochet ivory lace fabrics plus memorable doll faces. Newly featured are a unique finished head and shoulder plate (doll's body is *not* to be added), a vinyl reproduction of a Bru doll, or a "Marionette" (the logo of the *Louis Nichole Collection),* an "Angel doll," and other bridal, bridesmaid and flower girl dolls. The *Louis Nichole Collection* originated from his White House designs produced for Christmas decorations with the romantic flavor of the old world "while still being of his own time."

Porcelain "Marilyn Monroe" doll produced by World Doll, Inc. This model sells for $400 retail. *Photograph courtesy World Doll Co., Inc.*

Ideal's porcelain "Shirley Temple"™ is a collectors' edition that will retail for approximately $400. *Photograph courtesy Ideal Toy Company.*

ABOVE LEFT: One of several versions of the "Marilyn Monroe" dolls made by World Dolls, Inc. This model is shown with one of original costume sketches.

ABOVE: "Groucho Marx" by Effanbee is an almost life-like portrait of this famous comedian.

LEFT: *Presidents Washington* and *Lincoln*, from Effanbee's Presidential Series.

FOLLOWING PAGE: *Huck Finn* and *Mark Twain* are among the 1983 dolls introduced by Effanbee at the American Toy Fair.

See captions on page 194.

Ideal

At the Ideal Company they have introduced several porcelain dolls in limited editions. Their largest limited edition doll is "Shirley Temple" ™ "Raggedy Ann" ™ and "Raggedy Andy" ™ are characterized from the original artwork conceived by Johnny Gruelle. The dolls have porcelain heads, hands and feet, and stuffed cloth bodies. They also have three limited edition porcelain babies. Two are 14in (35.6cm) "Tiny Tears" dressed in antique crocheted outfits with molded hair, and a 14in (35.6cm) "Tiny Tears" with rooted hair and dressed in a crocheted antique romper outfit. The third baby is an 18in (45.7cm) porcelain "Thumbelina" attired in an antique beige crocheted Christening outfit. In vinyl, they are introducing "Shirley Temple" ™ in a 12in (30.5cm) and 8in (20.3cm) version. These dolls are dressed in costumes worn by Shirley Temple in the following movies: *Little Miss Marker, Wee Willie Winkie, Poor Little Rich Girl, Rebecca of Sunnybrook Farm, Susannah of the Mounties* and *Dimples.*

A new line, Victorian Ladies ™, will also be available in two sizes, 8in (20.3cm) and 12in (30.5cm). They have six different Victorian outfits. Nursery Tales are 8in (20.3cm) Fairy Tale character dolls. These are only available in this smaller version. The six Fairy Tales covered are *Mother Goose, Little Red Riding Hood, Little Bo-Peep, Cinderella, Snow White* and *Alice in Wonderland.*

There will be several collector edition baby dolls. A 14in (35.6cm) molded hair "Tiny Tears" attired in an eyelet Christening outfit and two "Thumbelinas" in Christening outfits. The 16in (40.6cm) "Thumbelina" will have rooted hair, and the 18in (45.7cm) "Thumbelina" will have molded hair.

International Playthings

International Playthings, the American distributor for Sasha dolls, proudly displayed "Kiltie," their limited edition doll for 1983. Only 4,000 of these human hair dolls will be made. "Kiltie" has painted gray eyes and wears a Black Watch tartan cotton dress with an amethyst necklace.

There are three new dolls in the 1983 Sasha family — a brunette with a blue ballerina dress and ballet slippers, "Baby Rosie" dressed for bed, and a blonde baby in a sleeping bag.

Also available from International Playthings are "Halfpenny" (pronounced haypenny) pocket dolls made with particular attention to details. They are available as stickpin dolls, individual and families, gift ties and book markers. "Halfpenny" dolls are available in three different faces with two outfits. This line includes a "Bella," "Amy" and "Charlie" doll 15in (38.1cm) tall. They have vinyl heads and cloth bodies and are dressed as English children. "Bella" has long dark braids; "Amy" is a blonde; and "Charlie" is a brunette boy.

Jesco Imports, Inc.

Jesco Imports, Inc., besides being the distributor for Corolle Dolls from France, are also the manufacturers of the Kewpie dolls. They acquired the original molds and production rights from the former owner, Joseph Kallus, in 1982. This year at Toy Fair they have introduced three lines of Kewpies. A 26¼in (66.7cm) vinyl Kewpie was introduced as a Memorial Edition to Joseph L. Kallus. She is attired in a red dress with white apron, white socks and black patent leather shoes. She will be packaged in a plain box decorated with some of Rose O'Neill's original artwork. All the dolls from the original Cameo molds will be marked "Cameo" and "Jesco" on their backs. Also available are three 16in (40.6cm) Kewpies dressed in red striped

dress with pinafore, pink organdy, and blue gingham. The 12in (30.5cm) Kewpies are dressed for a picnic, shopping, the beach, fishing, school and a birthday party. In this group the boy is differentiated from the girls by having his painted eyes looking to the right; the girl's eyes are painted looking to the left.

Fifteen new styles were also introduced in the Cameo/Jesco line. These dolls are 10in (25.4cm) tall storybook dolls. All the dolls have the same face, but different costumes and hair coloring. They represent characters of storybook fame.

Reeves International, Ltd. Suzanne Gibson Dolls

Suzanne Gibson dolls, distributed by Reeves International, Ltd., featured a Grandma and Red Riding Hood set as one of their 1983 limited productions. "Red Riding Hood," 16in (40.6cm), is dressed in the traditional red cape lined with the same printed fabric of her dress and carrying her basket of goodies. A uniquely designed "Grandma," 21in (53.3cm), wears a pink checked gown and night cap. She has long gray braided hair. Her removable cap converts into a wolf's head (designed by Suzanne Gibson and made by Steiff, the soft animal people) cleverly hidden under the cap, which can be slipped over the doll's head to transform Grandma into the wolf. Grandma stands 21in (53.3cm) tall.

Suzanne Gibson's "Mother Goose" has been redesigned this year with the goose being made much smaller than before.

Gibson's *Nursery Rhyme* series includes "Lucy Locket" in a floral dress, pantaloons, hat and purse; and "Jack and Jill" in matching blue and pink outfits, each carrying a bucket.

The Suzanne Gibson *Colonial Ladies* series each 21in (53.3cm) includes "Miss Abigail" with gray hair and wearing a gown of the 1777 to 1797 period, as worn by women of many classes. "Miss Penelope," a brunette with curls, wears a colonial gown of green printed fabric with box pleats and billowy sleeves, topped off with

a straw hat; "Miss Felicity," with blonde curls, wears a Watteau-style jacket over her colonial costume and an organdy hat.

"Mother Calico" is a special 1983 Signature Edition, each doll being signed by Suzanne Gibson. This 21in (53.3cm) blonde doll has a blue dress with white polka dots, a printed apron, white stockings and black shoes.

Another 1983 Signature Edition is "Danny" and "Danielle," blonde children dressed in blue velvet outfits trimmed in white lace and red ribbons.

"Clarissa" and "Eileen" are new little girls. "Clarissa" is a brunette with a yellow reversible rain outfit, while blonde "Eileen" wears a similar rain outfit in blue.

Other new dolls by Suzanne Gibson are baby dolls and drink-and-wet dolls.

Heidi Ott Dolls

Reeves International, Inc., are offering for 1983 the following Heidi Ott dolls: "Ruthie," a 19in (48.3cm) doll with blonde braided hair, dressed in a brown costume with a striped pinafore. "Rudi," a 19in (48.3cm) boy doll with reddish hair, dressed in a brown tweed jacket, black boots and hat. "Maya," a 19in (48.3cm) doll with brunette braids and dressed in a brown and yellow printed dress. "Mareia," a 13½in (34.3cm) doll with long brunette curls and bangs, wearing printed fabric dress and apron. "Dorina," a 13½in (34.3cm) doll with blonde braids and bangs, dressed in a blue striped costume, blue printed apron, and holding a basket of flowers. "Ursli," a 13½in (34.3cm) boy doll with brunette hair wearing a plaid shirt, brown pants, vest and cap. "Andrea," is a 13½in (34.3cm) brunette with curls wearing a pink printed fabric dress. "Viola," a 15½in (39.4cm) brunette doll wearing a red lace-trimmed dress. "Karin," another 15½in (39.4cm) brunette doll with braids and bangs, wearing a plaid dress and white sweater. "Bruno," a 15½in (39.4cm) boy doll with brunette hair, wearing a striped sweater and brown pants. "Denise," 15½in (39.4cm), has reddish hair and wears a blue dress and bonnet. "Marc," a 13½in

Page 193 - Clockwise from bottom left: Suzanne Gibson's limited edition of "Grandma and Little Red Riding Hood" was a showstopper at Reeves International's showroom. *Photograph courtesy Reeves International Ltd.* Jack Wilson of House of Nisbet shows off his firm's "My Princess" vinyl doll. Other new vinyl dolls from Nisbet are shown on the shelves behind Mr. Wilson. *Photograph by John Axe.* Sarah Doggart holds "Baby Rosie," a favorite from her *Sasha Doll Collection.* Beau James of International Playthings, Inc. (right) is the U.S. distributor. *Photograph by John Axe.* Nancy Villasenor and James Skahill of Jesco have revived the Cameo/Kewpie line of dolls. Featured between them is their Memorial Edition Kewpie, a tribute to the late Joseph Kallus, former owner of the Kewpie copyrights. *Photograph John Axe.*
Page 194 - Clockwise from top: Lenci's new "Golfer" carries his own golf club. *Photograph John Axe.* "The Edwardian Social Season" represented by four dolls made by Royal Doulton and dressed by House of Nisbet. "Benjamin," a new Max Zapf doll made in West Germany and distributed in the U.S.A. by FNR International Corp. *Photograph courtesy FNR International Corp.*

(34.3cm) boy doll, has brunette hair and wears a plaid shirt, gray pants and cap, and brown boots.

House of Nisbet

A completely new endeavor by the House of Nisbet Ltd. is their "My Little Girl" series of fashion dolls made entirely of vinyl and dressed in pretty clothes. There are three sets of these dolls, each 10in (25.4cm), 13in (33cm) and 16in (40.6cm) tall. The dolls are sculpted to show a family resemblance as they actually "grow" from child to girl to young woman.

The first group, *Parties and Romance Theme*, includes "Birthday Party" (No. 3101), "First Dance" (No. 3134) and "Debutante's Ball" (No. 3167). *Parasols and Sunshine Theme* includes "Garden Party" (No. 3102), "Afternoon Tea" (No. 2135) and "Promenade" (No. 3168) dressed in Summer prints and pastels.

Wedding Days Theme has "Bonnie Bridesmaid" (No. 3103), "Maiden-in-Waiting" (No. 3136) and "Bewitching Bride" (No. 3169).

Also new from House of Nisbet Ltd. is a 16in (40.6cm) "My Princess," a portrait doll of H.R.H. the Princess of Wales in her wedding dress. This doll is sculpted on a firm porcelain-colored vinyl body.

Royal Visit (LE 22) is the new Royal Family edition set and consists of Queen Elizabeth II (P1012) and her mother dressed to visit Charles, Diana and the infant Prince William. The Queen Mother is dressed in an embroidered pink gown; Queen Elizabeth II is dressed in blue, wears a tiara, and carries a gold purse.

Other new dolls included *Royal Wedding* models of Princess Diana (P 1005) in her wedding dress and Prince Charles (P 1004) in uniform. The Princess of Wales dressed in a green gown and holding Prince William (P 1008) and the Prince of Wales (P 1007) in a red and blue uniform, are also new this year.

The Archbishop of Canterbury (P 833) and Pope John Paul II (P 832) dolls will only be made during 1983.

Grace Kelly (P 1040) and Prince Rainier of Monaco (P 1041) are being made in a special signature set of 7,500. Dressed in their wedding attire, they commemorate their marriage on April 9, 1956. This is a special signature set made for collectors in the United States, and will be distributed exclusively by Reeves International, Ltd. of New York City.

"St. Nicholas in Europe" (B 335) is dressed in green and carries a red sack, and "Father Christmas in Britain" (B 334) wears a red suit and holds a brown sack.

"Teddy Roosevelt and Friend" (P 1042), is a special signature edition of 7,500 made to commemorate the 125th anniversary of President Roosevelt's birth. Teddy Roosevelt is wearing his army uniform and

is fitted with gold-rimmed glasses; he is holding his "Friend." House of Nisbet is distributed by Reeves International, Ltd.

Dollspart Dolls

A lovely rendition of Her Serene Highness, Princess Grace, in her wedding dress was a feature presentation of Dollspart's 1983 porcelain offerings. Dressed in white satin and lace, she stands 18in (45.7cm) tall. In their *Here Come the Brides* series are three 18in (45.7cm) dolls, each dressed in gowns typical of the country represented. The "English Bride" wears a gown of lace, tiered and surmounted by a white satin coat with a long train behind. The "German Bride" wears a simpler costume of white trimmed with pink flowers and ribbons. Japan's "Oriental Bride" is beautifully attired in a white kimono lined with rose satin. While it is not the traditional costume for a Japanese bride, it is never-the-less very effective.

Three 18in (45.7cm) dolls created by Robert Keene McKinley (see **DOLL READER**, February/March 1983) are new this year, too. Dubbed the *Tiffany Era*, they are "Mariam," dressed in a turn-of-the century black skirt and jacket with lavender blouse and feather-trimmed hat. "Rosemary" wears a lovely white dress with lace trim on the edge of the long skirt, cuffs and bodice; blue ribbons and belt have been used as accents; she also carries a lace-trimmed parasol. "Carolyn" wears an evening gown of pink accented at the shoulders with black straps and black lace. The doll's hair is set with elegant feathers and she carries a pink feather fan.

Faith Wick's "Mother and Child" is also new for 1983. Dressed in a night gown and peignoir of eyelet embroidered material, she holds a sleeping infant costumed in a Christening dress and cap of elegant design. This doll stands 18in (45.7cm) tall; the baby is 5in (12.7cm) long. Faith's "Baby Scarecrow," "Baby Clown," "Baby Plays Mommy" and "Baby Hobo," are all 18in (45.7cm) tall, and new for 1983. Reeves International, Inc., is the exclusive distributor of Dollspart porcelain dolls.

Zapf

Zapf dolls are produced in Rodental, Germany, and distributed exclusively in the United States by F.N.R. International Corporation. The nearly 80 Zapf dolls feature sleep eyes, kankalon and nylon hair, and soft bodies with the hand finished clothes. This year, they have introduced a series called *Colette*. These dolls feature human hair wigs, leather shoes and more detailed accessories. There are approximately 30 dolls available in this line. The babies have PVC heads, arms and legs. They are sweetly dressed as babies and toddlers.

The soft standing dolls have PVC heads, arms and legs and human hair wigs

and soft bodies. They are attractively dressed in traditional European costumes. New this year is a soft doll made completely of velour. She has painted eyes, real human hair and leather shoes. The dolls are dressed in peasant costumes with aprons. F.N.R. is also the exclusive distributor for the limited edition Armand Marseille dolls (no changes from 1982).

Lenci

The Lenci Doll Company, represented in the United States by Tide-Rider Inc., showed seven new classic dolls this year. There are two dolls in sport costumes. "Pluci" is the golfer with club in hand. He stands 22in (55.9cm) tall and wears black checked knickers. "Suzanne," 20in (50.8cm) tall, is dressed in a green tennis outfit and holds a tennis racquet. There are two new boy dolls. "Nanni," 22in (55.9cm) tall, is wearing a brown trench coat and hat. "Bubi," 22in (55.9cm) tall, is a blonde boy wearing blue shorts and a white shirt. The girl dolls are "Natonia," 20in (50.8cm) tall; "Claretta," 16in (40.6cm) tall; and "Piera," 16in (40.6cm) tall. "Natonia" wears a large pink bow in her hair accenting her blue dress with pink dots. "Clarette" is dressed in red and has her hair dressed in two pony tails. "Piera" is wearing a purple and white outfit with purple shoes and white hat. All of these dolls have the classic expressive face of the Lenci line.

Royal Doulton

Royal Doulton announced a new limited edition *Heirloom Doll* series, "The Edwardian Social Season." Four dolls comprise this set that represents important social occasions which occurred during Edward VII's reign. "Ascot," "Presentation at Court," "Lords" and "Henley" each stand approximately 14in (35.6cm) high and are dressed in splendid costumes, including accessories and fanciful headgear, that reflect a period in English history characterized by opulent dressing and lavish social events.

The costumes are fashioned by the House of Nisbet Ltd. The fine English bone china head and extremities are created by Royal Doulton artists. Each doll is limited to an edition of 2,500 worldwide.

"Ascot" is based on the prominent horse racing social event traditionally held in June about halfway through the social season. Elaborate hats and luxurious costumes were worn by women attending Ascot.

The social event which formally introduced women to society is captured by "Presentation at Court." This important affair provided the opportunity for young ladies to be presented to the King and thereafter be eligible to receive desirable social invitations.

ABOVE: Heidi Ott dolls were a smashing success at the Toy Fair this year.

RIGHT: Suzanne Gibson's "Little Miss Muffet" is one of several Gibson dolls distributed by Reeves International.

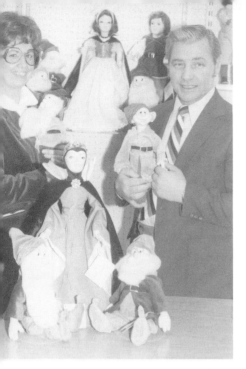

"Lords" captures the essence of the high point in the cricket season, while the rowing season social highlight is represented in "Henley." "The Edwardian Social Season" will be available by late spring of 1983

Kathy Ann Dolls

Kathy Ann Dolls, Imports distributed by Charles Zadeh, features Hans Gotz and Helmut Engel dolls from West Germany. Both of these doll lines are made of soft vinyl with either rooted or wigged hair. All outfits are designed by the owners of the firm Ana Kalinke and Kathy Berman. Featured are a 20in (50.8cm) "Klaus" and a 17in (43.2cm) "Kristal." A series of cloth dolls by Karin Serie is made with a cloth body, painted faces, human hair wigs, and leather or wooden shoes. Several hundred pieces of each of five dolls will be made in 1983. The dolls are 12in (30.5cm) "Anna," and her 16in (40.6cm) friends: "Kristen," "Knut," "Lisa," and "Lars."

Thomas Boland Company

The Thomas Boland Company, acting as manufacturers' representatives, featured two new artists, as well as Avigail Brahams. New to their line is Yolanda Bello, a Venezuelan artist who is making porcelain portrait dolls in limited editions. Her two series are child dolls taken from original photographs. A very limited edition of 100 dolls each are "Hollie," "Heather" and "Eric." "Hollie" and "Heather" are blonde girls with white fancy dresses accented with ribbon. "Eric" is dressed as a soldier in black trousers and a red tunic and wears a tall black hat. Also available are three additional child dolls in a series of 1,000 pieces each. They are elaborately dressed and have charming smiles on their faces. Their names are "Megan," "Connie" and

"Merile." This doll artist can also be commissioned to do an individual child doll.

Avigail Brahams has introduced two reproductions of her original dolls. They are both porcelain ballerinas. One is standing on her toes and is dressed in an elegant ballerina costume with silver ballet slippers. The second doll is a seated ballerina. These two dolls will be limited to 450 each.

Dolls By Jerri

This company features a new Walt Disney porcelain doll collection license, the *Snow White and the Seven Dwarfs Collection.* Each character is modeled exactly after the movie portrayal. The characters that make up this exciting set are "Snow White," the "Prince," the wicked "Queen," and the seven dwarfs ("Bashful," "Doc," "Dopey," "Grumpy," "Happy," "Sleepy," and "Sneezy"). All dolls from this collection are made of all bisque jointed bodies, except the dwarfs who have jointed soft bodies. Other new porcelain dolls added to the *Dolls by Jerri Collection* are: two black character dolls "Obadiah" and "Blossom," from the Mark Twain Collection; a beautiful bride doll; a little girl with apricot dress accented with beige lace; a stunning "Blue Boy" and "Pinkie" of the painting fame; "David at One Year," and the first English child born in America, "Virginia Dare."

Gorham

The Gorham Company has many new bisque dolls for collectors. With the American Greeting Company, they are introducing nine dolls in a *Holly Hobbie* ™ series. There will be eight girls and one boy dressed in that country-casual charm associated with *Holly Hobbie* ™. These

dolls are in various sizes. The new line also included four *Little Women* dolls — "Meg" 19in (48.3cm), "Jo" 19in (48.3cm), "Beth" 16in (40.6cm) and "Amy" 16in (41cm). All of the dolls are hallmarked and dated on their shoulder plates. Gorham also introduced a new *Bridal Doll,* "Jennifer," 19in (48cm) tall and beautifully attired in a splendid wedding gown. In conjunction with their china division, one of these dolls is being offered as a prize in a Bridal Sweepstakes. Of interest too, may be their new 8in (20.3cm) bisque *Dolls of the Month.* Each doll has a hanging loop on her back so it can be used as an ornament. All of the dolls are attired in long dresses that vary for the month they represent. Also new to their line is furniture sized for their dolls — chairs, a settee and a brass bed are their first offerings.

Bing & Grondahl

Bing & Grondahl have introduced for 1983 their first porcelain limited production. The doll, "Mary," is modeled after a popular porcelain figurine that they have been producing since the turn of the century. The mold will only be used in 1983, and then destroyed. "Mary" is made of a high lustre porcelain with cloth body and holds her own cloth baby doll. She is dressed in a white dress with a rosebud print. Her white cap has rosebud accents. She comes with her own wooden stand and is marked on her foot with the familiar Bing & Grondahl trademark.

Shader China Doll Company

Shader China Doll Company, Inc., have introduced several new reproduction dolls this year. They include a "Jester," "Julia," "Janie," "Josh" and "Constance." All are elaborately costumed.

197

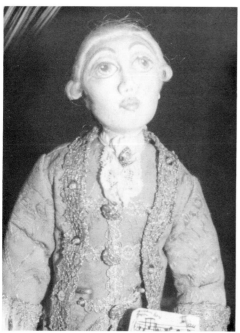

"Mozart" was one of Peter Wolf's dolls dressed in antique fabrics. The U.S. distributor for these dolls is Thomas Boland. *Photograph by John Axe.*

North American Bear Company's V.I.B.'s celebrate their arrival at the New York American Toy Fair with a candlelight dinner party. *Photograph by John Axe.*

The Gerber Baby

For 50 years people have wondered if the Gerber Baby was a boy or a girl. This question has finally been answered by Atlanta Novelty, distributors of the Gerber Baby. The *Gerber Baby Limited Edition Collectors' Dolls* for 1983 are a pair of porcelain baby girl and boy with soft bodies. They were sculpted by Neil Estern and produced by Ken and Stephanie Shader. The babies are dressed in costumes of nostalgic Old World charm. Brother's royal blue velvet suit and beret are trimmed in white lace, and sister's ruby-red costume, also trimmed with lace, is embroidered with pink rosebuds scattered on her skirt and bonnet. The "Gerber Babies" will be sold separately, or as a pair, and will be available in May of this year.

Mattel

Mattel has a line of Barbies that were made exclusively for department stores. They feature foreign Barbies. New to this line for 1983 are a "Hawaiian Barbie," a "Swedish Barbie" and a "Spanish Barbie." The "Hawaiian Barbie" comes with a two-piece swim suit, matching skirt and surfboard and sail. "Spanish Barbie" is dressed in a red ruffled dress, black mantilla, jewelry and flowers; she also carries a black fan. The "Swedish Barbie" is a blonde dressed in blue with lace bodice, white blouse and apron.

In their collector dolls series with Sekiguchi Company, Inc., they are introducing a limited edition "Sharlotte." She is a 20in (50.8cm) porcelain doll marked with a serial number on her neck. She has gray eyes with painted brown brows and lashes

and lovely dark hair. She wears a soft brown dress and matching bonnet accented with a generous amount of lace, satin and pearly buttons. The "Mariko" numbered limited edition series has four dolls dressed to represent drama, mime, music and art. Their magnificent ivory complexions have the appearance of fine porcelain. These dolls stand 14in (35.6cm) tall and have crimped colored hair that has been cut in a unique fashionable style. The dolls are cleverly dressed to represent their particular art.

"La Cheri" is issued in a limited edition of three 18in (45.7cm) sister dolls. One is a blonde doll with curled hair (#4726) dressed in a burgundy coat, matching French cap, petticoat-type dress and black stockings. The dark-haired sister (#4725) wears a pink pinafore with matching print dress and straw hat. Another blonde-haired sister (#4727) wears a white pinafore with Navy blue print dress and straw hat. Each doll wears a distinctive leather tag bearing a serial number to insure its authenticity as a limited edition. Also available are a pair of "Sala" and "Berg" dolls in a limited edition. "Sala," the girl, wears a pink pinafore over a plaid dress. She has long dark hair and wears a bell about her neck. Particular attention has been paid to her shoes and undergarments. "Berg" is dressed as an Alpine boy with brown vest,

hat, trousers and a plaid skirt. He carries a "sheepskin" bag and a horn. As in the La Cheri series, these dolls will also feature a leather identification tag.

German Toys & Crafts

GTC is the exclusive distributor of a new series of dolls by the German firm, Wernicke. Wernicke has been making dolls since 1912 in a small village in the Black Forest. The baby, "Nanneli," has a head of celluloid-like material, is dressed in a christening gown, and has a crying mechanism. Marked "Wernicke/BRIGITTE" to reflect the production of the doll for a specialty magazine from West Germany. The other dolls in this new collection are a young girl, "Martina," with a closed mouth, "Peter Boy" with an open mouth, a young girl "Beatie" with an open mouth.

GTC also announced three new sizes to their *Gustel Wied Collection.* The 64cm (25in) "Ulrike" has three models: model 8282-64 with red dress with blue flowers; model 8283-64 has a dark blue dress; model 8281-64 has a light blue German dress. The 64cm (25in) "Jutta" introduces several new models: 8272-64 with a dark brown dress with rows of flowers plus an over apron; 8271-64 has a pink dress with gray, black, and white stripes; and 8273-64 with a dark blue dress overprinted with

purple and white flowers, and a waist apron with printed flowers. Two other new sizes of the *Gustel Wied* are 55cm (22in) and 36cm (14in) that are the last year's faces shrunk down to a smaller size. For those wishing to create a family setting of dolls, one can do it with the *Gustel Wied* dolls. There is a new baby with a "Evi French lace buggy," a father, a mother, an older daughter, a boy, and a girl.

Lloyderson Dolls & Plush

Lloyderson International, Ltd., imports and distributes two of the most prestigious lines of Spanish dolls.

One line is from Famosa, the largest doll company in Spain, which featued 256 different dolls and accessories including Nancy, who has many additions to her vast wardrobe. Famosa began in Onil, Spain, as several small companies and cottage industries, which were combined into one facility in 1957.

One of the most exciting lines offered to doll collectors in 1983 is the *Marin Selection* Dolls. These dolls come from Chiclana, in southern Spain, where Jose Marin Verdugo began making dolls over 50 years ago. This company is famous for its dolls representing people dressed in regional Spanish costumes, and for dolls representing flamenco dancers.

The "Selection Dolls" from Marin consist of 12 models depicting the changes that occurred in women's dress from the 15th to the 20th centuries. Each doll is 16in (40.6cm) tall and even the hair style is unique and correct for the period the doll represents. These dolls are limited productions and are exceptionally well detailed and intricately attired. There are also six models in a limited and signed edition. Like the Selection Dolls, the Limited Edition Dolls have such accessories as tiny combs, fans and purses, but they are even more elegant and elaborate.

Other dolls shown by Lloyderson included the Mary Vazquez art dolls from Madrid, which have a vinyl base covered with felt. The limited edition porcelain dolls of Julie Good-Kruger are children representing the virtures of *Truth*, *Wisdom* and *Beauty*, and are

sculpted with life-like gestures and expressions. These models are limited to 50 examples each.

Pittsburgh Doll Company

The 1983 *Anili Doll Collection* features Italian felt dolls showing quite a diversity of styles. Small "Good Luck" figures, whimsical beings 6in (15.2cm) to 8in (20.3cm) include among the multitude, frogs, ladybugs and turtles. Other dolls include: monks, one of which is a 12in (30.5cm) "Fraticello;" *Midinettes Collection* 10 different models of 25in (63.5cm) long-legged boudoir-type dolls; several models of *Cenerentola*, a 27in (68.6cm) soft-limbed version of the Grugnetto; a new 23in (58.4cm) toddler Grugnetto "Marji" with articulated neck, hips and shoulders wearing a brightly trimmed black felt jumper with white blouse.

At press time, all dolls included here were indicated by manufacturers to be available during 1983. Sometimes unforseen factors cause delays in delivery and possibly decisions to not manufacture at all. You, the collector, have a unique responsibility. By purchasing dolls you cast your ballot and encourage manufacturers to provide what *you* are looking for. Collect the dolls that you are personally drawn to and made in the medium of your choice. Because of the multitude of decisions that you will have to make, one might be wise to have a game plan for the acquisition of the 1983 commercially manufactured dolls.

ABOVE: Mariko dolls, made in Japan, are a numbered limited edition series distributed in the U.S.A. by Mattel exclusively through department stores. *Photograph courtesy Mattel.*

ABOVE LEFT: Jose and Ana Marin Rodriguez of Marin Dolls, Chiclana, Spain, hold one of their exquisitely costumed dolls. *Photograph by John Axe.*

BELOW: 23in (58.4cm) "Marji" and a "Good Luck Frog" by Anili. *Photograph courtesy Pittsburgh Doll Company.*

TOY FAIR 1984

★★★★★★★★★★★★★★★★★★★★★★★★

by the Editorial Staff

The stars shone — not only on Broadway but at the 81st Annual American International Toy Fair in New York, New York in February — a star-studded event.

Unveiled at the Toy Fair were dolls depicting such celebrities as Elvis Presley, Madame Alexander, Judy Garland, Michael Jackson, Elizabeth Taylor, Grace Kelly, Louis Armstrong, Theodore Roosevelt, Winston Churchill, Peggy Nisbet, Bud Abbott and Lou Costello, Norman Rockwell, and members of the British royal family. And, of course, there is another *Shirley Temple*™ doll by Ideal. *Ginny* fans will be excited to learn that she is back in all her old glory with a new company and in a new medium — porcelain — as well as vinyl.

Alexander Dolls

The Alexander Doll Company, Inc., is proud to announce a 21in (53.3cm) doll of *Madame Alexander* dressed in an elegant pink evening gown. This crowning achievement by Madame is sure to be eagerly sought after by collectors. Because of the limited number that can be made it is anticipated that this doll will continue production past 1984. This doll was one of the finest in design, costuming, and theme in the 1984 American Toy Fair.

The sopranos of the *Opera Series* of 1983 are joined by *Salome* (1412) who is ready for her starring role in a cream chiffon with a purple velvet vest, velvet hat with gold lace accents and metal medallians. The *Portrait Dolls* will miss *Manet* which is rewardingly replaced by *Monet* (2245). Another masterpiece in a black checked dress with lace trim accented by a black

BELOW: The "Doll Reader™ Doll" (Model 3159). 15in (38.1cm) with vinyl head, torso, and arms on a cloth body, with miniaturized abridged copy of the April 1984 edition of DOLL READER™

ABOVE: *Supergold Elvis*, Issue Number One, in the *Elvis Presley Limited Edition Doll Series* is an 18½in (47cm) vinyl doll — limited production of 25,000 of these dolls dressed in this particular outfit.

OPPOSITE PAGE: The elegant 21in (53.3cm) "*Madame Alexander* Doll" (2290) was sculpted by the artist who sculpted the John F. Kennedy statue in Boston. *Madame* is attired in a floor-length pink evening gown, a cape with rhinestone accents and a rose corsage. She is carrying a sequined evening bag. Her gorgeous hair is held in place by a pink velvet bow highlighted with rhinestones. Her most unusual drop pierced earrings complete this remarkable doll of a remarkable lady.

1984 Alexander Catalog. All color catalog featuring the *Madame Alexander* doll plus all 1984 Alexander dolls in gorgeous color. This catalog is truly a work of art.

★★★★★★★★★★★★★★★★★★★★★★★★★

lace-trimmed red velvet jacket. Her outfit is completed by the lace-trimmed red parasol and maribou hat. The *Portraits of History* are joined by the couple, *Lord Nelson* (1336) and *Lady Hamilton* (1338). *Lord Nelson* has an admiral's hat with a light blue naval uniform jacket (with medals) and white sash. *Lady Hamilton* is stunning in her green velvet dress with spectacular lace trim. Accents are a floral corsage and lovely pearl necklace. Her red wig is a new shade. Also utilizing this new red wig is *Sargent* (1576) from the painting by John Singer Sargent. The violet floral hat goes with the full violet striped dress with ruffles and lace trim. The white parasol with a design complete this remarkable doll.

The 1983 dolls dropped are *Manet, Blue Boy, Little Lord Fauntleroy* and *Goldilocks*.

Changes limited to costumes include *Pussy Cat*, 14in (35.6cm) (3228) pretty pink print, 20in (50.8cm) (5232) print and solid pink dress and (6252) dotted blue dress with lace bodice; *Puddin*, 14in (35.6cm) (3935) pink box print and 21in (53.3cm) (6935) blue box print; and *Ballerina* style (1652) with a pink outfit and new tiara with pink satin ribbon and delicate flowers.

ABOVE: "Goldilocks and the Three Bears." This group is a joint venture using Suzanne Gibson's doll and Margarete Steiff Teddy Bears. Ms. Gibson designed the doll and bears' costumes, to appear as though they had just returned from a Sunday morning outing to discover Goldilocks in their home. This is a signed, limited edition set (No. 4003), and is sure to be a crowd pleaser.

LEFT: 14½in (36.9cm) *Judy Garland*, the 1984 *Legend Series* from Effanbee. The magic of this movie role comes to life.

ABOVE: 1984 Heidi Ott Dolls: **Front row, left to right:** 44.84 * G Grosse: ca 46cm; 31.84 Grosse: ca 35cm; 53.84 * G Grosse: ca 46cm; 45.84 * G Grosse: ca 46cm; 47.84 * G ca 46cm. **Back row, left to right:** 17.84 Grosse: ca 40cm; 30.84 Grosse: ca 35cm; 4.84 Grosse: ca 48cm; 46.84 * G: ca 46cm.

World Doll

Surely the most exciting Celebrity Doll for 1984 is World Doll's *Elvis Presley*. In the tradition of World Doll's 1983 sensation, *Marilyn Monroe*, the company has secured the rights to produce doll likenesses of Elvis Presley from Elvis Presley Enterprises, Inc. There will be several Elvis Presley dolls, each to be produced for only two years.

Issue Number One, *Supergold Elvis* in the *Elvis Presley Limited Edition Doll Series* is an 18½in (47cm) vinyl doll with molded hair and painted blue eyes. This doll is unusual in that it stands in a crouched singing position and the right hand, which holds a hand microphone, swivels at the elbow. The doll wears a white simulated leather jumpsuit that is trimmed in gold braid panels in the wheat design, a bright red scarf at the neck and white vinyl boots. Only 25,000 of these dolls will be produced.

ABOVE: *Elvis Presley*, Issue Number Two, the 21in (53.3cm) vinyl doll is a limited production of 25,000 dolls with this costume.

A collectors' edition of 4,000 pieces will be made of *Gold and Platinum Elvis*, an 18in (45.7cm) design with a porcelain head, hands and legs and a white simulated leather body. The *Exclusive Edition Elvis Presley Doll, Aloha Hawaii Elvis*, is 19½in (49.6cm) tall and is all-porcelain with the addition of a swivel waist. This doll also wears a jumpsuit, but it is studded with rhinestones and "jewels," has a real diamond in the belt buckle and has a miniature scarf made from one of Elvis Presley's own. The *Aloha Hawaii Elvis* also has a ticket from Presley's last concert and comes in a glass and mirrored oak framed case. This edition is limited to 750 pieces.

Effanbee

As in past years, EFFANBEE has introduced many new doll models of special appeal to collectors. The 1984 *Legend Series Doll* will be *Judy Garland* as Dorothy in the Wizard of Oz. The *Judy Garland* doll is 14½in (36.9cm) tall and has long dark braids and painted blue eyes. She wears an authentic and detailed costume from the 1939 musical film from MGM, including Dorothy's "ruby slippers," and carries her little dog *Toto* in a basket. Other celebrity and portrait dolls have been introduced. These are *Winston Churchill*, at 16½in (41.9cm), in the *Great Moments in History* series; *Theodore Roosevelt*, at 17in (43.2cm), in *The Presidents* series; *Louis Armstrong*, at 15½in (39.4cm), in the *Great Moments in Music* series; and *Becky Thatcher*, at 11in (27.9cm) in the *Great Moments in Literature* series from *The Mark Twain Collection*. Each of these dolls has molded and painted hair, with the exception of Becky who has a rooted wig, and all of the dolls have painted eyes and are dressed in characteristic costumes. As accessories, which are typical of each character, *Churchill* has a cigar in his hand, *Roosevelt* carries a saber and *Armstrong* has a trumpet.

The *Jan Hagara Collectible Dolls* series is expanded with a 15in (38.1cm) old-fashioned girl, *Laurel*, with curly hair. A new series of dolls created by an American artist is introduced. These are the *Edna Hibel Collectible Dolls*, *Contessa* and *Flower Girl of Brittany*, 11in (27.9cm) and 13in (33cm) respectively, both with rooted wigs and elaborate and detailed European costumes.

In addition to these new dolls many of Effanbee's continuing series of dolls have been expanded and changed. Several of the dolls in the *International Collection* and the *Storybook Collection* have new costumes; a new mold for a boy doll is introduced; and many of the models have darker skin tones, such as those who represent characters from the Latin American nations.

Thomas Boland & Co., Inc.

Thomas Boland & Company has an expanded line of originals for collectors this year. From Avigail Brahams, *Violetta of La Frawata* is an 18in (45.7cm) 500 piece limited edition. Peter Wolf has many new one-of-a-kind creations, such as *Greta Garbo* and characters from literature. Nerissa's dolls are fine 18in (45.7cm) porcelain ladies in a seated position; *Ashley*, with a cat head in the same format; and six 4½ to 5in (11.5 to 12.7cm) toddlers with porcelain heads and limbs on poseable cloth bodies. The Nerissa dolls are also hand-crafted in the artist's studio.

ABOVE: Peter Wolf's dolls, distributed by Thomas Boland, are all one of a kind. Each one is about 14in (35.6cm) tall. In front in a gold costume is film star *Greta Garbo*.

Coleco Industries, Inc.

In the May 1983 issue of DOLL READER™ (page 80) we introduced our readers to the Coleco version of the *Cabbage Patch Kids*™ — a full five months before its incredible impact on the doll market was even suspected. These remarkable dolls in still newer versions were presented again at Toy Fair 1984. Coleco, of course, is hoping that lightning will strike again, and in the same spot.

Coleco's 1984 *Cabbage Patch Kids*™ with new names and wardrobes are dis-

ABOVE: New from Coleco are the *Cabbage Patch Kids*^{TM}, *"Preemies."*

tinguished by the birthmark (signature of Xavier Roberts) on the "tush." Black in 1983, the 1984 birthmark is dark green. The 1984 packaging features a "1984" banner. New outfits include western, sporting and poseable action wear.

Designed with the *Cabbage Patch Kids*^{TM} philosophy of having individuality, Coleco is offering the *Koosa*^{TM} line. 16in (40.6cm) tall, with molded vinyl heads, rooted hair and soft cuddly bodies, they have dimpled knees and elbows, belly buttons and tails. All bearing Xavier Roberts' signature, they came wearing a collar and identification tags and each has registration papers. The owner selects a name for his *Koosa*^{TM}, sends it with the registration paper to the specified address and, in turn, will receive identification for the *Koosa*^{TM}, should it get lost. Each is packaged in a pet-carrier box complete with handle and air holes.

Coleco's *Preemies*^{TM} are infant *Cabbage Patch Kids*^{TM} ranging in age from newborn to six months. Having different skin tones, eye color and facial characteristics, each has individuality. Each has a belly button, birthmark (signature of Xavier Roberts), comes with a double name, birth certificate and adoption papers. All *Preemies*^{TM} wear a diaper and infant outfit. Additional outfits are available.

Dolls by Pauline

Dolls by Pauline features a 20in (50.8cm) *Alice* rag doll from *Alice in Wonderland*, carrying a white rabbit in the pocket of her pinafore. A 15in (38.1cm) black doll named *Tamara* joins the line, wearing a lace-trimmed yellow dress with bloomers. Filling out *Ling Ling*'s Oriental family series will be the 18in (45.7cm) mother, *Kim Ling*, and the 18in (45.7cm)

father *Kee Ling*. In addition to these new dolls, there are 20 new rag play dolls for children and collectors alike. Dolls by Pauline are distributed by Charles Zadeh.

Dolls by Jerri

Seventeen new character faces form the new 1984 quality porcelain doll line by this doll maker. The 19in (48.3cm) *David at Age 2* (841) grows one year older and reflects changes in face molding and a cowboy play outfit with pony-head stick, black leather boots with spurs, and cowboy hat. *Emily* (8416), a beguiling miss, is ready

for bed dressed in a long pink nightgown, fur bed shoes, security blanket and an all-wool Teddy Bear. The *Princess (Elissa) and the Unicorn;* completion of the *Little Women Series* with new *Laurie* (8410), *Jo* (8412). *Meg* (8413) and *Mamee* (8414); young misses all dressed up for parties *Molly* (8418), *Nichole* (843); *Charlotte* (8415) and *Camille;* the baby, *Carrie;* the whimsical clowns are *Eene* (8420), *Mynee* (8421), *Meenee* (8422), and *Mo* (8423); 13in (33cm) *All-American Kids* out for the Olympics, *Bobbie Jo* (girl) and *Billy Bob* (boy) limited to 1,000 dolls or December 31, 1984, whichever comes first; *Mickey Mouse*, a license from Disney.

Norfin Trolls

At the time of the interview, E.F.S. introduced many new models and extensive re-costuming of their 3¼in to 18in (9.6cm to 45.7cm) Norfin trolls. They came in a variety of styles including boys and girls, many of which have movable heads, arms and legs.

Also from E.F.S. are a family of four hedgehogs — mother, father, son and daughter. Ranging from 8in to 11½in (20.3cm to 29.2cm), they are made in Denmark of PVC and are costumed in shades of brown.

German Toys & Crafts

Featured for 1984 is a new girl doll, 17¾in (45.2cm) *Christine* with either blonde or brunette hair in three costume styles.

G.T.C. continued

ABOVE: *Christine*, 17¾in (45.2cm) is a new GTC, Gustel Wied girl doll with either blonde or brunette hair in three costume styles.

ABOVE: 16in (40.6cm) blonde version of the Barbara Cartland Heroine by Goldberger.

G.T.C. continued
Also new to the attractive selection of German vinyl dolls are *Tony* and *Hilga* at 21¾in (55.2cm) in corduroy costumes.

Goldberger Doll Mfg. Co., Inc.

The Goldberger Doll Mfg. Co., Inc. has addressed the collector market with two new models of the 11½in (29.2cm) *Prince Charles* and *Lady Diana* and a 20in (50.8cm) *Prince William* in a long christening gown.

The company has also introduced a 16in (40.6cm) lady doll in the Barbara Cartland Heroine Series. This doll is in two styles with either blonde or brunette hair and wearing a long taffeta gown trimmed with marabou feathers.

Gorham

Gorham features a new collection of dolls called *Petticoats and Lace* with wide-eyed French style faces and wearing soft pastel outfits. Included in this collection are 18in (45.7cm) *Lisa, Dawn* and *Courtney*, 16in (40.6cm) *Melissa, Victoria* and *Natalie*, and 14in (35.6cm) *Rebecca, Beverly, Tiffany* and *Frederick*.

Holly, the 19in (48.3cm) limited edition porcelain doll, has a Jumeau-style face, long elaborately styled light brown ringlets and brown paperweight eyes. She is hall-marked, dated and numbered and her music box plays "Winter Wonderland."

Odette is a 19in (48.3cm) prima ballerina with a Jumeau-style face looking like she just stepped out of the ballet. Her music box plays "Swan Lake."

The 8in (20.3cm) non-musical Story-book Dolls include *Heidi, Rebecca of*

Sunnybrook Farm, Cinderella, Red Riding Hood, Hansel, Gretel, Rapunzel and Alice in Wonderland.

Hans Götz Dolls

Imported from Rodental, West Germany, this line consists of about 75 dolls, approximately 80 percent of which are new for 1984. These fresh-faced children range in size from 11in (27.9cm) to 24in (61cm) and come in a wide variety of attractive and colorful costumes. Hans Götz Dolls are distributed in the United States by Kathy Ann Doll Imports and Charles Zadeh.

Hobby Enterprises, Inc.

The newly costumed Wernicke dolls limited to 300 each, signed and numbered, include child dolls, a baby with a mama voice and several other lovely models. They are vinyl, have human hair, glass eyes, leather shoes and all teeth are porcelain.

Among their exclusive Gotz dolls is the *Collector's Corner* series. The eight child and baby dolls have darker skin tones than other Götz dolls and are costumed with a more European look.

The Zanim and Zambelli collection features ten signed and numbered dolls limited to 1000. Among those new is 26in (66cm) *Ciri* in her white knit outfit with pink quilted bunting; 22in (55.9cm) *Penny* and 26in (66cm) *Patrick* have mulatto skin color and sport yellow and white knit outfits. Also of interest are 19in (48.3cm) *Kizzy* and *Oliver*, both with black features.

Hobby Enterprises, Inc., is the distributor for these dolls.

House of Global Art

Added to the House of Global Art's *Dolly Dingle* line are eight new models ranging from 12in to 16in (30.5cm to 40.6cm). Each is musical and limited to 5000. In addition to being costumed in party dresses, a pair have sailor costumes and two others are wearing nighties.

Ideal™ (CBS Toys)

Ideal™ CBS Toys has introduced several new celebrity dolls for 1984. *Shirley Temple*™, a vinyl collectible at 16in (40.6cm) with a choice of outfits from three classic films, *Heidi, Glad Rags to Riches* and *Stand Up and Cheer.* Each doll will be boxed in a "portrait" package having a photograph of Shirley Temple™ on the cover.

Abbott and *Costello*™ are vinyl, each with a six-piece poseable body. Reproduced in baseball costumes, the set will

come with a tape of the comedy team's radio routine, "Who's On First."

The Wizard of Oz set features dolls of Judy Garland, Ray Bolger, Jack Haley and Bert Lahr as *Dorothy, The Scarecrow, Tin Man* and *Lion* in a 9in (22.9cm) size. There is also a one-piece *Toto,* who stands 8in (20.3cm). These vinyl character dolls have six-piece poseable bodies and sculpted faces.

Three 12in (30.5cm) dolls and one 8in (20.3cm) doll star in the *Little Women* collection. Each doll with sleep eyes comes packed inside a "book" decorated with a still featuring all four characters from the MGM film of 1949. The dolls are *Jo* (June Allyson), *Beth* (Margaret O'Brien), *Meg* (Janet Leigh) and *Amy* (Elizabeth Taylor).

Sasha

International Playthings' most important doll for 1984 is the Limited Edition *Sasha Harlequin* whose accessories include a straw hat and a wooden guitar. She has a long blonde wig. *Sasha* and *Gregor* also have new clothing designs, one cute concept of which is the school outfits with the Sasha logo on her jumper and on his white shirt.

ABOVE: *Sasha* dolls, which are distributed by International Playthings. At the right above *Sasha* and *Gregor* with blonde hair in the *School* ensembles with the Sasha logo on the fronts.

ABOVE: Effanbee's 15½in (39.4cm) *Louis Armstrong*, No. 7661 from the *Great Moments in Music* series. Louis has painted hair and features, and he holds a trumpet and a handkerchief.

RIGHT: *Clementine*, a poured wax doll by House of Nisbet. This beautiful baby doll is modeled after Alison Nisbet Wilson's infant daughter.

BELOW: *Emily*, a porcelain doll by *Dolls by Jerri* with a security blanket and wool teddy bear.

BELOW: *Kewpie Bride and Groom.*

Karsuji, Inc.

Karsuji, Inc., introduces its new porcelain collectible doll, the *Karsuji Baby*. Wearing a specially designed dress with hand-crocheted booties, the *Karsuji Baby* is numbered, dated and signed by the doll maker, Cheryl J. Reeder. A certificate of authenticity accompanies the doll.

LJN

LJN Toys new celebrity doll for 1984 is the 11½in (29.2cm) *Michael Jackson* with sculpted hair and painted eyes wearing a dazzling rock star costume.

ABOVE: Nancy Villasenor, President of Jesco, Inc., with the 1984 *Scootles*. On the top shelf are the three 12in (30.5cm) versions of *Old Tyme Scootles;* on the bottom shelf are the 16in (40.6cm) *Scootles Carnival Kids.*

ABOVE: *Hans and Baerbel,* 18½in (47cm) are now being distributed for the first time in the United States by the newly revived Schildkröt Company. Three other sets of Schildkröt dolls include a boy and girl in authentic sailor outfits, a boy and girl in Bavarian folklore outfits, and a girl in pink overdress and boy with blue suspendered pants (both with blonde wigs).

Jesco

Jesco has added to its exciting *Kewpie* line of last year with new designs. The most charming of which is the *Bride* and *Groom* in the *Yesterday's Kewpies* series. New for 1984 are three models of *Old Tyme Scootles* and two models of *Scootles* as *Carnival Kids* — girl and boy version in matching costumes. Three designs of Cameo's *Miss Peeps,* from Joseph Kallus' original molds are also featured in the series of this whimsical baby doll from the past.

Schildkröt Dolls

The dolls from Kathy Ann Doll Imports that will generate collector interest are the celluloid 17in (43.2cm) children from

BELOW: The all-porcelain 16in (40.6cm) *Outstanding Ladies of Europe* by Marin of Spain. Each doll is costumed in gold, lame′, brocade, or other appropriate materials. From left to right, the models are *Marie Antoinnette, Queen Catherine,* and *Elizabeth I.*

BELOW: The Mary Vaz all-felt dolls for 1984. The dolls have acrylic wigs and painted features and they range in size from 11in (27.9cm) *May* to 27in (68.6cm) *Lena.*

ABOVE: The dazzling duo from Mattel Toys shimmer all the way to the Crystal Ball.

Schildkröt-Puppen of Germany. These dolls are cast from the original antique molds. The celluloid formula has an extra ingredient added to make it non-flammable. Two models have hand-knitted costumes made from the original patterns.

Lloyderson Dolls

Lloyderson Dolls has several attractive lines from various doll companies in Spain. Of special interest to collectors will be the porcelain models in a limited edition of 1,000 each from Marin. This is the outstanding *Ladies of Europe* 16in (40.6cm) designs in very detailed costumes that will sell for an attractive price. The porcelain molding is intricately detailed to the point of having separated fingers on the doll's hands. The 1984 models are *Marie Antoinette, Queen Catherine* and *Her Majesty Queen Elizabeth I.*

The Mary Vaz line of molded felt dolls has several new face models such as the open-mouth doll, *The Singer,* an unusual design.

Mattel Toys Inc.

1984 marks the 25th anniversary of the introduction of the *Barbie®* fashion doll. Since 1959 over 200 million *Barbie®* dolls and other members of her family have been sold worldwide. In addition, on the average more than 20 million *Barbie®* fashions are sold annually. *Crystal Barbie's®* ruffled ball gown and change-around stole looks like sparkling crystals. *Crystal Ken®* also celebrates this silver anniversary in a white tux and shiny vest. To work off the pounds after the celebration there is a *Great Shape Barbie®* with a full body leotard or *Barbie®* can relax in the *Barbie® Bubbling Spa.* The *Barbie®* models made for special sale include *Irish Barbie®* (7517), *Scottish Barbie®* (3263), *Eskimo Barbie®* (3898), *Swedish Barbie®* (4032), *Swiss Barbie®* (7541), *Spanish Barbie®* (4031), *India Barbie®* (3897), *Oriental Barbie®* (3262), *Hawaiian Ken®* (7495), and *Barbie®* (7470). Other Mattel Collector Dolls are 13in (33cm) porcelain *Flory Twins* (7556 girl and 7557 boy); 20in

(50.8cm) porcelain *Sharlotte II* limited to 800 dolls; two additions to the *Mariko* series, *Mariko Sailor* (7554) and *Mariko Dance* (7552) each of 2,000 piece editions; a *La Cherie* 18in (45.7cm) in warm European color; *Danielle* (7586) of 2,200 pieces; and two 14in (35.6cm) *Alpine* vinyl dolls — a boy (7590) and a girl (7589).

Old-Time Ginny Dolls

The ever popular 8in (20.3cm) *Ginny* makes another debut, this time for Meritus Industries, Inc. Looking more like the original *Ginny* by Vogue Dolls, this new all-vinyl doll comes in 12 different styles. An exciting new addition to *The World of Ginny*™ is the Chinese Porcelain Collection featuring three different styles of *Ginny* all done in Chinese porcelain.

Four limited edition *Ginnys* of fine porcelain are presented in *The Heritage Collection: Southern Belle, Party Time, Christmas Spirit* and *Holiday Deluxe.*

Once Upon A Time

New offerings from this reproduction porcelain doll maker, Kristine A. Caulie, include the following dolls: a 14in (35.6cm) Bru dressed in pink; a 27in (68.6cm) Cody Jumeau called *Vision of Spring* and wearing a white tulle dress with silk ribbon trim; and a 21in *Goose Girl* and *First Day of School* boy, both in European dress.

Signature Collection/ Dollspart

Among the 14 new collector dolls for 1984 from Dollspart are a *Velvet Collection; Here Comes the Bride* (Spanish, Dutch, American and Oriental); *Princess Diana;* and *Humpty Dumpty, Puss in Boots* and *Queen of Hearts* by Faith Wick. Of special interest to collectors may be *Buffalo Bill's Wild West Show,* in commemoration of the 100th anniversary of this happening. *Buffalo Bill* and *Sitting Bull* are all porcelain. *Belle Star* has a soft-stuffed body with poseable arms and legs. *Buffalo Bill's* costume includes a suit of suede cloth, matching hat and high boots. *Sitting Bull* in his feathered headdress wears an appropriate suede Indian costume including moccasins. *Belle Star* is very fancy in her burgundy dress with lace, ruffle and ribbon trim. A feather ornament decorates her curly coiffure. Each of these 18in (45.7cm) dolls is a numbered limited edition.

These dolls are distributed by Reeves International, Inc.

Suzanne Gibson

Suzanne Gibson Dolls from Reeves International features one of the most exciting concepts for collectors in 1984.

ABOVE: *Royal House of Dolls'* 1984 *Christmas Collection* consists of five dolls. Shown left to right are: 17in (43.2cm) *Sweetheart*, 15in (38.1cm) *Debutante*, and 13in (33cm) *Timmy*.

sister *Mary Rose*, *Oliver Cromwell*, *Mozart*, and others, including *Uniforms of Great Britain* and *Cries of London*. In addition there will be a new series of the American Ladies who became members of the British Aristocracy — *Jenny Jerome*, *Nancy Langhorne* and *Consuela Vanderbilt* — and the *Prince* and *Princess of Wales* in the Klondike costumes, a numbered edition limited to 5,000 dolls worldwide.

Robin Woods, Inc.

Joining the *At the Mardi Gras* series of clowns are three new clown dolls by Robin Woods. *Blossom*, with turquoise-green hair, wears a multi-colored clown suit and *Kubla*, with blue hair, also wears a multi-colored clown suit with sequins and braid trim. *Panjandrum*, created exclusively for Bloomingdales, is costumed in a pink suit with a multi-colored metallic vest. He has blondish hair.

Love, a limited edition doll inspired by Elizabeth B. Browning's poem, *How Do I Love Thee*, has banana curls and wears a green velvet dress and high-button shoes.

Another new offering is *City Child* in a white dotted swiss dress with lace and ribbon trim and wearing white high-button shoes. Inspired by the children of long ago, *City Child* carries a basket of flowers.

All of the Robin Woods dolls are signed and dated and are distributed by Charles Zadeh.

This is *Goldilocks* and *The Three Bears*. *Goldilocks* is 16in (40.6cm) tall. *The Three Bears* are made by Steiff and are 13½in (34.3cm) *Papa*, 12in (31.8cm) *Mama* and 9½in (24.2cm) *Baby*, all wearing outfits signed by Suzanne Gibson.

The Gibson *Nursery Rhyme* series of 16in (40.6cm) models, and the 8in (20.3cm) *International Dolls* and the baby and toddler lines also include many new designs. Prominent among these are *Hansel* and *Gretel*; a limited edition *Mexican Boy* and *Girl* (set); and *Geoffrey* and *George*, who wear wool Eton suits.

House of Nisbet

The House of Nisbet in 1984 announces the most comprehensive program of new products ever introduced in its 31-year history.

Highlights of the new Nisbet dolls include a replica of the first Nisbet doll created, a signed and numbered edition of the doll made in 1953 of *H.M. Queen Elizabeth II* to commemorate her Coronation. Nisbet is reviving the English tradition of poured wax dolls. The first two dolls in this series will be an 18in (45.7cm) portrait of *Mrs. Peggy Nisbet* and a portrait of

Alison Nisbet Wilson's infant daughter *Clementine*. The *My Princess* series in vinyl has been expanded to include a 16in (40.6cm) model of *The Princess of Wales* in the Klondike costume she wore on her tour of Canada. The *My Little Girl* series in vinyl now features the 10in (25.4cm), 13in (33cm) and 16in (40.6cm) models in two new costume themes — *Winter Wonderland* and *Ballet Rehearsals*. The Nisbet *Royal Baby* series is also announced and features two 18in (45.7cm) designs of *H.R.H. Prince William of Wales*.

A very special vinyl doll from Nisbet is sure to appeal to collectors. This is the Kate Greenaway girl which is the logo for the **DOLL READER**™. The 15in (38.1cm) *Doll Reader*™ *Doll* will hold a miniature, abridged version of the April 1984 issue, scaled to the size of the book she holds in the **DOLL READER**™ logo. Also in vinyl is a 15in (38.1cm) fashion doll, known as the *Alison Nisbet Doll*.

The *Nisbet Miniature Celebrity Dolls*, the 8in (20.3cm) hard plastic dolls for which the company is famous, will have many new designs for 1984, including a "secret" which cannot be announced yet. New individual dolls will include *Sherlock Holmes*, *Dr. Watson*, *Dr. Martin Luther King, Jr.*, *Bozo the Clown*, Henry VIII's

Royal House of Dolls

The Royal House of Dolls celebrates its 70th anniversary with a new *Royal Family* collection which for the first time includes a "king." *His Royal Majesty*, 17in (43.2cm), is costumed in a lovely royal blue velvet cape trimmed with gold braid and white maribou feathers. His red velvet tunic is elaborately trimmed with gold braid and sequins and a white satin shirt and trousers complete his outfit. 15in (38.1cm) *Her Royal Majesty* wears a lovely gold flowered brocade gown and her cape matches the king's. Both of their heads are adorned with crowns. There is an accompanying 13in (33cm) *Prince* and *Princess* appropriately dressed.

The 1984 *Royal Christmas Collection* consists of five dolls exquisitely costumed in silver metallic brocade. 13in (33cm) *Timmy* and *Missy* co-ordinate with the collection, *Missy's* gown being trimmed in red satin and lace. 17in (43.2cm) *Sweetheart's* gown is also trimmed in red satin and she wears a red satin bow in her hair. There are two *Debutantes*, a 15in (38.1cm) and a 17in (43.2cm). The smaller with a "jeweled" tiara carries a white maribou feather boa. The other *Debutante* also has a boa and a lovely feather-trimmed hat.

Rumbleseat Press Incorporated

These four dolls are the last in the series of Mary Moline's Norman Rockwell dolls. 10½in (26.7cm) *Laura* was fashioned after the original artwork appearing on the cover of the April 1918 *Red Cross Magazine*. *Santa Claus*, 12in (30.5cm) seated, was designed from the cover of the December 1976, *The Saturday Evening Post*. 12½in (31.8cm) seated, *Molly* was inspired by the Rockwell artwork from the cover of the May 1922 *The Library Digest*. She wears a blue dress, white apron and is sewing on an American flag. Last in the series is a likeness of Norman Rockwell, himself, modeled from his self-portrait on the Summer 1971 issue of *The Saturday Evening Post*. He wears a blue jacket and tan trousers.

Shader's China Doll Inc.

Two gorgeous brides are among the new offerings from Shader. The most spectacular was 16in (40.6cm) *Francoise* elegantly gowned in satin and lace with lace and pearl trim on her dress. Her bridal bouquet contains antique flowers. *Helene* at 15in (38.1cm) was also a beautifully costumed bride.

Five clowns, from 12in (30.5cm) to 16in (40.6cm) are introduced. *Jack, Timmy, Geoffrey, Lenny,* and *Kurt* all come in brightly colored clown suits with equally bright trim and ostrich maribou feathers for hair in a variety of colors.

ABOVE: 20in (50.9cm) *La Modestina* by Lenci. This all-felt beauty has big, round side-glancing eyes and a dark blonde wig. Her multicolored felt dress is trimmed with organdy, and she carries a hat box.

RIGHT: 19in (48.3cm) *Christopher Robin* by R. John Wright. The doll has a dark blonde mohair wig.

BELOW: 20in (50.8cm) *Marill* with blonde hair, blue and white print dress, white with blue print pinafore, white shoes and stockings.

R. John Wright

Noted doll artist R. John Wright introduced a fabulous felt *Christopher Robin* at 19in (48.3cm) with a dark blonde mohair wig. This doll leads his companion, an 8in (20.3cm) bear, with his left hand.

Lenci — Tide-Rider

For 1984 Tide-Rider has four new Lenci models. *Modestina*, a 20in (50.8cm) girl, has side-glancing eyes and her mouth has a surprised look. She has a multi-colored felt and organdy dress and carries a modestina hat box. *Bobby* is a 22in (55.9cm) baseball player who holds a wooden bat. His outfit is a red felt hat and shirt, mustard colored pants and red and white striped hose. *Ketty* at 18in (45.7cm) has blonde hair and wears a pink felt dress with navy blue trim. *Loretta*, like the *Modestina*, is another 1984 mold from an

antique Lenci. She is 12in (30.5cm) and has a blonde wig with wound braids over her ears and wears a pink felt costume.

Tristar

Tristar International has expanded its celebrity doll series with four new movie models added to the *Marilyn Monroe* series from Twentieth Century Fox films. The new dolls are *Elizabeth Taylor* in costumes from MGM's *Cat on a Hot Tin Roof* and *Butterfield 8* and *Grace Kelly* dressed in the MGM film costumes from *Mogambo* and *The Swan*. Each doll is 11½in (29.2cm) tall.

Zapf

Included in Zapf's extensive new line for 1984 are 23⅛in (58.7cm) *Katja* and 20in (50.8cm) *Marill*. All costumed in pert little dresses, these dolls have PVC heads, arms and legs; combable and washable nylon hair, sleep eyes and soft bodies.

Zapf dolls are distributed in the United States by FNR International Corporation. Not only were many dolls of the famous introduced, but the 1984 Toy Fair re-introduced several old familiar friends. All in all, a truly exciting array of dolls from which to choose — something for everyone!

American International 1985 Toy Fair

Something old...Something new Something borrowed Something for you

by the Editorial Staff

New York — February 11-20 - 82nd Annual Toy Fair

Traditional doll making techniques that have not been used for years by manufacturers have been revived.

Like the dolls of years ago, manufacturers are once again constructing dolls with posable heads that can be positioned at many different angles. There are also more dolls with complete stringing of the jointed components which also allows for greater posability and positioning. The vinyl used in the dolls from many of the manufacturers is also more rigid, permitting the dolls to stand better as well as making them more durable and long-lasting.

Applause has released three new porcelain *Cabbage Patch Kids*® limited to 15,000 each. These 16in (40.6cm) dolls are hand-finished, hand-assembled, and each may be registered with the original owner's name. *Della Frances'* costume is a maroon velvet dress, white blouse, lace-trimmed socks and patent shoes. She has champagne colored hair in a ponytail. Green-eyed *Timothy David* wears a gray wool jumper and cap, white shirt, red bow tie and saddle shoes. In a turquoise lace-trimmed satin dress is *Melanie Susanne*. There will be two more editions of three dolls each in 1985. © 1985 Cabbage Patch Kids® is a Registered Trademark of and Licensed from Original Appalachian Artworks, Inc., Cleveland, Georgia, U.S.A. All Rights Reserved.

Effanbee has produced a first for them, a "living legend" for their "Legend Series," *Lucy* modeled in the likeness of Lucille Ball. Costumed as she appeared opening her television series, "Here's Lucy."

Dynasty vinyl 19in (48.3cm) *Krystle*, Nolan Miller fashion drawing and *Alexis* in a red form-fitting gown. Joyce Christopher is sculptor. Distributed by World Dolls.

Left: *Samantha* is the first in a series of limited edition Christmas dolls from Lenox. She is 16in (40.6cm), dressed in silk and velvet. Distributed by Lenox.

Right: *Tammy*, a porcelain doll sculpted by Jerri McCloud. Her ornate hair and dress is complemented by a basket, and she holds "Teddy-Rabbit." Distributed by Dolls by Jerri.

Clockwise:

Top Left: Black dolls by Mary Vaz, 22in (55.9cm), Doris & Leroy have posable head and dark brown eyes. Distributed by Lloyderson Dolls.

Above Right: Mary Todd Lincoln, 12in (30.5cm) by Suzanne Gibson. Distributed by Reeves International, Inc.

Below Right: Prince Gregor. 1985 Sasha Limited Edition doll. Photograph by Sara Doggart. Distributed by International Playthings.

Below Left: House of Nisbet *Royal Children* Limited Edition set with *Princess Diana* in a day dress, *Prince William* in a sailor suit and *Prince Harry* in a cradle. Distributed by Tide-Rider, Inc.

There were thousands of newly introduced dolls for a variety of tastes. Celebrity dolls, fashion dolls, art dolls, limited edition and production dolls, novelty dolls and baby dolls. Success breeds imitation and the successes of the last few years have resulted in many look-alikes.

And also something for you: Doll Reader® announced "The Dolls of the Year Awards" (DOTY)™. This first of what will be an annual program will permit consumers to vote for *their* "Dolls of the Year." For the first time doll collectors, parents and children will vote for each of the 12 categories including play and collector dolls. The balloting will be from nominees voted on by the International Doll Academy (IDA), an organization of 70 experts from around the world who will consider dolls introduced in 1985. More information about DOTY will appear in future issues of the Doll Reader.®

The Hobby House Press, Inc., staff covered all new dolls shown at Toy Fair; however, space limitations restrict our reporting to the following dolls.

Mme. Alexander Dolls

Those who were not fortunate enough to obtain the *Madame Alexander* doll in an evening gown (#2290) will find this doll available. The "First Ladies" series has seen the introduction of the fourth set: *Lucy Hayes* 1877-1881 (#1420); *Lucretia Garfield* 1881-1881 (#1421); *Mary McElroy* 1881-1885 (#1422); *Frances Cleveland* 1885-1889 (#1423); *Caroline Harrison* 1889-1892 (#1424); and *Mary McKee* 1892-1893 (#1425). These 14in (35.6cm) dolls come replete in the high Victorian fashion with fancy hairdos. The new Portrait Doll is a 21in (53.3cm) *Morisot* (#2236) dressed in a tiered ruffled taffeta and tulle over a crinoline petticoat. *Morisot* has a very elaborate hat. Another new doll, the 14in (35.6cm) *Renoir Girl with Watering Can* (#1577) is dressed like the painting. "The Dolls from the Opera" series adds the 14in (35.6cm) *Isolde* (#1413). The new dolls in the "International Dolls" (8in [20.3cm]) are: *Philippines* (#554); *Panama* (#555); *Peru* (#556); and, *Bulgaria* (#557). The all-color *1985 Madame Alexander Catalog* will be available (early April) at $4.95 from Hobby House Press, Inc.

214

Associated Dollmakers

Associated Dollmakers, Inc. has two lines of dolls from renowned artists. All of these dolls have posable heads and inset eyes.

Yolanda Bello Creations feature an 8in (20.3cm) "Americana Series" of seven little girls dressed in authentic period costumes. The 14in (35.6cm) "Little Miss Doll Collection" is eight little girls in detailed costumes such as *Sunday School Girl* and *Junior Bridesmaid*. *Baby Laura* is four versions of a 22in (55.9cm) baby. These dolls are all-vinyl with rooted hair.

The **Avigail Brahms Creations** are lady dolls with such delicate tinting and features that the vinyl construction appears to be fine bisque. Heading this series is *Sara Bernhardt*, at 17in (43.2cm) in a long brocade gown. In the same size are two dolls who have been designed with the cooperation of the American Ballet Theater. These are *Odile, the Black Swan*, from "Swan Lake" and *Giselle* from "Giselle." Each doll is authentic in costume re-creation and pose. These dolls are limited to 1985 production.

Avigail Brahms has also designed three 21in (53.3cm) "Dancers in Action" and a 17in (43.2cm) *Bride* and *Bridesmaid*, all with elegant and elaborate costumes that feature many authentic miniature accessories, such as a little blue garter on the *Bride*'s right leg.

Berjusa

Berjusa is the Spanish doll company who has produced the battery operated life-size *Minene* dolls that are so popular with collectors. A new anatomically-correct boy and girl called *Just Born* were shown at Toy Fair and word-of-mouth publicity made them one of the most talked-about items of the show. The all-vinyl dolls look just like a newborn baby and they have a

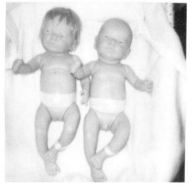

Just Born boy and girl dolls made by Berjusa of Spain.

Michael Langton's *Cowboy* doll.

....vel with a gauze pad over it, as the baby is "just born." These dolls are 14in (35.6cm) and 21in (53.3cm) long and they have inset eyes. The boy has molded hair, the girl has rooted blonde hair that is inset with only a few strands to each hole, which makes the head appear realistic. The detailing on these dolls, which include fat little wrinkles and folds, is charming and natural. (Distributed by Barval Toys, Inc.)

Thomas Boland

The most artistic, creative, original and unique dolls at Toy Fair are those from Thomas Boland & Co. of Chicago. The following are some highlights of some of the artists featured in the Boland Exhibit.

Michael Langton's fully-articulated hardwood dolls are 20in (51cm) to 22in (56cm) tall. The rugged, weathered features of his cowboys and workers attract a great deal of attention for the character and emotion his carvings capture. Each head is hand-carved and finished.

The production of the artists represented by Thomas Boland & Co. transcend perfected craftsmanship as it is also recognized as the fine art it is. Each doll is unique and is a treasure itself. As the Boland artists become even more universally recognized their work will increase more in value because of the high artistic quality that is its essence.

Manhattan Sandcastle *Merman* doll, by William Arthur Wiley, is all-porcelain, fully jointed with glass eyes, and stands 26in (66cm) tall. This is a limited edition of just 99 dolls. Mr. Wiley is represented by Thomas Boland & Company.

Cabbage Patch Kids® Twins, by Coleco. © 1985 Cabbage Patch Kids® is a Registered Trademark of and Licensed from Original Appalachian Artworks, Inc., Cleveland, Georgia, U.S.A. All Rights Reserved.

Right: Faith Wick is the sculptor of the "Alice in Wonderland" series of 16in (40.6cm) dolls by the R. Dakin Company. Included are Alice, Mad Hatter, White Rabbit.

Manhattan Sand Castle by **William Arthur Wiley.** Mr. Wiley's dolls are all-porcelain with glass eyes and they are in an edition of 99 examples. They are various characters from Fairy Tales, all sculpted with great detail and emotion. The *Candy Witch,* with her cruel, piercing eyes has a mean wart on her lip. *The Merman* is highly muscled with a strong masculine face. His "fish" portion is of composition and each scale is hand painted. *King Midas' Daughter* is 14k gold over porcelain.

Nerissa has a new series of 9in (22.9cm), 15in (38.1cm) and 21in (53.3cm) toddlers with fired clay heads that have intaglio eyes. The bodies, arms and legs are fabric. The dolls and all accessories are hand-crafted by Nerissa.

Peter Wolf has several new models of his one-of-a-kind, including a devastating *Carmen Miranda* and a pair of *Monkey Musicians* from cast resin compounds.

Avigail Brahms dolls feature the "Heroines of the Ballet," such as the all-porcelain *La Sylphide* dressed in her original costume under an exclusive license with the American Ballet Theater. The "Opera Dolls," made in conjunction with the Metropolitan Opera are characters such as *Musetta* from "La Boheme" and *Aida* from "Aida" in replicas of their original costumes.

Susan Wakeen's 15½in (39.4cm) all-porcelain "Littlest Ballet Company" dolls are six charming and whimsical boys and girls attired for dancing roles. Each doll has glass eyes and human hair wigs.

Cabbage Patch®

Coleco has introduced a number of new *Cabbage Patch Kids®* dolls and accessories for 1985. Their World Travelers include dolls in costumes from Spain, China, Holland, Scotland and Russia. Each has its own travel bag and, of course, airline tickets, a travel brochure and a souvenir T-shirt. Fashion conscious Cabbage Patch Kids® have a new wardrobe including "fur" coats with "designer" linings, sportswear and costume slippers. What playtime wardrobe would be complete without at least one of the six new T-shirts available, each having a slogan such as "Why Me?" Some have baby teeth, others eyeglasses.

In 1985 once in approximately 100 Cabbage Patch® births will be twins. A top-of-the-line offering, the twins have clothing of fancy fabrics, lace and embroidery. A special twin stroller is available for daily outings.

A new line of 5½in (14cm) *Cabbage Patch Playmates®* come with a change of clothes — other costumes being available.

Every kid wants a pony. *Cabbage Patch Kids®* did too so a *Show Pony* has been introduced, available alone or with a *Cabbage Patch Kid®* dressed in a Western outfit.

Birthmarks (signature of Xavier Roberts) on 1983 *Cabbage Patch Kids®* "bottoms" was black, 1984 was dark green and in 1985 it is dark blue.

R. Dakin & Company

For 1985 R. Dakin & Company, famous makers of plush toys, has introduced a series of dolls called the "Elégante Doll Line." These dolls were designed by Faith Wick and Helen Kish.

Three of the offerings are 16in (40.6cm) characters from "Alice in Wonderland" in vinyl. There are *Alice*, the *White Rabbit* and the *Mad Hatter*. **Faith Wick** based the designs for these dolls on the John Tenniel line drawings from the original edition of the book, adding her own feelings and colors. Faith Wick has also created other vinyl characters for Dakin: *Pip*, a 16in (40.6cm) Pierrot who has five extra masks to wear; *Merlin* from "Knights of the Round Table" at 21in (53.3cm) in a gold lamé costume; *Elvin*, a 13in (33cm) woods elf who shows Mrs. Wick's Scandinavian background; and, *Susanna* and *Lily*, two 16in (40.6cm) peddler dolls, a favorite Faith Wick theme.

From **Helen Kish** Dakin presents two all-vinyl dolls. *Annie Laurie* is a 20in (50.8cm) baby in a white eyelet dress and *Meggie* is an 8½in (21.6cm) freckle faced little girl who comes in three different costumes.

Dakin's entry in the celebrity doll field is *James Dean*, an all-vinyl doll of the actor who achieved tremendous popularity in films in the early 1950s. 1985 is the 30th Anniversary of the death of this star who is still a worldwide legend. The *James Dean* doll is expected to be released by mid-year.

Pierre Cardin

Making its debut at Toy Fair, the Pierre Cardin Collection includes three different types of faces, ten headdresses and a wardrobe "Haute Couture" of fourteen models. These rag dolls have classic, romantic and modern faces. Approximately 25in (63.5cm) tall, they are made of 100% cotton fabric. Their clothing of cotton, velvet and tulle is designed by Pierre Cardin — cocktail dresses, school dresses, weekend dresses and more. Accessories include jewelry, ribbons, flowers and shoes. A distinctive feature is the synthetic wigs, styles including short and long hair, plaits and buns.

Dolls by Jerri

The porcelain Dolls by Jerri® has several 1985 featured offerings. In the "Walt Disney Collection" there is a *Mickey Mouse*. Three elegant lady dolls are *Audrey*, in an 1885 English walking dress; *Yvonne*, who wears an Empire style gown; and, *Annabelle* in an 1853 antebellum gown. Each is limited to a production of 300 dolls. Several new child dolls have been introduced in the Jerri line. Among these are *David*, a three year old made up as a clown; *Tammy*, who wears an over-sized hat; *Samantha*, who is all dressed up in her mother's clothing and shoes; and, *Elizabeth*, the most poignantly sculpted of the group who has

a cute character face with a pursed mouth and whose dress has a Teddy Bear print in the pattern.

Dollspart Dolls

The Signature Collection™ is porcelain doll creations by Dollspart. This year Dollspart has introduced six new dolls based on the *Saturday Evening Post* covers by Norman Rockwell. Each doll is all-porcelain with an applied wig and it is jointed at the arms and legs. Each of the six models also has various accessories. The six "cover dolls" are *Croquet*, a lady dressed in a long white dress who has a croquet mallet in her hand and two croquet balls at her feet; *Bedside Manner*, a little boy with a bottle of medicine and a spoon for a sick all-bisque puppy wrapped in a blanket; *Christmas* is Santa holding a yellow plume and a Christmas list seated at a wood desk; *The Prom Dress* is a teenager dressed in jeans holding her prom gown in front of a full-length mirror; *The Shiner* is a feisty young lass in long braids who has a black eye and who is seated on a wood bench; *Triple Self Portrait* is the famous *Post* cover from 1960 which in doll form is Rockwell painting at his easel and looking in a mirror. This last set includes the easel, two wooden stools, the mirror that is topped with an eagle design and various artist's tools.

The standing dolls are about 16in (40.6cm) tall and each doll in the set retails for an affordable price, which is amazing considering all the details on the doll and the accessories that accompany it. (Distributed by Reeves International)

Below: "Triple Self Portrait" the February 1960 cover of the *Saturday Evening Post*, an all porcelain doll by Dollspart Dolls. Distributed by Reeves International Inc.

Right: *Naomi*, a 19in (48.3cm) Helmut Engel doll with a Hermann Teddy Bear in her pocket. Distributed by Kathy Ann Dolls, Imports, Inc.

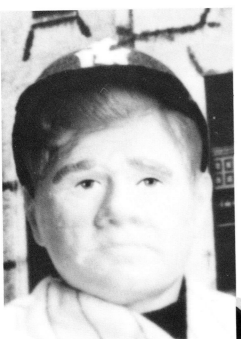

Below: *Erica*, a 17in (43.2cm) celluloid Schildkröt doll. Distributed by Kathy Ann Dolls, Imports, Inc.

Steiff and Suzanne Gibson have created a smaller size version of the 1984 Limited Edition set *Goldilocks and the Three Bears*. Distributed by Reeves International, Inc.

Babe Ruth, the "Sultan of Swat," is Effanbee's 1985 doll for their "Great Moments in Sports" series.

Effanbee

Effanbee has produced a first for them, a "living legend" for their "Legend Series," *Lucy* modeled in the likeness of Lucille Ball. Costumed as she appeared opening her television series, "Here's Lucy," she wears a formal tuxedo jacket complete with tails, tap pants, red tie and matching cummerbund. *Lucy* carries a gold topped black cane and wears a top hat on her carrot-red curly hair.

"Great Moments in Sports," a new series for 1985, features the well-known baseball player, *Babe Ruth*. Suited up in a pin-striped Yankee baseball suit, the 15½in (39.4cm) *Babe* holds a replica of his bat.

Eleanor Roosevelt, 14½in (36.9cm), is the second doll to be added to the "Great Moments in History" series. As a companion piece, *Franklin Delano Roosevelt* has been released in "The Presidents" series. This 17in (43.2cm) doll has its teeth clenched on the ever-present cigarette holder. *Tom Sawyer* joins the "Great Moments in Literature" series.

New in the "Storybook Collection" for 1985 are the following 11in (27.9cm) dolls: *Dorothy, Cowardly Lion, Tin Man, Straw Man, Santa Claus, Mrs. Claus, Old Woman in the Shoe* and the *Little Milk Maid*.

Effanbee is now a Disney licensee and has produced four Disney dolls, exquisitely designed and closely modeled from the classic characters: *Prince Charming, Cinderella, Poor Cinderella* and *Mary Poppins*.

Three all-time nursery rhyme characters have been introduced in the "Once Upon a Time Collection:" *Humpty Dumpty, Pat-a-Cake* and *Tooth Fairy*.

Effanbee intoduces two new Jan Hagara collectibles, 15in (38.1cm) *Lesley* and 17in (43.2cm) *Larry*.

Little Old New York, a limited production series has been introduced along with four 18in (45.7cm) exquisitely attired ladies in the "Age of Elegance" series which are also limited production.

GAMA 5

GAMA 5 has developed a new process (GAMA 5's exclusive patent) for implanting doll hair which allows "Little Mothers" to play hairdresser, shampooing and styling their GAMA 5 doll's hair. Until now many strands of hair were implanted into a doll's head, approximately 200 implants in a 16in (40.6cm) doll. With this new technique nearly 3,000 implants are done in the same size head with only 2 to 4 strands in each implant. This gives the doll more realistic looking and manageable hair. These dolls come in four sizes, 12, 16, 20 and 24in (30.5, 40.6, 50.8 and 61cm). Some are sold with wardrobes, others with wardrobe and doll in an attractive white suitcase. GAMA 5 doll clothing can be identified by the "gold" bow trademark attached.

The dolls, clothing and suitcases are all manufactured in the GAMA 5 factory in France. They have vinyl head and limbs, soft bodies and sleep eyes. (Distributed by Pottier Import Co. Inc.)

German Dolls

Kathy Ann Dolls, Imports, Inc. has a large selection of dolls imported from various German firms. The most notable for 1985 are: from **Götz** several vinyl dolls are strung with elastic and they have posable heads. Among these are 18in (45.7cm) *Elsa* and *Eric* with brown hair and eyes, five 19in (48.3cm) little girls with long rooted hair and dressed in little girl pinafores and smocked dresses, and a group of six 15in (38.1cm) and 16in (40.6cm) toddlers with six joints, which includes a swivel waist. Three 16in (40.6cm) babies, *Amy, Allison* and *Audrey* have vinyl heads that are secured with a tie draw string so that the dolls' bodies can be machine washed. **Schildkröt** has a new 17in (43.2cm) celluloid girl, *Erica*, for collectors who wears a pink knitted sweater with matching high stockings, all decorated in pompons. *Erica* is based on the original 1926 Schildkröt (turtle mark) design and is made from the original mold. The most exciting of the **Helmut Engel** dolls is 19in (48.3cm) *Naomi*, a little girl with long dark hair who carries a Hermann Teddy Bear in the pocket of her white eyelet trimmed pinafore.

Caroline, a 16in (40.6cm) bride doll by Gorham. Original bisque face and musical works that play "We've Only Just Begun."

Horsman's 18in (45.7cm) re-creation of the 1920s *Dimples* doll with hard vinyl and christening outfit.

Dolly Dingle a porcelain doll distributed by House of Global Art.

Suzanne Gibson Dolls

The standard lines of Suzanne Gibson dolls, such as the 8in (20.3cm) *International Dolls* and the baby and toddler dolls include many new models and clothing design changes. There are also two new exciting offerings for 1985 that incorporate several unique concepts.

The Special 1985 Suzanne Gibson-Steiff combination is an 8in (20.3cm) *Goldilocks and the Three* (Steiff) *Bears. Goldilocks* wears a long pink dress trimmed in lace, *Papa* is 9in (22.9cm) and he wears a vest and bow tie and a straw hat, *Mama* is 7in (17.8cm) with an apron, lace collar and lace trimmed bonnet, and *Baby* is 5in (12.7cm) and is wearing a sailor suit. All the Steiff bear costumes were designed by Suzanne Gibson and each bear is fully-jointed.

Another new honor was bestowed on Suzanne Gibson. The **Smithsonian Institution**, after a ten year search and study project to find an artist who could properly design the Inaugural Gowns for dolls from the gowns of the Presidents' wives that are exhibited in the Smithsonian, chose Suzanne Gibson to interpret the gowns for dolls. The **First Ladies dolls** will be 12in (30.5cm) tall in all-vinyl. The dolls are all from the same mold and individuality is achieved with hair treatment and eye color. The Smithsonian wants all the dolls to be identical because they are actually "mannequins" for the authentic gowns in miniature. The first four models are *Martha Dandridge Custis Washington, Mary Todd Lincoln, Dolley Payne Todd Madison* and *Grace Anna Boodhue Coolidge.* The models in the Smithsonian follow this same concept for displaying the originals of the First Ladies gowns. Suzanne Gibson is working closely with curators from the Smithsonian to insure that each First Lady doll will wear a completely accurate copy of the gowns the Presidents' wives wore during the Inauguration ceremonies and so that these gowns and all accessories will be complete in every detail. The dolls will have wigs that are sewn on a cloth foundation to further establish accuracy of style. (Suzanne Gibson dolls are manufactured and distributed by Reeves International.)

Gorham

A new collection of Nursery Rhyme Dolls has been introduced by Gorham. Six musical dolls with original porcelain faces, hands and feet and exclusively designed outfits bring to life these nursery rhyme characters. Each 16in (40.6cm) doll is hallmarked and gift packaged. The series includes *Jack and Jill, Miss Muffet, Little Bo Peep, Mary Quite Contrary* and *Mary Had a Little Lamb.*

Also featured is Gorham's new 16in (40.6cm) musical pride; *Caroline.* Her lovely bridal gown is white taffeta and Belgian lace with a full train, tiered and trimmed with rosebuds. She plays "We've Only Just Begun."

Gorham also introduced *Sweet Inspirations,* a collection of ten soft body dolls and Around the World International Dolls.

GTC

Eva-Maria Reick of GTC has created a series of four fully-jointed all-porcelain dolls representing the Four Seasons as commemorative dolls in dedication to her mother, Gustel Wied, who passed away ten years ago. The 18in (45.7cm) dolls recapture her mother's childhood in 1910 when she was 14 years old. The costumes are fashioned in the tradition of that time. Each doll is limited to an edition of 500 pieces and is accompanied by a booklet about the life of Gustel Wied with a cover drawing appropriate to each season by Eva Maria Reick. (Manufactured/distributed by German Toys & Crafts)

Horsman

Horsman Dolls Inc. is celebrating its 120th birthday as a doll maker this year. To commemorate this special event, they have introduced a new line of dolls. A five-year program has been established to offer a different Horsman unique nostalgia doll from years past. This year they are offering *Baby Dimples,* first made circa 1928. This 18in (45.7cm) doll has a soft body and vinyl head, arms and legs. Costumed in an ecru batiste christening dress and bonnet, *Baby Dimples* is sure to delight doll collectors of all ages as well as children who love to play with doll babies. She will be made for only one year.

House of Global Art

New editions of *Dolly Dingle* and *Billie Bumps* are featured by House of Global Art. These 14in (35.6cm) limited edition musical porcelain dolls are dressed in sailor suits. *Dolly Dingle* plays "Over the Waves" and *Billy Bumps* plays "Row Your Boat."

12in (30.5cm) *Merry,* a musical limited edition doll, has been added to the *Victoria Ashlea Originals*™ porcelain doll series. Exquisitely dressed for Christmas, *Merry* plays "We Wish You a Merry Christmas."

New also this year is a 12in (30.5cm) porcelain Googly bride available in black or white. Featuring a music box which appropriately plays "The Wedding March," this bride has been added to the *Victoria Ashlea Originals*™ collection.

Jesco

Jesco has added several new designs to the **Kewpie** and **Scootles** collections. The *Bride* and *Groom* from the *Kewpie Bridal Party* are now accompanied by a *Flower Girl* costumed in pink and a *Ring Bearer* who is all dressed up in formal wear. The series *Kewpie Party Time* is three 16in (40.6cm) charmers in fancy "party" dresses. Four new 12in (30.5cm) *Kewpies* are *Goes Nite Nite*, a blue sleeper outfit; *Goes to the Ballet* is a pink tutu; *Goes to Grandma's* includes a little suitcase; and *Goes to Play Tennis* has a small racquet with her tennis costume. A new 36in (91.4cm) *S.S. Kewpie* wears a cute sailor costume and is a limited edition of 3,000 dolls. For 1985 two 16in (40.6cm) *Scootles* are appropriately attired as *Cheerleaders*.

Jesco reports that the famous **Nancy Ann Storybook Dolls** have been acquired by the company and that by mid-summer these popular collectors' dolls will be recreated in a "Days of the Week" series and will be packaged in reproductions of the original polka dot boxes.

Scootles 16in (40.6cm) dolls attired as *Cheerleaders*. Distributed by Jesco.

36in (91.4cm) *S.S. Kewpie* in sailor suit limited to 3,000 dolls in 1985. Distributed by Jesco.

Lavinia, a 24in (61cm) recreated by Lenci, very ornately dressed. Distributed by Tide-Rider.

LJN

LJN Toys is not certain yet about the manufacture and distribution of the *Boy George* doll. The company says that the doll will be distributed in Europe and that it will have limited distribution in the United States if it is produced. For celebrity doll collectors LJN has four play dolls 4½in (11.5cm) figures of the main characters of the television show "V" and five bendable 5½in (14cm) figures of stars from the World Wrestling Federation. The wrestlers are Hulk Hogan, The Iron Sheik, Andre the Giant, Big John Stud and Jimmy "Superfly" Snuka.

Lenci®

In 1984 Lenci of Italy produced *La Modistina*, the first repeat of a classic Lenci design using the "surprised eye" model. In 1985 three new 20in (50.8cm) models use this design and each is limited to 999 examples. These are *Charlotte*, *Sirenetta* and the cutest of the three, *Scolaretta*, a little school girl with big brown eyes who carries a book bag in her right hand. *Lavinia* is a fabulous 24in (61cm) "bed doll" with elongated limbs and a blonde wig. She wears a pink organdy dress that is trimmed with dozens of felt flowers. There are also two 12in (30.5cm) little girls - *Luigiana* and *Franca* in felt little girl dresses, typical of Lenci quality. (Distributed by Tide-Rider, Inc.)

Lloyderson

Lloyderson Dolls, renowned for its imported dolls from Spain, has created a charming trio of soft-sculpted dolls, *The Emigrants*. The group is a 22in (55.9cm) *Father*, a 20in (50.8cm) *Mother* and an 18in (45.7cm) *Young Boy Traveler*. These dolls are costumed as European peasants who journeyed to the "Land of Hope."

Marin

The most famous doll company in Spain is Marin. The 18in (45.7cm) all-porcelain line now includes two kings -*Louis XV* and *Henry VIII*. These dolls are loaded with intricate detail and are dressed in velvets, silks and brocades. A new Marin line is six vinyl models of 9in (22.9cm) ladies in period costumes from the 15th through 20th centuries and each doll is authentic and minutely detailed. For collectors who like dolls in authentic regional costumes Marin has designed 14 pairs of 10in (25.4cm) dolls in vinyl, called "Couples in Miniature." Each man and woman is totally authentic and minutely detailed. All items of clothing and accessories are in accurate scale, such as the miniature candles on the table with the couple from *Israel* and the basket held by the lady of the *Argentine* couple. (Distributed by Lloyderson Dolls)

Mattel

Mattel means *Barbie*®! For 1985 there are many new *Barbie*® styles, costumes and accessories, all with a high degree of play value and collectibility. *Barbie's*® "trendy younger sister" *Skipper* has been re-designed and she now has the look of a young teenager. One series of new *Barbie*® fashions is the "Collector Series" of four Oscar de la Renta gowns made of luxurious fabrics for *Barbie's*® most opulent evening wear yet. For the *Barbie*® "Dolls of the World Collection," which is only distributed through the better department stores, a *Japanese Barbie,*® robed in a long kimono, has been added. These dolls are discontinued: *India Barbie,*® *Eskimo Barbie,*® *Scottish Barbie*® and *Oriental Barbie.*®

Also new is a *Barbie*®-related family called "The Heart Family." The *Mom* and *Dad* are made from *Ken* and *Barbie*® molds. Both dolls are packaged with a small *Baby* who has rooted hair - blonde on the girl and brunette on the boy. The family of four is also packaged together as a "Deluxe Set."

Among *Barbie's*® many new accessories, a notable item is *Prince* her furry standard poodle who wears a beret.

Right: Barbie® has a new fashion ensemble designed by Oscar de la Renta.

Countess Maria, 18in (45.7cm) Marin doll, a limited edition Outstanding Ladies of Europe. Distributed by Lloyderson Dolls.

Mighty Star

Mighty Star, Inc. has an all-vinyl doll of special interest to collectors. This is the 14in (35.6cm) *Dolly Dingle* who has three different costume variations and each doll is packaged in a box featuring original *Dolly Dingle* art work. The dolls have painted eyes and rooted, dark blonde hair.

Molly Dolls

Molly handmade small character dolls are a brand new import from Ireland. This collection of nine fine costume dolls, reminiscent of the 19th century, are *Molly Malone, The Aran Knitter, The Immigrant* and *The Dublin Flower Girl.* The dolls have porcelain heads, hands and feet with soft bodies. Each has been attired in carefully chosen fabric which has been hand-tailored into an authentic detailed costume. The dolls' stands are made exclusively from Irish turf (peat). (Distributed by Blythe, Imports)

House of Nisbet

The House of Nisbet dolls from England distributed by Tide-Rider, Inc. have many new models each year. Of special note for 1985 are the following.

In the Nisbet 8in (20.3cm) series new models are *Queen Mother* (85th Birthday Edition), *Princess Margaret, Princess Michael of Kent, The Duchess of Kent, Princess Alexandria, Florence Nightingale, Madame Curie, Mrs. Indira Ghandi, Doris Day* (as *Calamity Jane*) *Vera Lynn* (as the *Force's Sweetheart*), *Robin Hood, Tiny Tim* and *Bob Cratchet* and several others.

There is a new 18in (45.7cm) vinyl *Prince Harry.* Other new vinyl dolls include *Doris Day* and *Vera Lynn* in 16in (40.6cm) sizes, four new models of the 15in (38.1cm) *Alison Nisbet Doll,* 10in (25.4cm) dolls representing *England, Ireland, Scotland* and *Wales,* Louis Nichole designs of two 10in (25.4cm) and two 13in (33cm) costume dolls.

The House of Nisbet is offering a reward of £1000 for the first collector who can produce an example of the very first Peggy Nisbet doll, which was made in 1953 in china. This is an 8in (20.3cm) doll that commemorated the coronation of H.M. Queen Elizabeth II and is dressed in the Coronation robes. A "Replica Edition" model of 5,000 dolls worldwide is being offered in 1985. This doll is based on the sketches that remain and the memories of Mrs. Peggy Nisbet, her son Peter and her daughter Alison. (Distributed by Tide-Rider, Inc.)

Heidi Ott

Dolls with new faces and jointed bodies have been added to the Heidi Ott line. These newly molded heads are even more beautiful and more realistic looking than before. From their expressive eyes and mouths to their posable bodies, these dolls in their finely made clothes reflect the talents of this exceptional artist. These new dolls range in size from approximately 12in (30.5cm) to 19¼in (49cm). (Distributed by Reeves International, Inc.)

Heidi Ott 1985 doll, K17.85*S, 19¼in (49cm). Distributed by Reeves International.

The new "June Bride Collection" from Royal House of Dolls includes 11in (27.9cm) *Flower Girl*, 15in (38.1cm) *June Bride*, 17in (43.2cm) *Groom* and 15in (38.1cm) *Bridesmaid*.

Royal Doulton

Commemorating another royal event, Royal Doulton's *H.R.H. Prince Henry*, second son of Prince Charles and The Princess of Wales is 12in (30.5cm). The limited edition (2,500) doll is swaddled in a Scottish woolen christening shawl and bonnet by the House of Nisbet Ltd. A 3in (7.6cm) silver christening spoon surmounted with the Royal Doulton lion and crown accompanies the new prince doll.

Royal House of Dolls

Leading the new offerings by **Miss Elsa** for Royal House of Dolls this year is a stunning *Vienna*, the first in a new "Night at the Opera" limited edition series. Elegantly attired in heavy brocade, this 15in (38.1cm) all vinyl doll is limited to 2,000 dolls.

Shannon, the choreographer for the Dallas Cowboy Cheerleaders, is another new limited edition collectible doll. This 15in (38.1cm) vinyl doll (2,000 limited edition) comes dressed in a formal gown with a cheerleader outfit included.

The "Royal Bridal Collection" has both a winter and spring bridal party, each complete with a 17in (43.2cm) *Groom*. *Alaska, Ohio, Delaware* and *Kentucky* are the states which have been added to the "*Mary Jane* Growing Up in the USA" series. A 15in (38.1cm) *Lilly* joins the ballerina line and, of course, there is the 1985 limited edition "Christmas Collection.". As an added attraction this year, names have been given to the Ladies of Grandeur, Royal Ballerinas, Rosebud Collection, Polka Dot Collection and the Christmas Collection.

Silvestri

Faith Wick has designed a most unique collection of dolls for Silvestri based on Alice in Wonderland. These fully articulated 27½in (69.9cm) porcelain dolls include *The Mad Hatter, Alice, The White Rabbit, The Queen* (of Hearts), *The Cheshire Cat* and *The Dutchess* with the pig baby (a two-sided figure with a baby on one side and a pig on the other). *The White Rabbit* is covered with rabbit fur from the underarms down while the other figures in the collection are exquisitely costumed in silks and satins. A second collection consists of the same dolls but in different costumes and in a 23in (58.4cm) size. There will be a few additional characters in this collection.

World Doll, Inc.

Leading the tour of the 1985 celebrity dolls from World Doll is the 21in (53.3cm) vinyl *Elvis Presley* with rooted hair - a commemorative issue for Elvis' 50th birthday. The third and fourth editions of the "Celebrity Collection" are *Alexis* and *Krystle* from the TV show "Dynasty." The vinyl dolls are 19in (48.3cm) tall. *Alexis* is a stunning portrait of Joan Collins and she is wearing a red form-fitting gown. *Krystle* is an astonishing likeness of Linda Evans and she wears a black beaded gown. Both dolls also come as $10,000 porcelain editions that include diamonds and furs. These dolls were sculpted by Joyce Christopher, who has done all of the characters in the "Celebrity Collection," beginning with *Marilyn Monroe* in 1983.

The "Movie Greats Collection" from World is Clark Gable as *Rhett* and Vivien Leigh as *Scarlett* from *Gone With the Wind*. *Rhett*, attired in a morning suit, is 21in (53.3cm) tall; *Scarlett*, whose gown is the green sprigged version she wore to the 12 Oaks party in the film, is 19in (48.3cm). The dolls are also accurate portraits of the film stars and they were designed by Niel Estern. The heads of the dolls are attached as a socket so they can be posed in many different positions. *Rhett*'s arms are designed to be placed at *Scarlett*'s waist as she looks up at him and her arms are designed to be placed at his shoulders, in a dancing position. A 17in (43.2cm) *Rhett* is also available in porcelain.

One innovation that World has used for the dolls in the celebrity lines is that the legs on *Rhett, Scarlett, Krystle* and *Alexis* have molded shoes. This allows for far more accuracy and detailing as well as permitting the dolls to stand better. The over-all effect is very attractive.

World Doll has also secured a license to produce the famous *Campbell Kids*. There are a 15in (38.1cm) Boy and Girl in porcelain and a 17in (43.2cm) in vinyl, all with wigs. Eugene Doll & Novelty, the parent company of World, also has a line of *Campbell Kids* in vinyl with painted hair in 17in (43.2cm) and 12in (30.5cm) sizes with two different costumes each.

Eugene Doll, among its many offerings, has a large baby, inspired by "Dynasty." This is *Krystina Carrington*, who has blonde hair and blue eyes and who wears a rhinestone necklace and who has her birth announcement packaged with her.

Sasha

The year 1985 marks the 20th anniversary of the founding of Sasha dolls by Sasha Morgenthaler. To mark this anniversary a re-creation of the first *Sasha* doll, No. 1 Sasha, a 16in (40.6cm) doll will be made with black hair and the blue corduroy dress. The 1985 limited edition doll, for the first time a boy, is *Prince Gregor* (LS 185/2) limited to 4,000 pieces. Newly introduced were the *Sasha* girl (LS 115/2) with a blue tunic and blonde hair, *Sasha* girl (LS 116/2) with a party dress and honey blonde hair, and *Baby Ginger* (LS 515/2) with a knit sweater and trousers and red hair. Distributed by International Playthings.

Vogue® or Ginny®

With the successful re-introduction of *Ginny* in 1984, Vogue Dolls,® Inc., has brought out an undressed 8in (20.3cm) vinyl *Ginny* this year. An assortment of 12 ensembles for party and play will be offered separately.

Ginny also comes fully dressed in 12 different costumes, something for every occasion. In addition, *Ginny* will have her own bed, vanity, wardrobe — and her very own pony.

Famous Pairs include *Ginny* as a *Bride and Groom, Hansel and Gretel,* and *Jack and Jill.*

A most unique offering is the "Ginny Calendar Series" featuring *Ginny* in 12 beautiful ensembles holding the flower of the month and a birthstone charm.

Ginny represents the Four Seasons as a porcelain doll in lavish appropriate costumes while the "Heritage Collection" features five variations in fine porcelain: *Southern Belle, Party Time, Christmas Spirit, Holiday Deluxe* and *Birthday Party* featuring *Ginny* on a porcelain carousel horse. The "Heritage Collection" will be a limited edition series.

One of the more exciting releases for collectors in the line is the re-creation of the *Coronation Ginny* dressed in furs, velvet, satin and lace with a crown and sceptor.

Ginnette, Ginny's baby sister is offered in vinyl in three outfits and also in porcelain in a christening outfit. (Manufactured/distributed by Meritus Industries, Inc.)

This sampling of new doll introductions provides you with a starting point for your quests. Because the fun is in the "discovery" of dolls that meet your personal taste, we wish you "happy hunting."

INDEX